OPEN SOURCE LEADERSHIP

Reinventing Management
When There's No More
Business as Usual

RAJEEV PESHAWARIA

Research Team: Adel Jayasuria, Nadine France, Michael Eric Kossler

New York Chicago San Francisco Athens London Madrid
Mexico City Milan New Delhi Singapore Sydney Toronto

1 2 3 4 5 6 7 8 9   LCR   22 21 20 19 18 17

ISBN   978-1-260-10836-1
MHID   1-260-10836-8

e-ISBN   978-1-260-10837-8
e-MHID   1-260-10837-6

Library of Congress Cataloging-in-Publication Data

Names: Peshawaria, Rajeev, author.
Title: Open source leadership : reinventing management when there's no more
    business as usual / Rajeev Peshawaria.
Description: New York : McGraw-Hill, 2018.
Identifiers: LCCN 2017025069I ISBN 9781260108361 (alk. paper) I ISBN
    1260108368
Subjects: LCSH: Leadership.
Classification: LCC HD57.7 .P469 2018 I DDC 658.4/092--dc23 LC record
    available at https://lccn.loc.gov/2017025069

McGraw-Hill Education books are available at special quantity discounts
to use as premiums and sales promotions or for use in corporate training
programs. To contact a representative, please visit the Contact Us pages at
www.mhprofessional.com.

To Mohini and Ram Gopal Peshawaria
who left too early

To Kusum and Rajendra Kumar
who filled the void

To Vandana Peshawaria, without whom
I wouldn't be here today

To Rahee, Salim, and Kabir Peshawaria
who inspire me to keep going

CONTENTS

ACKNOWLEDGMENTS

This book would not be possible without the contribution, help, and encouragement from a lot of people. It is impossible to list all of them here because much of the work is inspired by the numerous conversations I have had with participants of my programs, seminars, and senior management retreats over the years. The best part of my job as a leadership consultant and educator is the opportunity to interact with and learn from so many smart people all over the world. Thank you all for sharing your wisdom so generously. This book now takes our collective work out of our workshops to a broader audience globally.

There are a few names I must call out. First of all, I must thank my agent Lucinda Blumenfeld and my editor Donya Dickerson because without their faith in this project, this book would not have seen the light of day. Next, my research team comprising Adel Jayasuria, Michael Kossler, and Nadine France did an amazing job of building out our hypothesis into a compelling story. Not far behind was Salim Karan Peshawaria, who contributed to and improved significant parts of the book.

In the early stages of the project, Michele Adelene Sagan was part of the team that helped shape the global study. Toward the end, my assistant Deanna Teh worked tirelessly to get the manuscript ready as per McGraw-Hill guidelines. Wong Siew Li, Rahee Ghosh Peshawaria, and Kabir Raman Peshawaria provided critical feedback after reading the manuscript, which significantly helped improve the text. I am also thankful to Philip Steggals and his team at Kadence for their diligent work as we collected and analyzed data from 28 countries, and the Mohammed Bin Rashid School of Government Dubai (MBRSG) for the Middle East study.

Last but not least, I want to acknowledge the biggest source of inspiration behind this work—Tan Sri Dr. Zeti Akhtar Aziz, former governor of the Central Bank of Malaysia, and chairperson of the board of directors of The Iclif Leadership and Governance Centre. Whatever I have learned about leadership until today has been possible mostly by observing unconventional and large-hearted leaders like her.

FOREWORD

In Silicon Valley, there's a saying that the only way you make money as an entrepreneur and investor is by being "contrarian and right."

If you're only right, but not contrarian, it's unlikely you'll be able to achieve a major impact because everyone else is attempting the same thing. You'll be ignored in a marketplace of sameness. If you're only contrarian but not right, well—that's called failure.

To be contrarian *and* right is to be Jeff Bezos announcing that he was going to sell books online, on Day 1 of Amazon. To be contrarian and right is to be Oprah Winfrey vowing to create a talk show and media empire that would make her one of the richest people in the world. In both cases, and countless others, their visions were met with skepticism. It didn't seem possible. It didn't seem likely. Their ideas were flawed. Yet, it was the very unpopularity of their ideas, at the start, that enabled them to outmaneuver complacent competitors and achieve market dominance.

This book, by one of the most thoughtful thinkers today on leadership development, is full of ideas that are definitely contrarian, and *may just turn out to be right*.

Let's look at one example. In the social media age, prevailing wisdom holds that companies and governments everywhere are being overturned by bottoms-up forces. Anyone with a Twitter account is empowered to speak out and help overthrow established governments (think Arab Spring). Crowdsourcing enables large numbers of amateurs to work together and produce news that rivals the quality of what comes out of established news organizations (think Wikipedia).

As a result, many business leaders draw parallel lessons to the world of leadership and management advice. They think that giving their employees the loudest voice possible is essential, and that decision making ought to be as democratic as possible. After all, decision-making culture in business ought to mirror the social media–rich age we are living in, right? Consider the adoption of "Holocracy" by companies like Zappos to see this mindset in its extreme: there are no real managers or corporate hierarchy at companies that practice Holocracy. All decision making is truly democratic.

Rajeev Peshawaria argues that leaders who think this way are badly mistaken. He writes, "To drive breakthrough results in today's age of speed, top-down autocratic leadership is indeed required." *Autocratic* leadership in . . . the age of Facebook? Yes. Here's the nuance: "do the naked autocrat dance whereby [as a leader, you] practice autocracy of values and purpose, and compassion, humility, and respect for people at the same time." It's complicated, but Rajeev captures your attention through a genuinely contrarian thought.

Rajeev is on a mission to make you think. He's on a mission to make you a better leader. Do not read *Open Source Leadership* expecting clichés that affirm all of your intuitions. Read it to open your mind to different ways of acting in a changing world that demands nothing less.

Time to go restart your career, restart your company, and perhaps restart your mind. The era of open source leadership is upon us.

BEN CASNOCHA
Former chief of staff to the chairman of LinkedIn, and coauthor,
with Reid Hoffman, of *The Start-up of You: Adapt to the Future,
Invest in Yourself, and Transform Your Career* and *The Alliance:
Managing Talent in the Networked Age*
Silicon Valley—June 2017

INTRODUCTION

The world's largest taxi company owns no cars, and employs no drivers directly. The world's largest hotel service owns no properties and employs no housekeeping or room-service staff. Communication has been WhatsApp*ed*, memories Instagram*med*, jobs Bangalore*d* and life itself Facebook*ed*. Almost everything we knew as normal in both business and social life has changed dramatically in just the last 15 years. We now live and work in the age of 24/7 connectivity where knowledge is free and abundant, ordinary people more empowered than ever before, everything fully transparent, and leaders completely exposed and naked.

Global population doubled from three billion to six billion between 1960 and 1999, and is expected to reach nine billion by 2050. On one hand, the population explosion is creating significant pressure in terms of food, water, communal harmony, and other basic necessities; on the other it is creating an abundance of talent and innovation. Thanks to 24/7 connectivity, we can now source talent and innovation far easier and quicker than ever before in human history.

Welcome to the twenty-first century where everyone and everything is completely open and connected, and where scarcity and abundance coexist.

Even while the very nature in which people work, interact, and transact has already changed beyond recognition, and current times are posing unprecedented challenges and opportunities, the most widely used frameworks and practices for personal career and organizational success seem to have remained unchanged over the last 50 to 75 years. Many of these practices were insufficient even in stable times, let alone in the brave new world of today and the fast-evolving world of tomorrow.

Of the following statements, which would you agree with?

- The consumption-led growth formula of the last 100 years will enable global well-being and success in the twenty-first century.
- A democratic, all-inclusive style of leadership is better than an autocratic style.
- The traditional theory and practice of effective leadership still applies in today's uber-connected and uber-populated world.
- Setting stretch goals universally for all employees will spur high performance throughout the organization.
- People leave managers, not companies.
- Measuring and proactively managing the engagement of all employees drives productivity and profitability.
- Isolating innovation to incubators and other pockets of an organization will produce new breakthroughs as quickly as needed in the new economy.
- Leadership succession must be planned; future leaders must be identified and groomed deliberately.

While they may have served us well for quite a while, in this book I will argue that these ideas have outlived their useful lives, and offer updated thinking better suited to enable effective personal and organizational leadership for today's transformed landscape. We must shed myths of the past and adopt future-ready ideas. Over a 30-year career in business, and particularly the last two decades as a leadership, management, and strategy consultant and educator, I have worked with hundreds of senior management teams as they have led their businesses, and coached thousands of executives individually. There is no shortage of smarts within these teams and individuals, but are they inventing new personal and organizational frames of reference fast enough to succeed in today's new world? Having lived, worked, and researched in the United States, Europe, Asia, and the Middle East, I have seen the same tendency everywhere—individuals and organizations are still trying to compete and succeed using tools and frameworks built for times where knowledge was scarce, talent seemingly limited, and privacy still possible.

Consider just one example: communication (Table I.1). Until 1995, snail mail, telegram, telex, fax, and expensive international phone calls were the ways in which people communicated. Since long-distance contact was difficult and inadequate compared to what it is today, knowledge and location were great competitive advantages in business. However, in just the last 15 to 20 years we have started taking things like free voice and video calling, email, instant messaging, and 24/7 connectivity for granted. The amount of freedom and empowerment these communication channels provide individuals and employees is unprecedented. Yet, large companies still use management tools and practices designed in the industrial age when knowledge was at a premium and individuals had far fewer livelihood choices. Management's role then was largely to organize systems, processes, and people in ways that reduced costs and increased efficiency.

Today change itself is changing at a pace never seen before, with much of the acceleration happening in the last 15 years. Yet, instead of replacing outdated management and leadership practices to better compete in the new reality, many senior executives complain about the poor work ethic and values of millennials. In the twenty-first century, life and business have become "open source" with the advent of uber-connectivity and uber-population. To succeed and thrive in this new era, our thought and action must also become open source. Only those

TABLE I.1 The Emergence of the Open Source Era

	1976	1996	2016
World Population	4.1 billion	5.8 billion	7.4 billion
Communication	Snail mail, telegram, telex, phone, fax	E-mail, snail mail, video conferencing, phone, fax	Twitter, WhatsApp, Skype, E-mail, 24/7 mobile connectivity
Knowledge	Scarce, an advantage	A bit less scarce but still an advantage	Free and abundant, a commodity
Location	A competitive advantage	Still important	Largely irrelevant
Travel	Difficult and expensive	Difficult and expensive	Cheaper and easier (Uber, AirAsia, NetJets)
Goods and services	Scarce, hard to source	Still scarce and hard to source in many parts of the world	Abundant and easily available anytime, anywhere
Skills for professional success	Science, technology, engineering, and math (STEM)	Still STEM—left-brain skills rule the roost	Design, aesthetics, relationships—right-brain skills
Predominant need of individuals	Financial/job security	Financial freedom	Meaning more than money
Talent	Scarce	War for talent	Abundant and easily available through crowdsourcing

who adopt a mindset of changing faster than change itself will survive. We have already seen examples of this at the product innovation level. Organizations that are unafraid of cannibalizing their own products before others make them obsolete (think Steve Jobs and Apple) are the ones that win and thrive. But there aren't enough examples of innovation in people management practices. Going forward, as STEM-based knowledge (left brain acumen) becomes more commoditized, innovation on the people management front will distinguish winners from losers. More so than ever before, it is time for both established and aspiring business leaders to question conventional wisdom and adopt *open source thinking* around these five fundamental questions/challenges:

Powerful Personal Leadership in the Twenty-First Century

1. What style of leadership is best for creating break-through success in today's environment?
2. How must leadership be redefined/reincarnated in the open source era?

Leading the Organization to Outperforming Competition

3. How can we inspire, manage, measure, and reward performance at a time when a significant section of the workforce is opting for free agency rather than traditional full-time employment?
4. How can we measure employee engagement and effectively address the gaps?
5. How can organizations innovate quickly and more often, and create a pipeline of future visionary leaders at the same time?

Amidst all the rapid change, however, there is one thing that has stayed constant—the 80:20 rule, aka the Pareto Principle. Roughly speaking, the 80:20 rule posits that *80 percent of the effects come from 20 percent of the causes*. From macroeconomic conditions to micro-level business practices and personal patterns, 80:20 is omnipresent and omnipotent, but it is almost unacknowledged in much of contemporary management practice. In Chapter 1, I will describe the open source era in detail and highlight just how much has changed in the recent past. Before that, let me now briefly introduce the five challenges, which I will further elaborate with suggested solutions (using the wisdom of 80:20) in Chapters 2 through 6.

1. What Style of Leadership Is Best Suited for Creating Breakthrough Success in Today's Environment?

Conventional wisdom says that an all-inclusive democratic style of leadership is best suited for driving innovation and breakthrough success. While I am in full praise of diversity and inclusion, and generally against a dictatorial style of leadership, my research data shows that conventional wisdom may not be the preference of most employees. In a research experiment spanning approximately 16,000 people in 28 countries, one of the questions we asked respondents was to indicate their level of agreement with the following statement: *When it comes to achieving breakthrough success for the organization, a significant amount of top-down/bold leadership is required.*

Our data shows that over 75 percent of respondents agree or strongly agree with the statement. In other words, respondents are saying that if you want to create breakthrough success in today's fast-changing environment, you need to be willing to embrace an autocratic style, particularly when driving a vision forward. According to this data, the Steve Jobs phenomenon is not an anomaly.

Chapter 2 provides details of the global study, the case for top-down leadership, and offers practical guidance on how to overcome the challenges associated with it. Key questions we will try to answer are:

- In an age where ordinary people are so empowered and leaders completely exposed/naked, is it even possible to use top-down autocratic leadership?
- If top-down leadership is indeed the need of the hour, how can one practice it without antagonizing today's free and empowered workforce?

2. How Must Leadership Be Redefined/ Reincarnated in the Open Source Era?

At a time when population explosion is creating unprecedented challenges across planet Earth, and universal connectivity has made nearly everything transparent and available at the speed of light, how should one think about leadership? What does leadership even mean in this uber-connected and uber-populated world?

For far too long, leadership has been confused with:

- **Followership.** Leadership is typically seen as repeating the behaviors and practices of successful leaders. Hence the huge current focus on competency modeling and case study based education.
- **A position of authority.** Pick up any dictionary and look up the words *boss* and *leader*, and the root cause of the problem is obvious. We tend to define the two words almost identically. The 2010 Arab Spring and other similar phenomena tell us that in the age of uber-connectivity and freedom, "boss-ship" simply will not work.
- **Genetics.** There is a widespread belief that leaders are born, not made.

The first thing we need to do is remove this confusion. In order to create an environment in which the next generation(s) can thrive, we need to take today's challenges head-on. We need to recognize that current thinking around leadership will not be adequate to do so, and redefine leadership away from followership, authority, and genetics toward a burning desire to make a difference. When we adopt this new way of looking at leadership, we will become creators of a better future, and must be prepared to face stiff resistance along the way. The resistance will become stronger as we begin our journey, but we must not give up. Our resolve to stay the course will need to be stronger and firmer than the resistance, and we will need to find a way of developing this strength. *This firm resolve to create a better future is leadership.* Leadership is not a position or title, it is making the choice to continue to struggle and never give up. The primary difference between a leader and a nonleader is that the latter gives up in the face of resistance. The ability or force that prevents leaders from giving up is therefore the main ingredient of leadership. In *Too Many Bosses, Too Few Leaders*, I called this force *leadership energy*, and described it briefly. In Chapter 3 of this book, I will decode it in more detail. The likes of Mahatma Gandhi, Nelson Mandela, and Martin Luther King drew their power from their leadership energy, not from their position or title.

At the end of the day, leadership is about choosing to create a better future, and embracing a path that involves significant risk, loneliness, and unpopularity. So most "sane" people do not opt for it. Rather than asking how one can become a leader, the more appropriate question might therefore be, how many people opt for it? You guessed it—80:20! Individuals and organizations will be better off accepting the fact that only about 20 percent of people will choose leadership as defined here, and that is more than enough. Far more important than trying to figure out how one *can* become a leader is the question of whether or not one *wants* to in the first place.

3. How Can We Inspire, Manage, and Reward Performance at a Time When a Significant Section of the Workforce Is Opting for Free Agency Rather Than Traditional Full-Time Employment?

Since the dawn of the Industrial Revolution, thinking and tools for managing employees toward high performance have largely remained the same. Common practice around managing individual performance says all employees must be given stretch goals at the beginning of each year, managers must closely monitor performance and give regular feedback to ensure employees put their best foot forward every day, and performance must be measured and rewarded based on the preset stretch goals.

There are several problems with this approach. First, this system places the onus of enabling performance mostly on the shoulders of managers rather than employees themselves. Essentially, we have been treating people like machines that must be constantly programed, monitored, and controlled for optimal performance. Second, even while the existence of the performance bell curve is well acknowledged, we conveniently forget all about it in the beginning of the year and expect *all* employees to uniformly write stretch goals and perform at the highest level. According to the bell curve theory (which is derived from the 80:20 rule), performance in any group of people distributes itself along a bell-shaped curve in which 20 percent are top performers delivering 80 percent of the results, 60 percent are average performers, and 20 percent are poor (bottom) performers. Consequently, when people are stacked along the bell curve at the end of the year, both managers and employees are left feeling cheated. In today's reality, where the very nature of work has been democratized, it is time to turn this logic upside down. What if instead of stretch goals, employees were given goals that only specified the minimum level of performance outcomes required, and left everything else loose or undefined? What if instead of stipulating an annual limit, employees were allowed to take as much vacation as they wanted? What if we reduced supervision and management of employees to the bare minimum? In other words, what if we adopted an open source performance management system driven by self-management?

What then about the role of the immediate manager? Gallup and others have told us for decades, "People leave managers, not companies," essentially suggesting that the biggest influence on employee motivation is the employee's manager. This assumption is probably the reason why the current (outdated) performance management system puts much of the onus of employee motivation on the shoulders of immediate managers. By this logic, managers must do whatever they can to motivate their employees, because they can in fact motivate employees.

My research data points exactly in the opposite direction. It shows that the primary source of an employee's motivation is *not* his or her manager. But most companies still focus their management development efforts on teaching their managers tricks and techniques to motivate their employees.

An open source performance management system as described above would particularly benefit women. If a high-performing woman wants to take her foot off the pedal for a few years because she wants to take care of a young baby, she would not be frowned upon under such a system. Once her baby is old enough and she feels it is time to step on the gas again, she may. She decides!

"But if you allow employees to get away with just the minimum, the organization will suffer. Who will do all the work that needs to get done?" This is the counterargument against creating an open source performance management system. The truth is that with or without such a system, performance will distribute itself along the 20:60:20 curve anyway. By acknowledging it, you set the right expectations and let people contribute as much as they want without stress or stigma. As the knowledge-is-free-and-abundant digital economy matures further, companies might have no choice but to give more freedom.

In Chapter 4 we will discuss the pros and cons of open source performance management in more detail, and show how minimizing supervision can maximize organizational performance.

4. How Can We Measure Employee Engagement and Effectively Address the Gaps?

While companies evoke the bell curve to justify their year-end compensation and promotion decisions, they tend to forget about it when conducting annual employee engagement surveys. The same survey is sent to all employees regardless of performance level, and feedback data is aggregated in terms of high and low scoring items. In other words, if it is true that performance falls on the 20:60:20 curve, the voice of the top 20 percent gets drowned under the weight of the rest who are not as good. Furthermore, the best performers are so busy that they often do not fill out the survey in the first place, whereas the underperformers not only find the time to fill it out, they complain the most while doing so. As a result, senior management does not get an accurate picture of actual engagement levels across each segment of the bell curve. By addressing average scores with well-meaning but ill-informed measures thereafter, senior management ends up unknowingly promoting mediocrity instead of excellence.

In Chapter 5, I will show how and why a values-based 360-degree feedback process is far superior to an annual engagement survey. For those that still want to conduct annual engagement surveys, I will offer a much better alternative than the current one-size-fits-all model.

5. How Can Organizations Innovate Quickly and More Often, and Create a Pipeline of Future Visionary Leaders at the Same Time?

According to the 80:20 principle, only a handful of people will have the ability and motivation to innovate. Acknowledging this fact, companies typically choose their so-called innovators and put them to work in innovation incubators. Before long, large amounts of money and time are spent on such isolated incubators with no guarantee that the chosen few will actually have the best ideas or the ability to see them through.

How can anyone predict who the 20 percent are and where they live? In the open source twenty-first century, one must use open source leadership and crowdsource innovation from in- and outside the organization. To understand this phenomenon, consider what General Electric did recently in its aviation (aircraft engines) business. It ran a global contest for designs to reduce the weight of engine brackets by 30 percent, and offered a prize of $20,000 for the best design. To GE's surprise the winning design came from a small town in Indonesia, and reduced the weight by a whopping 84 percent. Now how's that for exceeding your innovation KPI by 180 percent at the cost of just $20,000? And who would have thought that the world's biggest aviation giant would achieve such a breakthrough for so little, and more importantly from small- town Indonesia? Open source leadership enables the *democratization* of innovation by crowdsourcing it, thereby significantly increasing the chances of success.

Similarly, when it comes to succession planning and developing and retaining the next generation of leaders, it is time for companies to rethink conventional practices. Succession planning typically begins with plotting employees on a nine-box grid on which one axis represents current performance and the other axis is future potential as shown in Figure I.1.

Employees that end up in the top right-hand box of the grid are considered part of the succession pool. HR departments then draw up spreadsheets showing several possible successors for each key job, and create special development programs to prepare the deemed "successors" for those positions. These special programs often require participants to work on extra

FIGURE I.1   Traditional Succession Planning

projects over and above their day jobs, to solve important issues while showcasing their leadership at the same time. The programs are considered win-win arrangements, wherein participants "learn by doing" and get a chance to showcase their abilities to senior management, and the company gets to solve problems and exploit new opportunities. In theory everyone is happy, and the board of directors is impressed with management's succession planning efforts.

Again, there are several issues with this approach. First, in today's uber-connected free world, how can we say that the so-called chosen ones will actually remain with the company after such programs? Since there is no longer the promise of long-term employment, why should employees be forever grateful for all the investment in their development? Second, most high performers are already very busy and stretched while delivering on their performance goals.

Participating in development programs that require them to put in even more hours on special projects puts additional burden on these high performers' already full plates. It is not that they don't welcome opportunities for career progression;

they just don't have extra bandwidth for hypothetical work. So, many of the chosen few end up unhappy about being included in such succession pools. And finally, the rest of the employees—those not chosen for such accelerated development—end up unhappy too because they see no hope for their careers in the company. What is intended as a win-win initiative ends up being lose-lose.

Chapter 6 first takes a deep dive into building long-lasting capability for brisk innovation through external crowdsourcing. Next, it shows why it might be time to dismantle the traditional succession planning machinery, and how internal crowdsourcing is a much better strategy for developing a leadership pipeline for the future. As you will see in this chapter, crowdsourcing kills two birds with one stone—more frequent innovation *and* leadership succession planning—and it does so with minimal or no cost to the organization.

Figure I.2 serves as a road map for the book that we will revisit in each chapter.

CONTEXT

1. The Open Source Era

OPEN SOURCE PERSONAL LEADERSHIP

2. The Naked Autocrat Creates Breakthrough Results

3. Leadership Energy, Not Competencies

OPEN SOURCE ENTERPRISE LEADERSHIP

4. Minimum Supervision, Maximum Performance

5. No More Engagement Surveys

6. Crowdsourced Innovation and Leadership Succession

FIGURE I.2 Open Source Leadership Roadmap

Throughout the book, I will also introduce you to some leaders who epitomize the concepts of this book. Learning about their life stories was one of the more enjoyable parts of writing this book for me. I hope you enjoy reading them as much as I enjoyed writing them.

This book could get uncomfortable for some individuals, executives, management (and even corporate boards), as it reveals several inconvenient truths around current practices that need to be inversed. It is, however, urgently required for those seeking to get—and stay—ahead in the open source era.

Rather than being a "how to" recipe book for success, this book is a "think" book. Leadership is more of an art than a science, so readers will need to think carefully about how the ideas in this book fit in with whatever they are trying to accomplish, and paint their own canvas by mixing colors according to their own preference. Whether leading their own careers or leading the organization, I hope that this book poses thought-provoking insights and dilemmas for readers. Pablo Picasso once said, "Computers are useless. They only give you answers." It is with the right questions that leaders first imagine, then create, a better future. So rather than answers, this book provides questions.

PART 1

Context

CHAPTER 1

The Open Source Era

CONTEXT
1. The Open Source Era

OPEN SOURCE PERSONAL LEADERSHIP
2. The Naked Autocrat Creates Breakthrough Results
3. Leadership Energy, Not Competencies

OPEN SOURCE ENTERPRISE LEADERSHIP
4. Minimum Supervision, Maximum Performance
5. No More Engagement Surveys
6. Crowdsourced Innovation and Leadership Succession

Klaus Schwab, founder and chairman of the World Economic Forum, describes the technology driven changes to business and society as the Fourth Industrial Revolution. In his 2017 book of the same title, he lists the previous three revolutions roughly as follows:

- The first revolution used water and steam power to mechanize production.
- The second used electric power to create mass production.
- The third used electronics and information technology to automate production.
- The fourth is building on the third and is blurring the lines between physical, digital, and biological spheres.

Each revolution created massive disruption in business and society. Those that adapted and innovated quickly (Like Thomas Edison, Henry Ford, and others) not only survived, they created tremendous well-being and wealth. Most others were displaced and left panting. Can you imagine being the owner of a business delivering goods by horse carriage when the railroad was invented? A similar displacement is under way now. While some are reaping huge benefits, many are being left behind because they don't have either the right skills for the new economy, or the innovative leadership mindset to acquire them quickly enough. Both individuals and organizations today stand on the edge of either extinction or renewal. In later chapters I will lay out both personal and organizational strategies for powerful leadership in today's reality, which is both daunting and exciting at the same time. First, I believe it is important to revisit the lessons of history. While the context and extent of the current revolution is different and larger, the wisdom gained from past experience will help us better comprehend the profound changes unfolding as we speak. So, let us take a brief tour of history, beginning with the advent of the twentieth century.

1900 to 1950: From Artisanal Labor to Factory Work

The first half of the twentieth century shattered the social, economic, and political norms of the previous centuries and cemented many of the management practices we still use a hundred years later. World Wars I and II brought the beginning of the end of the great European empires, cracked open the door for women and minority groups to enter the workplace, and provided the first inklings of the urbanization that would define the latter half of the century. It was also the very beginning of the rapid growth of global population. In 1900, there were 1.6 billion inhabitants on the planet, which had jumped to 2.5 billion by 1950, despite the vast loss of life in the two World Wars.

1900 to 1950 cemented the separation between work and home life, a separation we are reconsidering over a century later. For most of the nineteenth century the workplace had been indivisible from home life. Men, women, and children worked where they lived and pitched in when required. The majority of farming remained family-owned and small-scale, and production was artisanal, handmade, and small-batch. However, the rise of the railroads in the latter half of the nineteenth century brought with it the creation and separation of jobs that had never existed before, particularly in finance, as U.S. tycoons created influential transport, shipping, and steel companies and employed thousands of blue-collar and office workers. The railroads also allowed for large-scale movement of goods and workers crossing the country in search of employment.

In 1900, much of the Western workforce (38 percent) was still defiantly agricultural, with another third in mining, manufacturing, or construction. Only five percent of factories in production used electricity to power their machines, and less than 10 percent of private homes had electricity. Work remained split along gender and class lines; only 19 percent of working-age women were in the workforce, while less than 14 percent of the wider workforce had graduated from high school. Men with college degrees earned on average 62 percent more than those with a high school diploma.

World Wars I and II solidified the transition from agriculture to manufacturing. As the majority of young males went to the trenches, women's participation in the U.S. workforce doubled. Munitions factories were by far the largest employers, a trend repeated in World War II. In postwar America, manufacturing provided 34 percent of all "nonfarm" employment in 1950, alongside 14.9 percent in retail trade and 13.3 percent in government. Services, at 11 percent, were a small but soon to be rapidly growing sector of the employment market.

Communication was slow by the standards of today, but had been revolutionized by newspapers, telephone, telegram, and radio. Radio in particular opened up marketing and advertising to a mass audience, and companies could start pushing their goods and services instantly to previously untapped audiences. Telephones were limited to one-on-one discussions but allowed for greater communication between buyers, sellers, and suppliers. However, location remained a key asset for any company or business owner; in 1900, only 0.11 of every 1,000 Americans owned a car, and shopping was limited to local shops and suppliers.

The best example of the changing workplace in the first half of the century is the Ford Motor Company. The company templated the shift from artisanal labor to factory work under the watchful eyes of Henry Ford and Frederick Taylor, whose "scientific management" theories enabled Ford's assembly line model. Influential thinker Gary Hamel, in fact, believes that management as a concept may have been the greatest invention of the twentieth century, with its ability to organize people and resources in a way not really seen before. Taylor applied the principles of mechanization to the workforce, establishing standard times and production standards for each factory task. His writing emphasized the laziness and stupidity of the average factory worker, who he believed required detailed training, supervision, and an authoritarian style of management.

Ford's Model T brought automobiles to the masses. In 1908, he hired Taylor as a consultant to streamline construction. At the time, a team of skilled workers took 12 hours to build a single car, which remained in a stationary central position as workers brought and attached each component. Taylor and Ford broke down construction into individual actions and rearranged the line, with the workers stationary rather than the vehicle. The speed of the new assembly line (down to 93 minutes per car) allowed Ford to bring down prices and make the Model T accessible to the mass market.

1951 to 1990: The Birth and Practice of Modern Management

The latter half of the twentieth century laid the groundwork for many of the workplace realities that we are still grappling with today. The postwar job-for-life model was steadily eroded, and the global population started to boom. This period also heralded the beginning of the technology that has so disrupted our lives, and if you looked closely enough, you could begin to see the wheels of change spinning a little faster.

The post–World War II years began with a new era of prosperity, superior healthcare, and a "baby boom" that more than doubled the global population in 40 years, from 2.6 billion in 1950 to 5.3 billion in 1990. Immediately postwar, workers benefited from economic stability, increased purchasing power, and so-called "jobs for life." The automation of many household tasks, the civil rights and women's movements, and postwar migration began to diversify the white, male-dominated Western workforce. These decades also heralded the shift away from manual labor to service-based employment. In 1956, workers in white-collar roles outnumbered blue-collar workers for the first time, and by 1967 the economic contribution of jobs dealing with the production of information accounted for 46 percent of U.S. gross national product.

This change in employment was reflected in a shift in management theory, which began to recognize the complexity of motivation, challenge, and reward for employees and define the role and responsibilities of a manager beyond simply keeping employees in line. Peter Drucker's influential *The Practice of Management* outlined five core roles for managers, which included objective setting, organizing the group, motivating and communicating, measuring performance, and developing people. The idea that workers were motivated by personal challenge, recognition, and advancement rather than pay or punishment represented an enormous shift in thinking. The war for talent increased as economies grew and flourished, and workplaces began to offer benefits outside of salaries.

These decades also presaged a new age of technology and the beginning of a shift toward globalization enabled by the new communication tools. Between 1945 and 1960 computers moved from purely military use to electronic data processing machines for office use. They remained fairly discreet entities throughout the 1960s and 1970s, used by an individual worker to facilitate a job rather than as a tool for communication. In the late 1970s the invention of the LAN (local area network) broke new ground as computers within an initially limited area were linked up. LAN networks were first used to share storage and printers, but eventually expanded to include tens if not hundreds of computers, despite the restrictions of early wired models.

Other new forms of communication were having an enormous impact. Television opened new options for advertising and communication to a mass audience, while the increasing prevalence of home telephones also led to a rise in telemarketing and the use of the facsimile or fax. It's important to note here, though, that while the options for communication seemed to expand quickly, they still grew at a much slower pace, relatively speaking, than anything we experience today. To illustrate this point: it took 76 years for the telephone to reach half of the U.S. population. In contrast, the smartphone achieved the same coverage in under 10 years and is rapidly eating into *another* market, the desktop market, with share rising from 17 percent in 2013 to 29 percent only a year later.

IBM is a good example of the wider trends that occurred throughout this period, and an interesting comparison to what would come later. Founder Thomas Watson Sr. established the company in 1914 and adopted three "basic beliefs"—respect for the individual, exceptional customer service, and the pursuit of excellence in all tasks—that translated into progressive, nondis-criminatory hiring policies and pro-family workplace activities. Watson believed that job security was good for business, and until the 1980s not one IBM employee was made redundant, a fact that seems entirely astonishing now. In the 1960s, Thomas Watson Jr. reiterated his father's beliefs. During those years IBM flourished, providing, leasing, and servicing the System/360 mainframe computer.

IBM weathered the economic shocks of the 1970s while other U.S. companies began to feel the squeeze of the Vietnam War, skyrocketing inflation, unemployment, and the rise of Japan and Germany as industrial powerhouses. Between 1973 and 1995, U.S. wages fell 15 percent and family income stagnated. Government policies favored deregulation and privatization of previously state-owned industries. Seeking ways to cut costs, companies began to investigate outsourcing labor to cheaper locations. The 1990 "Washington Consensus" outlined 10 policy prescriptions for developing countries (particularly in

South America) that focused on market liberalization and state nonintervention. Workers were no longer protected by the state, and unions began to lose their influence.

In the 1980s, IBM's mainframe business began to lose traction with the rise of the PC and competition from Apple, Hewlett-Packard, and Sony. The company hired its first "outsider" CEO, who rejected many of the values that the Watson dynasty had established. Fast running out of cash in the face of global competition, in 1993 IBM laid off 60,000 members of its global workforce, at the time the biggest redundancy in U.S. corporate history. This massive shift marked the death of lifetime employment as practiced by most successful large corporations of the time. From now on, employees would have to think more entrepreneurially about their jobs and careers. By 2015 this mindset was to become the very difference between survival and extinction.

1991 to the Present, and Beyond: The Open Source Era

And now we come to the recent past, present, and beyond. As I mentioned briefly in the Introduction, this era is defined by two major megatrends: uber-connectivity and uber-population, both of which present huge opportunities and daunting challenges at the same time.

Uber-Connectivity

The 1990s and beyond are dominated by the exponential rise of information technology, automation, and 24/7 connectivity, which have facilitated the globalization of the business landscape and a shift in economic dominance from West to East. Free-trade agreements made goods production and service provision vulnerable to outsourcing, and job insecurity and short-term, contracted, or contingent positions are now the norm. The separation between work and life established during the Industrial Revolution is again breaking down as mobile technology allows workers to contact the office anytime, anywhere and globalization demands that employees function within a 24-hour marketplace.

The 1990s were the final nail in the coffin of the "job for life" model. Companies in the 1970s had vastly overestimated their sustainability and future success, and the 1980s recession meant corporations fired well-trained and experienced employees en masse. As the global economy picked up again in the 1990s, newly streamlined organizations were able to pick and choose from the surplus of skilled talent, ushering in and cementing the "free agent" model. By 2014, the United States had 28 million temporary workers, representing 20 percent of the entire workforce, while by 2012, some 20 percent of short-term assignments lasted less than 12 months.

At the same time, many jobs were outsourced to the East. An estimated 2.1 million U.S. manufacturing jobs were eliminated or relocated between 2001 and 2011 as China became the "factory of the world." This trend is no longer confined to manufacturing; white-collar roles are increasingly outsourced as well. In recent years, 13 out of every 100 computer programming jobs have been shifted offshore, while automation in the workplace is making human workers obsolete. When was the last time, for example, that you spoke to a bank teller? It is reasonable now to say that no job is "safe," and the breakneck pace of change demands that workers keep endlessly refreshing their skill sets to maintain relevance.

All these changes would not have been possible without the growth of connectivity, which has revolutionized almost every aspect of the workplace. The advent of the local area network we saw in the 1970s was the first step in the development of the Internet (launched in 1991), and now the ubiquitous 3G/4G mobile broadband (launched in 2001). This sharing technology revolutionized the way workers communicate with each other, as well as with customers, clients, and the public, across time and space in ways not previously imaginable. No longer is location a prized asset; companies can reach customers and clients across the globe with the click of a button. The two biggest disruptors over this period are possibly the advent of the smartphone and the birth of social media platforms. Both have brought information to the public in astonishing ways. Many of the smartphones and tablets we currently use have more power than the supercomputers that only decades ago filled an entire room. Information now moves at the speed of light across viral platforms like Twitter and Facebook, which users can access anywhere, anytime.

Before I suggest ways in which organizations will have to adapt to survive this new world order, let's take a look at the technological, business, and social trends that are going to reshape the landscape as we know it.

Technology: The Brave New World

In the new millennium, digital life is becoming difficult to distinguish from "real life," and the line will only get more blurred. Mobile phone sales are outpacing seemingly old-fashioned PC or laptop purchases six to one, while 43 percent of the global population is currently connected to the Internet. A recent World Economic Forum report posited this mind-bending question: could it be that in only a decade or two Internet connectivity is considered not a privilege, but a basic human right?

Consider this. Implantable technology (already seen in pacemakers and cochlear implants) is predicted to become ubiquitous. By 2022 it is estimated that 10 percent of people will be wearing clothes directly connected to the Internet. This will be alongside the supercomputer already in many people's pockets: global smartphone subscribers are anticipated to hit 3.5 billion by 2019. Who you are in "real life" is going to become indistinguishable from who you are on the Internet, and establishing and managing your digital presence will become just as important as what you choose to wear or how you choose to physically present yourself.

Alongside the data generated by individuals, "the Internet of things" (IoT) is predicted to skyrocket. Literally everything that can be digitally connected, will be. This will mean greater communication and ever more data-driven devices, in your home with smart appliances and in your city with smart traffic lights, services, utilities, and roads. More than 10 percent of cars on the roads will be driverless by 2026. While this isn't the focus of this book, this will raise (and already is raising) questions about surveillance and the right to privacy, as well as legality, ownership, and accessibility of the torrent of data being collected every moment of the day. Organizations both public and private are going to have to find ways of building public trust in data collection and application.

Big data is an ongoing theme. We are already seeing debate raging over the use and abuse of data. This can only become more critical and pertinent. Ninety percent of the world's data has been collected in the last two years, and the amount of information being collected is doubling every 1.2 years. Data analysis can and will become increasingly sophisticated and sought-after as consumers seek ever more customized products. Big data will also become the basis of decision making. It is predicted that in 2023 governments will start to use big data as a replacement for the traditional paper-bound population census.

If driverless cars don't seem like enough science fiction for you, yes, the robots are coming. According to *Deep Shift: Technology Tipping Points and Societal Impact*, a September 2015 report by the World Economic Forum, the first artificial intelligence machine will sit on a corporate board of directors by 2026. If that isn't startling enough, robots are going to continue to make inroads into previously unassailable jobs. We might be used to blue-collar manufacturing jobs being outsourced to the robot world, but the white-collar world is going to feel the impact too. Robots already account for 80 percent of the manufacturing of a car—prepare for that statistic to get even higher.

Finally, 3D printing is going to disrupt just about everything, particularly manufacturing, healthcare (including 3D printed transplantable organs), and consumer products. The last one is most interesting considering the themes that will come up later in this chapter. Already 3D printing can be done anywhere, and is cropping up in shared tech cafes and laboratories around the world. It creates opportunities for consumers to print products locally, at home or in an office, rather than going to a traditional shop or ordering online. It is already being used in making wind turbines, toys, and a whole host of other products. Over time, 3D printers will use many different materials such as plastic and aluminum, and replace entire factories to produce (print) complex products such as cars. This raises interesting issues about employment—what will happen to people who work in shops, manufacturing, and even services?

Employment: The Pressures on the Workplace

In the face of all this technology, what of us mere human workers? There are a number of trends impacting on the workplace over the coming decades. Technology is only one of them, alongside major shifts in demographics, motivation, mobility, and the kind of work we will be doing.

The millennial generation best exemplifies the early twenty-first-century workplace. The "digital natives" will shape the workforce as the century evolves, with limited or nonexistent loyalty to any one employer, expectation of more than one career path, prioritization of development and work-life balance over finances, and a preference to communicate electronically rather than face-to-face. Equally, their focus on ethical business and social and environmental responsibility is going to put businesses under pressure to live up to their sustainable and ethical demands, both as employees and as consumers.

Yet by 2025 the over-65s will be the fastest-growing demographic group on earth, making for a uniquely multigenerational workforce. While most people expect to retire by 65 years of age, a lack of planning and pressure on state pensions may force many baby boomers to stay in the workforce longer than expected. Employers are going to have to grapple with the complexities of the multigenerational workforce. At the same time, the baby boomers' purchasing power offers enormous potential for companies to provide unique, targeted goods, services, and experiences catering to their requirements, particularly around healthcare.

Organizations too must face the rise and rise of entrepreneurship and free agency, putting their offerings of "traditional" employment under pressure. The entrepreneurs and free agents of today and tomorrow are young, increasingly female, and are launching businesses because of financial necessity, or to sidestep the "decaying social contract" between employer and employee. Entrepreneurship is particularly popular in rapid growth markets, with the percentage of people aged 18 to 64 establishing new businesses at 27 percent in sub-Saharan Africa, 19 percent in Latin America, and 12 percent in Asia-Pacific, compared with only 8 percent in Europe.

Similarly, a lot of people who were earlier available for traditional full-time jobs now prefer free agency. Consider Uber. Uber neither employs any drivers nor owns any cars, yet it is one of the largest taxi companies in the world today. An Uber driver:

- Decides when he wants to work and when not. If it is his partner's birthday in the middle of the week, he has the option of not taking a customer and taking his partner out to lunch instead. He blends work-life boundaries rather than "managing" them.

- Realizes that her income depends directly on how much she drives.
- Realizes that the continuation of his contract with Uber depends largely on the customer ratings he gets after each ride. In other words, he must self-manage performance on the job.
- Has the flexibility of switching to another mobile app–based taxi company if offered a better deal, or working with more than one company at the same time.
- Knows that with technology-enabled infrastructure (Internet-enabled home office, Wi-Fi enabled coffee shops, 24-hour print and copy shops, reasonably rentable executive suites, and overnight delivery services), she has the perfect self-employment ecosystem at her disposal, allowing her to offer her services to businesses other than taxi operations. It is now possible to be an Uber driver, an Instacart shopper, a paid blogger, and an Airbnb host at the same time. In other words, she has discovered the joys of being a free agent.

Traditional full-time employers have historically found it hard to provide much freedom to their people. The more companies grew in size, the more rules and policies they introduced. In today's free agent gig economy, they will need to rethink this traditional approach and invent ways to make full-time employment as attractive, if not more so, than free agency. I will return to this need with concrete suggestions in several chapters starting with Chapter 2.

Mobility and the Shift from West to East

Western countries may try to fill gaps in their workforce by recruiting from the East. The exponential rise in tertiary education across the developing world has created a new class of young, highly skilled workers who are interested in seeking opportunities outside of their home countries—we'll explore this more when discussing the global population explosion. That said, it doesn't mean that young workers will immediately look to the West, but may instead look to their own home countries as their economies continue to boom.

That young workers are looking to their home countries rather than to the West is indicative of another huge trend. The gulf between mature and developing economies is predicted to shrink. Growth in key developing markets is expected to taper but remain strong, as in China (+5.9 percent), India (+6.7 percent) and sub-Saharan Africa (+5.8 percent). In particular, the growth of the middle class in these markets will increase their consumer power and these formerly "developing nations" will instead become hubs for global business. By 2025 the cost of manufacturing goods in China is predicted to be the same as that of the United States. Manufacturers will need to look further afield for cheap, low-skilled labor, moving the manufacturing bases to the next tier of developing economies in Africa, the Middle East, and South America.

The trend in mobility will also manifest in a way that we've already mentioned. The increasing sophistication and complexity of mobile technology is predicted to produce more efficient ways of collaborating remotely. An estimated 60 percent of the U.S. workforce today works in a role where physical location is no longer relevant. Additionally, almost 50 percent of managers in the United States, United Kingdom, and Germany are allowed to work remotely. This will only keep growing.

New Work

Finally, the sweeping change in our economic and social lives is going to change the very work that we do. Many of the jobs that people will be doing in 5 to 10 years don't currently exist, and 475 occupations in advanced countries are at risk of being automated in the next 20 years. An example of this new world of occupations is the data scientist, a role that was only coined in 2008 when organizations began to deal with the information generated by online technology. Businesses are drowning in data they have no idea how to interpret, and the data scientist was created to fill a previously unrealized need.

As we have seen, technology has reduced the need for actual human workers. While manufacturing still accounts for 30 percent of U.S. GDP, the number of Americans actually employed in the sector has declined dramatically as automation has taken over. It reflects the same trend in agriculture, where technology has hastened the end of the small family farm and the rise of industrial scale farms that require few, if any, human workers. Services are already being moved offshore, or automated through apps, software, or online tools. This raises a crucial question that must be answered: How can workers prepare themselves to work in jobs that might not yet exist?

Uber-Population

The Earth is experiencing a population explosion. This exponential rise in human life is a testament to the advances in healthcare and standards of living over the last century, but it also carries profound implications for the way we live now, and the way we must live in the future.

The soaring population offers both exciting opportunities and daunting challenges. On one hand, a growing global population offers companies new markets to grow their businesses, and an abundance of talented people to hire. On the other, resource depletion and the threat of climate change will disrupt how we manufacture, transport, and consume goods and services. It is worth exploring the complexities of the population explosion in greater depth, before outlining how the leadership of our organizations must adjust to take advantage of the best and mitigate the worst of this rapid change.

The Population Explosion

In 1804, global population reached one billion for the first time. Only 205 years later, Earth's population reached seven billion, with much of that growth occurring since 1960. The Earth's population is estimated to hit nine billion by 2050, with the majority of growth expected in Africa and East Asia. The Indian subcontinent will jump from 1.6 billion people (2014) to 2.2 billion in (2050), and sub-Saharan Africa from 899 million (2014) to 2.2 billion (2050). Countries like Yemen, Somalia, Nigeria, Pakistan, and Bangladesh are anticipated to see the most growth, and in 2028 India will overtake China as the most populous country in the world. In contrast, the West is likely to see modest growth, or even population shrinkage.

Population models had until recently assumed that the global population would peak at nine billion midcentury and then decline. However, a 2014 report by the United Nations Population Division and the University of Washington (Seattle) instead found that world population stabilization was unlikely in the twenty-first century. Their analysis suggested that the population would instead reach 10.9 billion in 2100. Asia was likely to remain the most populous continent, but the main driver of this growth would be Africa.

Running parallel is the expectation that the majority of individuals across the globe will be urban. Currently 54 percent of the global population lives in cities, expected to rise to 66 percent by 2050. Again, the vast majority of urban growth over the next 20 years will occur in Africa and Asia, while 122 of the 750 current biggest cities in Europe, Japan, and China will shrink by midcentury.

The impact of this increasing urbanization is mixed. Cities use a disproportionate amount of natural resources to function.

The infrastructure upgrades and construction needed to cope with the influx of people will be enormous. In addition, while urbanization offers many rural dwellers the possibility of a better life, for many the move is harsh. In 2014, nearly one billion people lived in urban slums, bearing the brunt of traffic congestion, air pollution, crime, unsafe water, and inadequate sanitation. These hopeless living conditions have the potential to erupt into social unrest.

Yet it is also important to acknowledge that the population explosion and urbanization has birthed a young, educated, and productive labor force. This burgeoning middle class is the result of agricultural and economic policies since the 1970s that have pulled millions out of extreme poverty and given young people in developing countries access to higher education. From 1990 to 2010 the gross enrollment ratio in tertiary education globally rose from 13.6 to 29.2 percent.

The Population Explosion and the War for Talent

So, what does this mean? The population explosion is going to increase the global pool of skilled workers, but will this actually have a positive impact on the war for talent, or just take the battle international?

In recent years, the portion of young people with a tertiary education has grown significantly, particularly in the West. However, this is counterbalanced by two factors: one, that Western populations are predicted to stagnate or shrink, and two, the rapid economic growth of emerging markets. As these markets move from low-cost manufacturing to skills-based economies, they will compete with the established Western multinationals for their own skilled workers.

China is a case in point. Between 1979 and 2014, China's annual real GDP grew nearly 10 percent, representing a massive global economic shift, and hauling 679 million people out of extreme poverty. China's economic growth was based on a manufacturing boom, predicated on the surplus of low-cost labor. In 2010 China overtook the United States as the world's largest manufacturer (on a gross value added basis), and in 2015 it was named by the IMF as the number one economic superpower in the world.

However, China's demographics and role as the "world's factory" are changing. From 2005 to 2014 Chinese wages rose by 309 percent, and by 2014 were at $763 per month (or 72.2 percent higher than Mexico). It is no longer "cheap China"; a Booz & Co. study in 2010 found that 83 percent of companies located their manufacturing in China for access to the large, educated, urbanized middle class consumer market, rather than for low-cost labor. Demand for workers is now outstripping supply, particular for young talented managers in Chinese and multinational organizations. In addition, the rise of Chinese organizations like Huawei and Haier, alongside prominent Chinese banks, are making skilled workers question whether working at the Chinese subsidiary of a Western business is actually better than working at the headquarters of a multinational Chinese-owned business.

It's a trend likely to repeat in other emerging markets, although the situation is more complex. At present, Bangladesh, Kenya, Morocco, and Nigeria will contribute a third of the estimated growth in the labor force, and currently supply greater numbers of college-educated workers than can be employed in local industries. Yet these are also important new markets for multinational companies, and increased foreign investment, entrepreneurship, and growing industry will close the talent gap.

It's worth noting, too, that increased population does not necessarily mean an increase in the kind of skills that employers are seeking. What it does mean is that employers will ratchet up the battle over those workers who do exhibit those skills, and that uber-connectivity will enable them to source talent from wherever it exists.

The Impact on Resources

While this book focuses on personal and organizational leadership rather than the environment, it is important to provide a quick outline of the impacts of the population boom on our natural world. The predicted scarcities make for alarming reading, and underscore the need for new ways of looking at and leading through the twenty-first century.

Since 1980 collective human demands on our natural resources provided by the planet have exceeded the Earth's regenerative capacity by 30 percent. This is particularly marked in the resources we use to feed, water, and warm ourselves, and is predicted to only get worse as the population grows. Water is the greatest concern. As a species, we drink on average four liters of water per person per day, but the food we eat requires 2,000 liters of water per day to produce. During the last half of the twentieth century the irrigated land used for food production tripled, which in turned tripled the amount of grain produced—70 percent of which is used for livestock feed. Clearly, this growth is unsustainable.

At present 18 countries, making up half the world's population, are pumping water over and above levels that can be replenished. These countries include India, China, the United States, Iran, Pakistan, and Mexico. According to the World Bank, 175 million Indians (15 percent of the population) are being fed with grain produced with unsustainably sourced water. This has grave implications for both food production and prices. More than one commentator has mentioned the likelihood of "water wars" as a result of shortages. In India, the states of Tamil Nadu and Karnataka are already fighting over the Cauvery River, while Punjabi landowners have used bulldozers to sabotage an unfinished canal designed to take water from the Sutlej River to Haryana.

Alongside water scarcity, land use is of concern. Just as harvests are shrinking in some countries due to water depletion, they are shrinking as a result of land overuse and soil erosion. Countries including Mongolia, Lesotho, northwest China, and the Sahel in Africa are developing into "dust bowls." Demand for agricultural land is predicted to double at least by 2050, and triple by 2100, ratcheting up pressure to clear some of the world's last remaining forests and rainforests. Roughly 20 percent of the Amazon rainforest has been cleared for soybean farming and cattle ranching, with another 22 percent weakened by logging and road building. Clearing or weakening half the Amazon rainforest may be the tipping point after which the remainder of the rainforest cannot be saved, also releasing roughly the equivalent of 15 years of human induced carbon emissions into the atmosphere.

Despite the numbers of people pulled out of extreme poverty in the second half of the twentieth century, the number of extremely poor in Asia, the Middle East, and Africa actually rose by 130 million between 2005 and 2009, and the number of malnourished people rose to over 1 billion. These alarming statistics are at least in part the result of the massive diversion of grain to fuel the ethanol industry.

At the same time 80 percent of the world's oceanic fisheries are being fished at or beyond their sustainable yields. While solutions including fish farming have been mooted, they also come with an environmental cost and require yet more land and water to produce the soy and cornmeal used as fish food. At present, we have no known way of providing food for the estimated nine billion residents of Earth by 2050, based on current land usage.

Finally, our energy use is scheduled to skyrocket. By the end of the twenty-first century we will need to triple energy production to meet demand at current rates. According to *The Guardian* columnist George Monbiot, this translates into 23,000 new nuclear power stations, 1,800 more of the world's largest dams, and 14 million wind turbines. Monbiot also notes that our urban transport needs will similarly rise, which not only increases air pollution and our demand for cheap oil, but may also increase the chances of the quick spread of pathogens and pandemics.

Our Unsustainable Economic Model

Clearly, the challenges of the future will require new ways of leadership. In light of the grim predictions of our resource-scarce, highly populated future, is it now relevant to reconsider the economic system that has got us here?

In his book *Consumptionomics* (2011), Chandran Nair argues that the adoption of the Western model of consumption by the developing world is impossible to achieve without ruining the planet in the process. He believes that Asia in particular must model new ways of living that place resource sustainability and care at the heart of government policy. To be effective, organizations must be forced to account for the cost of resources in their financial results.

Nair was inspired to write *Consumptionomics* following the 2008 financial crisis, when Asian consumers were encouraged to spend their way out of the Western-fueled recession to drive up global demand. At the same time the 2009 Copenhagen Climate Conference was highlighting the unsustainability of Western-style consumption. Nair recognized the disconnect: if the environment is in near-calamity due to Western consumption habits, what will happen when China, India, and the rest of Asia's middle class start living the same way, let alone the growing populations in Africa? He also recognized that Asia will bear much of the brunt of any potential environmental disasters, including rising sea levels, flooding, and water, air, and land pollution.

Nair uses poultry to demonstrate the potential impact. As observed in 2011, Americans eat nine billion birds per year, while Asia (with a population 13 times the size) eats 16 billion birds annually. If Asia followed American consumption patterns, the continent would consume 150 billion birds each year by 2050, with associated pressure on land, water, and grain requirements.

Using industrial capitalism's economic and technological tools to solve the world's climate and environmental problems will not work, because they focus on maintaining the system that caused the problem in the first place. Economic models to "fix" or mitigate climate change, including cap and trade and carbon credits, have roundly failed or been exploited and ignore the fact that climate change is not a static problem. The population is growing, consumption of natural resources is increasing, and economic schemes that strive to maintain the status quo in the face of these ecological pressures miss the point entirely.

Technology might offer some solutions, but it is more often used to justify things remaining the same. Take cars in China. In 1990 China's car industry produced only a few hundred thousand vehicles per year, yet by 2009 it passed the United States to become the world's largest car market, with 13 million vehicles sold. The U.S. Department of Energy estimates that in the late 2020s China will have around 330 million cars on the road, and anywhere between 470 and 660 million by 2050. Clearly the fuel requirements for running this fleet are enormous, not to mention the impact on air quality, infrastructure, and urban congestion. While the growth of zero emission vehicles is posited as an answer to the problems caused by this surge in traffic, it ignores the glaring fact that even zero emission cars must be built, fueled, and driven on congested roads. Technological advances themselves may be part of the problem. High-speed financial transactions fuel growth in consumption by offering consumers new ways of spending. This financial speed "accelerates the speed at which decisions can be taken to exploit resources," without consideration of the true costs.

Consumptionomics makes the case that the West can also afford to have a fundamentally different attitude to climate change, in the context of the shrinking Western population. Nair uses the equation I = PAT, in which Impact on environment = Population size + Affluence + Technology, or the level of environmental impact per unit of spending (the equation was first formulated in the 1970s by Paul Ehrlich and John Holdren). The West can focus almost solely on adjusting T, in the context of a stable or shrinking P, to maintain the existing level of A. Technology is the easy fix to lower the environmental impact given the stability of the rest of the equation.

The developing world doesn't have this luxury. Grappling with the desire to emulate Western affluence alongside a skyrocketing population, it is impossible to lower T through short-term technological fixes alone. This explains why Western solutions to environmental problems are so ineffective in the developing world. They are based on an industrialized model that fails to account for the differences in context.

It is clear that tackling the challenges imposed by the population explosion and seizing the opportunities it entails will require leaders of deep emotional strength and vision. As we will discuss later in the book, creating and implementing transformative change will come up against intractable and fierce resistance.

Where Do We Go from Here?

As I see it, both exciting opportunities and daunting challenges are unfolding at an unprecedented scale as we speak. I am no expert in connectivity, population explosion, or climate change. My aim in this chapter was neither to predict future megatrends nor prove that climate change is real. Instead, by summarizing what is going on around us, I wanted to contextualize the environment in which we live and work today, and raise a few questions:

• Are our career development and leadership models adequate for personal, organizational, and global success going forward?

- Have our business leadership and management practices kept pace with the rate of social and business change?

The answer to both questions, unfortunately, is a big *no*. Our management models are designed to manage the workers of over a century ago. The majority of current management tools, including task design, pay-for-performance, divisionalization, and task management were all invented in the first part of the twentieth century. While there has been modification on the fringes, the pace of evolution of management theory has slowed markedly over the last 50 to 60 years, just as the pace of change of technology, society, and work has ramped up. We need to develop new management strategies that not only reflect the workplace of today, but have the flexibility to adjust to the rapidly changing work of tomorrow. Specifically, we must look at both personal and organizational leadership frameworks as they exist today and devise new, open source paradigms to replace them.

Personal Leadership in the Open Source Twenty-First Century

To lead businesses in these complex yet exciting times will demand a new style of leadership that speaks directly to changing trends and is brave enough to leave behind outdated management dogma. Leaders in this new world will require a strength of vision and emotional resilience far beyond what is popularized in current leadership models taught at most business schools.

Leading the Organization in the Open Source Twenty-First Century

Thanks to uber-connectivity and uber-population, organizations are now in competition with approximately 7.5 billion people across the globe who are empowered by technology and driven by speed. Surviving and thriving in the open source era will require the full energy and imagination of all employees. Traditional "carrot and stick" methodologies will not work.

The shift in economic power from West to East and rapid-growth economies, the democratization of knowledge, and the ever-increasing pace of change means that competitive advantage is rarely found and quickly lost. Individuals and organizations will not only need to keep up with the Joneses, but to get there first. Organizations will only thrive if they can find new ways of sourcing innovation, at ever-faster speeds. Old-style, in-house innovation labs will no longer be enough. Fortunately, the population explosion alongside the possibilities of globalized communication means that organizations have greater access to potential innovators than ever before, should they find effective ways of tapping into it.

Likewise, developing the leaders of tomorrow will become even more important than ever before. Here again, traditional models of succession planning will need to give way to open source methods.

Over the next five chapters I will look at these challenges in greater detail and propose new and sometimes counterintuitive ways for organizations to adjust and thrive. There are no half measures. We've seen the scale of change to our lives and our work over the last century and can only begin to imagine the changes we will see in the future. This demands bold and unconventional thinking. In the next two chapters we will establish a much-needed redefinition of personal leadership in the context of the open source era. To begin with, in Chapter 2 let's take a look at what leadership style will be best suited for these times.

CHAPTER SUMMARY

- We now live and work in the open source era where everyone and everything is connected, ordinary people are highly empowered, and leaders stand completely exposed and naked.
- Uber-connectivity and uber-population are the two megatrends shaping the twenty-first century.
- Implantable technology, driverless cars, robots, IoT, big data, and 3D printing are just some of the ways in which life will change in the coming years.
- Digital natives will drive and shape economies.
- Digital natives prefer free agency over full-time employment. They have much more freedom and flexibility compared to their parents and grandparents.
- Many more traditional jobs will disappear, but plenty of new jobs will also be created.
- Global population will hit nine billion by 2050, creating huge pressure on natural resources such as food and water.
- If the Western model of consumption-led growth is replicated in Asia and Africa, it will lead to disastrous consequences for planet Earth and generations to come.
- We need new and bold forms of leadership to tackle both daunting challenges and exciting opportunities posed by the open source twenty-first century.

Questions for Reflection

1. In what ways is my business or profession changing?

2. What might replace my job or business in the near future?

3. What steps can I take now to remain viable?

PART 2

Open Source Personal Leadership

CHAPTER 2

The Naked Autocrat Creates Breakthrough Results

CONTEXT

1. The Open Source Era

OPEN SOURCE PERSONAL LEADERSHIP

2. The Naked Autocrat Creates Breakthrough Results
3. Leadership Energy, Not Competencies

OPEN SOURCE ENTERPRISE LEADERSHIP

4. Minimum Supervision, Maximum Performance
5. No More Engagement Surveys
6. Crowdsourced Innovation and Leadership Succession

In Chapter 1, I outlined a new landscape of work and life. Over the next three chapters starting with this one, I raise the questions:

- What kind of personal leadership is best suited for the open source era?
- Will traditional frameworks of personal leadership still enable success today and tomorrow?

Perhaps the biggest inconvenient truth of the current times is this: we've been idealizing democratic and all-inclusive leadership far too much, when the need of the hour is—and always has been—autocratic, top-down leadership.

If you're like most people, your first reaction to this statement is probably one of disbelief and even disgust. Having seen what the likes of Stalin, Hitler, Idi Amin, and others did during their dictatorial reigns, how could anyone say something like this? Allow me to explain.

As we've said all along, speed is everything today. It is no longer enough to have great innovations and ideas. Individuals and organizations must also move at lightning speed to implement them before someone else does. The cost of not moving fast enough is death. Consider Kodak. In 1998 Kodak had 170,000 employees and sold 85 percent of all the photo paper consumed worldwide. Within three years, its business model was obsolete and the company went bankrupt. In his thought-provoking LinkedIn post, Marco Ronnie Seiler, a hotelier with 20-plus years of global leadership experience, asserts that what happened to Kodak will happen to many more companies over the next 10 years, and at a pace faster than ever before. "Did you think in 1998 that three years later you would never take pictures on paper film again?" he asks. What's sad about Kodak is not just that it did not respond fast enough to a changing world. The worst part is that the digital camera itself was invented at

Eastman Kodak by Steven J. Sasson in 1975! The first camera had only 10,000 pixels and shot black-and-white photos that took 23 seconds to capture. While the first camera was initially a commercial disappointment, it eventually followed Moore's Law (that digital processing speeds will double every two years) and became mainstream in just a few short years.

As Seiler rightly points out in his post, the same phenomenon is about to happen to artificial intelligence, healthcare, cars and transportation, 3D printing, and jobs. "Welcome to the fourth industrial revolution," he says. Artificial intelligence is already helping computers beat the best chess and Go players in the world. IBM Watson is now helping diagnose cancer with an accuracy four times greater than human nurses. By 2020 you may no longer need to own a car at all, because you will be able to call one on your phone whenever you need one. Our kids might never need a driver's license. Insurance will become one hundred times cheaper with far fewer accidents. In a few years, a medical device called the Tricorder X will work with your phone to take your retina scan, blood sample, and breath to analyze 54 biomarkers to identify almost any disease. Ultimately, Seiler says, "if you think of a niche you want to go in, ask yourself, *in the future, do you think we will have that?* If the answer is yes, how can you make that happen sooner? If it doesn't work with your phone, forget the idea. And any idea designed for success in the twentieth century is doomed to failure in the twenty-first century."

John Chambers of Cisco agrees. In his 2016 *Fortune* article "How to Get on the Right Side of the Digital Divide," he argues that unless countries act fast enough to accelerate growth, they risk falling into a long-cycle recession. He asserts that countries that "get" digitization—the intelligent connection of people, process, data, and things—will thrive in terms of innovation, competitiveness, and job creation. He claims that while most world leaders are tackling symptoms such as trade and tax policies, those that are getting it right are focusing on the core issue of digitization. He cites France as an example, which has an impressive plan to transform into a digital republic by creating 1.1 million digital jobs between 2017 and 2019, and $719 billion in GDP growth by 2026. He also cites leaders in Israel, India, the United Kingdom, Germany, and the Middle East as other examples of people who "get it" and are building massive digital ecosystems for growth. "In India, Prime Minister Narendra Modi is working to build architectures that can support the Digital India vision, which leverages information and communication technology to deliver citizen services, virtual education, remote healthcare, and more. If that vision is successfully implemented, India will completely transform the way governments, citizens, and businesses interact, creating unprecedented economic value," Chambers says.

With the world changing as fast as we speak, how can anyone afford to be slow and still thrive? This brings us back to the question of democratic versus autocratic and top-down leadership. Will the time-consuming democratic consensus process deliver what is needed, fast enough? Or do we need something that provides faster results?

Typically, if we ask someone what kind of boss he or she would like to work for—a democratic or autocratic one—the most likely answer will be the former. However, history shows that people love working for and admire autocratic top-down leaders. Take just a few examples: Walt Disney, Henry Ford, Steve Jobs, John Chambers, Lee Kuan Yew, Nelson Mandela, and Mahatma Gandhi. According to Vivek Wadhwa, Disney, Ford, Jobs, and Chambers were all autocrats. Wadhwa is Distinguished Fellow at Carnegie Mellon University's College of Engineering, and has held positions at Stanford Law School, UC Berkley, Harvard Law School, and Emory University. In his 2016 *Washington Post* article he describes them as follows:

- *Walt Disney would ask employees for their ideas through surveys but would then dictate his requirements. When employees didn't perform, he would fire them immediately. He had a clear vision, was coherent and moral, and demanding. Disney did end up becoming excessively autocratic and losing touch with what made him successful. Yet he touched the hearts and minds of billions all over the world and created one of the greatest companies of its time.*

- *Henry Ford was known as a tough leader who had a hand in every major decision. He was so demanding of his employees that he monitored their activities outside of work. He was, however, resolute in vision. Ford defied his investors when they demanded he build a car for the wealthy, and increased average wages to $5 a day while reducing the work day to eight hours. He ended up revolutionizing transportation and setting new standards for the workplace.*

- *Steve Jobs ruled with an iron fist and demanded absolute secrecy and loyalty from his employees. He was egotistical and moody. Yet Jobs had a brilliant vision, unwavering determination, and uncanny understanding of what consumers wanted. He built the world's most valuable company and set new standards for technology design.*

- *The greatest technology innovator of today, Elon Musk, is a highly imperfect human being who makes extreme demands and sets unrealistic public deadlines for his employees. Yet he is single-handedly changing several industries—including space, energy, and transportation.*

- *Leaders need to step aside when they have peaked, as Cisco CEO John Chambers did last year. He too was an autocrat who said to the* New York Times *"I'm a command-and-control person. I like being able to say turn right, and we truly have 67,000 people turn right."*

Why do so many people continue to willingly work at Disney, Ford, Apple, Tesla, and Cisco? How did these leaders create so much value, even while they were autocratic? Similarly, why did the people of Singapore listen to and willingly follow their nation's founder and first prime minister Lee Kuan Yew, even though he was well known for his autocratic style of leadership? Why did the people of South Africa, who were thirsty for blood and revenge, instead listen to Nelson Mandela when he preached forgiveness and reconciliation? In Clint Eastwood's 2009 movie *Invictus*, a pivotal scene depicts Mandela's autocratic leadership style very well. On finding out that the black-dominated South African Sports Committee had decided to change the name of the national rugby team from Springboks to something else, and to drop the green and gold colors of their uniform, Mandela (played by Morgan Freeman) cuts short a meeting with foreign delegates and rushes to the sports committee meeting venue to successfully persuade the group to change their decision. Even though the group had just voted unanimously to remove the "symbols of apartheid" from rugby, why did they listen to him and reverse their decision? And why did the people of India follow Gandhi even though his nonviolent path to independence differed significantly from the popular desire to fight the British with guns and knives?

Looking at these and countless other examples over the years started me thinking. Is democratic leadership really as effective as it is made out to be in leadership literature? Ask any leader who has ever come up with a radically different vision for the future, and he or she will tell you how hard it was to implement it. All you get is resistance. With that in mind, and with breakneck speed all around, does one then risk missing the bus by spending precious time on consensus building? And if it is indeed true that democratic inclusion is the best form of leadership, then how do the above examples from history fit in? Could it be true that to drive breakthrough change, autocratic leadership was always needed, and that today's breakneck speed has simply amplified the need?

To find out, my colleagues and I designed a research experiment conducted in 28 countries covering approximately 16,000 senior and mid-level executives. Rather than simply asking up front which leadership style respondents felt was more effective, we decided to give them something to think about first. We provided a list of famous leaders comprising Aung San Suu Kyi, Jack Ma, Steve Jobs, Abraham Lincoln, Nelson Mandela, Mahatma Gandhi, and Lee Kuan Yew, and asked them to identify what they had in common. From a list of 11 leadership behaviors, we wanted them to choose the top three commonalities. Five of the 11 behaviors were democratic and all-inclusive, five were top-down and autocratic, and one was a mix of both. In our questionnaire, the behaviors were mixed up in one list and were not labeled as one or the other, but for ease of reference here, I have marked them with a *D* for Democratic or *T* for Top-Down/Bold:

1. Used a democratic style of leadership to achieve their vision—D
2. Took incremental steps to cautiously implement their vision—D
3. Dared to be different and willing to challenge general opinion—T
4. Enlisted everyone's approval and acceptance of an idea before moving ahead—D
5. Were bold risk-takers that pursued unpopular or unconventional ideas to break new ground—T
6. Remained firm in their course of action despite setback and resistance—T
7. Envisioned audacious ideas that didn't yet exist to create a better world—T
8. Listened to find middle ground in the face of opposing viewpoints to preserve harmony—D

9. Had long-lasting energy to see their plans through without giving up amidst challenges—T
10. Relied on consensus and support from others to make a difference—D
11. Listened to the views of others but made their own decisions of what is right—D + T

In country after country, the T behaviors were most frequently selected as the top three commonalities. There were no significant differences by country.[*] Figure 2.1 shows how they stacked up.

Next, we asked the same question in reference to today's business leaders. We asked respondents to tell us what today's business leaders need to do most in order to drive breakthrough success. We gave respondents the same list of 11 behaviors and asked them to rank order them in the same way as the previous question. Again, the T behaviors dominated the top of the list, as shown in Figure 2.2.

Finally, we asked an agree/disagree question. We asked respondents to indicate their level of agreement with the statement: "In order to drive unprecedented success for the organization in today's fast paced environment, a significant amount of top-down leadership is required." Seventy five percent of our global respondents agreed or strongly agreed (Figure 2.3).

While we had a hunch that respondents might admire top-down autocratic leadership (even though they might think otherwise), we were surprised by the one-sidedness of the data. For example, we had expected to see some differences by country, gender, and age group. But no, each country, gender, and age group consistently returned the same results. Figure 2.4 shows the extent of agreement with the need for top-down leadership by country.

---

[*] See Appendix for country by country snapshots and an overall description of the research methodology.

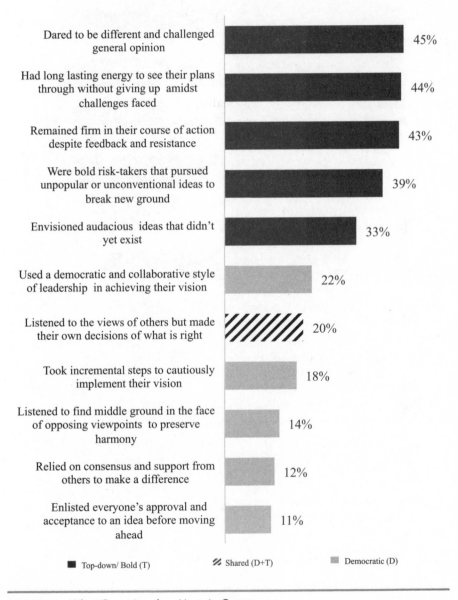

FIGURE 2.1   What Great Leaders Have in Common

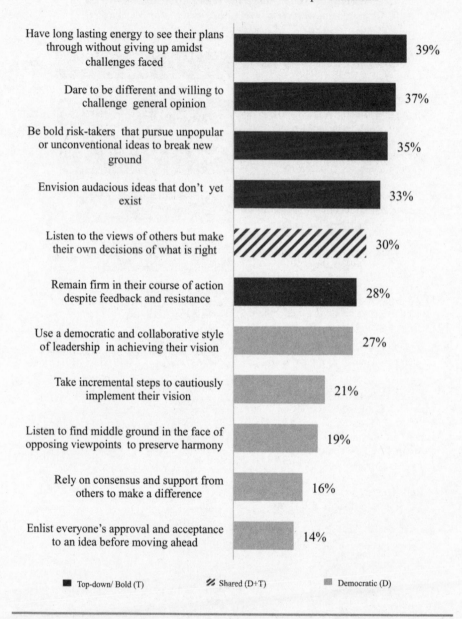

In order to drive unprecedented success in today's fast paced environment, business leaders most need to... Top 3 Statements

Have long lasting energy to see their plans through without giving up amidst challenges faced — 39%

Dare to be different and willing to challenge general opinion — 37%

Be bold risk-takers that pursue unpopular or unconventional ideas to break new ground — 35%

Envision audacious ideas that don't yet exist — 33%

Listen to the views of others but make their own decisions of what is right — 30%

Remain firm in their course of action despite feedback and resistance — 28%

Use a democratic and collaborative style of leadership in achieving their vision — 27%

Take incremental steps to cautiously implement their vision — 21%

Listen to find middle ground in the face of opposing viewpoints to preserve harmony — 19%

Rely on consensus and support from others to make a difference — 16%

Enlist everyone's approval and acceptance to an idea before moving ahead — 14%

■ Top-down/ Bold (T)   ▨ Shared (D+T)   ▨ Democratic (D)

FIGURE 2.2 What Business Leaders Most Need to Do

In order to drive unprecedented success for the organization in today's fast paced environment, a significant amount of top-down leadership is required. To what extent do you agree with this statement?

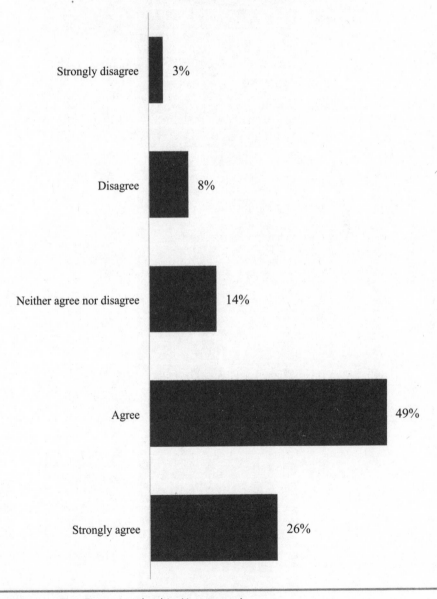

FIGURE 2.3 Top-Down Leadership (Aggregate)

In order to drive unprecedented success for the organization in today's fast paced environment, a significant amount of top-down leadership is required. To what extent do you agree with this statement?

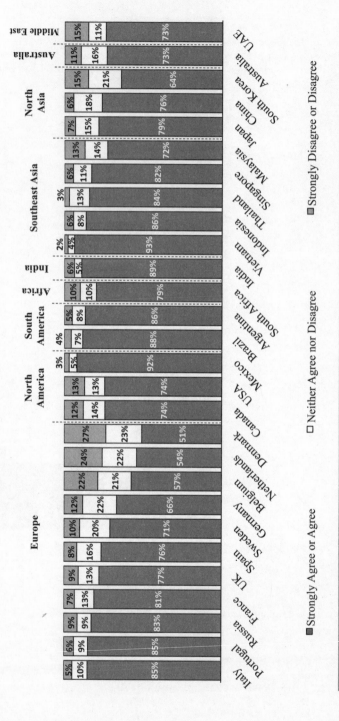

FIGURE 2.4 Top-Down Leadership (by Country)

The data was collected and analyzed independently by Kadence International, a reputable market research organization. Appendix 1 outlines the research methodology and provides an overview of the data by country.

Of course, acknowledging this data causes more problems than it solves. When we shared the first cut with our colleagues, several concerns emerged. "Are we now promoting autocratic leadership?" asked one. "Will this data be misunderstood, and will it give bosses license to justify their dictatorial behavior?" asked another. As we grappled with these concerns, another big question emerged: *In today's day and age when ordinary people are so empowered and bosses completely exposed and naked, is it even possible to lead with an autocratic style?*

It became obvious that we needed to understand the data more deeply, and tread carefully. With recording devices in their pockets, and social media reach at their fingertips, most people are more empowered than ever before. They can expose any and every action of their bosses at the drop of a hat. In the old days, it was easy for bosses to deny having said or done anything that was regrettable. Today, it is almost impossible. One simply needs to look at electoral politics as an example. The 2016 U.S. presidential election is an excellent case in point. There was no shortage of video clips and other fact-checking devices that made it impossible for Hillary Clinton or Donald Trump to deny their actions or misspoken words. Both stood completely exposed throughout their campaigns. In this environment, how can anyone get away with autocratic leadership? Yet, the data strongly suggests that it is the need of the hour. Welcome to the twenty-first-century leadership dilemma!

In the past, dictators and autocrats could use their authority and power to do what they wanted. It is becoming increasingly impossible to do so in the open source era. India Against Corruption, the 2010 grassroots movement created and led by ordinary citizens in India, shook the ruling Congress government and changed the country's political landscape once and for all. Until then, corruption was accepted as part of life and political leaders were seldom questioned. The power of the crowd made it very clear that from then on, corrupt leaders were on notice, and people demand higher standards of integrity from their leaders.

Former Uber engineer Susan J. Fowler's now famous February 2017 blog about rampant sexual harassment prompted NDTV.com to post a Bloomberg story with the headline "Uber CEO, with Tears in His Eyes, Apologizes for Company Culture." In the same month, a video posted by a driver who was berated by the CEO went viral, causing Uber even more PR trouble.

In April 2017, United Airlines had David Dao, a 69-year-old Kentucky physician, physically dragged off a plane upon his refusal to be bumped off due to overbooking. Almost immediately after the incident, videos of the incident recorded by passengers on their cell phones went viral, causing United one of its worst reputational disasters and costing the CEO his chairmanship.

The examples of Uber and United Airlines above, and the 2011 Arab Spring that toppled several totalitarian regimes in the Middle East, are great reminders of how vulnerable leaders, governments, and businesses are today. It is clear that using force or position power might not even be an option anymore. Yet, our data and practical experience strongly suggests that in order to drive breakthrough results in today's age of speed, top-down autocratic leadership is indeed required. So, what do we make of this strange paradox? The answer to this question lies in getting back to the question I raised earlier about Lee Kuan Yew, Mandela, and Gandhi. Why did their people listen to and follow them despite their autocratic behaviors? What was the difference between them and ruthless dictators like Hitler and Stalin?

Lee Kuan Yew, Mandela, and Gandhi practiced a form of autocratic leadership that was actually net positive. They realized that in their positions, every step they took and every word they uttered was in full public view. In this sense, they were naked and scrutinized by people 24/7. As leaders, on one hand they wanted people to like and respect them; on the other they knew hard decisions were needed to create a better future for all. So, they had to master the dance of the naked autocrat, which I explain below.

Five Keys to Positive Autocratic Leadership

In the open source era, leaders can apply autocratic leadership by practicing the following principles toward positive autocracy:

1. Earn the Right to Use Autocratic Leadership

Lee Kuan Yew, Mandela, and Gandhi were true leaders according to the definition and criteria of real leadership we discussed briefly in the Introduction and will revisit in detail in the next chapter. They wanted to build better futures for their people. The key word is *better*. They had tremendous leadership energy that was derived from a values-based purpose. People deeply believed that the three of them were each working solely to create a better future. Singaporeans were willing to forgo some liberties because they strongly believed that Lee Kuan Yew had their best interest at heart. So great was the trust between him and his people that people allowed him to be autocratic. The case was the same with Mandela and Gandhi. In other words, unlike ruthless dictators who used force, Lee Kuan Yew, Mandela, and Gandhi had *earned the right* to use top-down, autocratic leadership.

Earlier I quoted Marco Ronnie Seiler's question, "If you think of a niche you want to go in, ask yourself: *in the future, do you think we will have that?* If the answer is yes, how can you make that happen sooner?" The first part of Seiler's question helps uncover *what* the leader should do, and that is the relatively easy part. The second part—how can you make it happen sooner—is the hard part because it deals with the *how*. To make it happen sooner, leaders needs to look in the mirror and make sure they are comfortable with their values and purpose, and if their values and purpose will resonate with people. In the open source era, leaders earn the right to use top-down leadership by getting the essence of their leadership energy right—by establishing the right values and purpose.

2. Be Autocratic About Values and Purpose While Remaining Humble, Respectful, and Considerate with People

Mandela, Gandhi, and Lee Kuan Yew each arrived at their values and purpose slowly, deliberately, and thoughtfully. In Chapter 3 we will see exactly how this is done. Because of their deliberate thoughtfulness, they were sure that they were on the right track. Gandhi decided after much careful consideration that his purpose would be to obtain India's independence from British rule, in a nonviolent way. "For this purpose, I am prepared to die, but there is no purpose for which I am prepared to kill," he would say. Mandela was sure that the better future for South Africa was possible only through forgiveness and reconciliation, not revenge and bloodshed, and was not prepared to compromise on those values under any circumstances. Lee Kuan Yew recognized that discipline was sorely needed to make Asian nations prosperous, and there was little time to lose. All three recognized that democratic leadership alone was inadequate to bring about positive change, and that a certain amount of push was needed even without consensus. Again, unlike ruthless dictators, they did not use power to force people into submission. They balanced the need for autocratic action with respect, humility, and consideration. The biggest key to their success at using autocratic leadership was that *they were autocratic about their values and purpose while being considerate, humble and respectful with their people at the same time.* It is perfectly possible to do both. As Lee Kuan Yew famously said, "If there was a good reason why it is 'no,' then it must remain a 'no,' but the man must be told politely. You lose nothing by being polite."

In fact, in today's open source era, leaders have no choice but to live their values all the time. Because leaders are held in high esteem by their followers, even one slipup is one too many. The very people that put you on a pedestal with their love and admiration bring you down ruthlessly if you betray their trust. In this sense, leaders carry a tremendous responsibility on their shoulders, and are naked. So how can they be autocratic when they are naked? The only answer is to constantly do the *naked autocrat dance* whereby one practices autocracy of values and purpose, and compassion, humility, and respect for people at the same time (Figure 2.5). This is the paradox of twenty-first century leadership, and leaders need to learn the art of finely balancing the two seeming opposites.

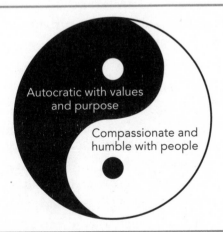

FIGURE 2.5 The Naked Autocrat Dance

3. Provide "Freedom Within a Framework"

I first heard the phrase "freedom within a framework" in 2006 at Coca-Cola where I was chief learning officer. Neville Isdell had just come back to the company from retirement with a mandate to turn the storied ship around. Given the breadth of Coke's operations, he knew he couldn't lead the turnaround with a centralized command and control strategy. He also knew that what was good for one market was not necessarily good for another country even in the same neighbourhood. Yet, he was convinced that the only way the global giant would be successful again is if the entire company adhered to some common principles. So, he laid out a broad, values-based framework, and told his top 150 people that they had full freedom within the framework. They could use whatever local strategies they needed, provided they played by and within the framework. Results were spectacular, and Coke began to get its mojo back in no time. Gandhi, Mandela, and Lee Kuan Yew practiced the idea of *freedom within a framework* too. While their values and the values-based purposes they pursued were nonnegotiable, for everything else they provided full freedom to their people. As long as the values were adhered to, how results were obtained was left to people to decide in their own way. Business leaders today need to do the same.

It is common knowledge that large companies tend to get overly bureaucratic over time. As business grows in size and scope, so does the number of employees. This growth in business and headcount highlights the need for consistent customer and employee experience, which in turn drives the formulation of internal rules, policies, processes, and procedures. Generally speaking, the larger the organization, the bigger the internal regulation or bureaucracy. Initially these rules and policies bring about a sense of order, transparency, and consistency and provide a backdrop for effective decision making and behavior. However, there comes a point when the internal bureaucracy becomes so cumbersome that the organization loses its agility and fails to innovate or respond to the market fast enough. This is because many companies, without realizing it, become too inwardly focused. While rules and policies become outdated fairly quickly, many companies are slow to update or change them in a timely manner. Eventually, many go into extinction because of this inertia; of the original Fortune 500 list published in 1955, 87 percent were gone by 2001.

In today's market, speed is everything. A key question facing large companies therefore is how to remain nimble and agile in an ever-changing landscape. While all ecosystems require some rules for effective functioning, rigid internal policies and processes get in the way of producing positive outcomes. One way to solve for this dilemma might be to lead more with values and less with rules because:

- The shelf life of values is much longer than that of rules and policies.
- Values tend to be broader than specific rules—they provide principles or guidelines for behavior rather than strict boundaries.
- A company's rules and policies usually stem from its values, or at least they should. As long as employees do not violate the values while conducting business, everything should be fine.

A simple example will illustrate the idea. A company's rule book might say that employees must show up at work punctually at 9 a.m. every day. To enforce this rule, many companies introduced the punch card system, which records arrival and departure times of employees. The same company's values might include things like:

- Think and act like an owner.
- Provide excellent customer service at all times.
- Strive for excellence to produce the best possible outcomes for the company.

It is no secret that with 24/7 connectivity, business has also become 24/7. Employees in different time zones routinely work at odd hours of the night to meet customer needs in another time zone, or to attend global conference calls. So as long as someone is living the values diligently and delivering satisfactory results, how important is the 9 a.m. punctuality rule? And what's wrong with a manager allowing his or her staff flexibility as long as there is no letup on productivity, integrity, and overall results? It is ironic that on one hand companies expect their employees to think and act like owners, yet on the other they impose rules upon rules, leaving no room for creativity.

This example uses a relatively simple issue to demonstrate the *freedom within a framework* idea, but the principle of values-based decision making and performance management can be equally applied to complex business situations. To begin with, it requires proactive focus on the part of management to make sure that the "letter of the law" quadrant (Figure 2.6) does not get too big and cumbersome over time (Figure 2.7).

In general, managers and companies will be much better off if they create a culture where the "spirit of the law" quadrant is bigger (Figure 2.8). To operationalize this, business leaders will need to sit down with their teams to evaluate the current state of play within their organizations, and figure out what actions, behaviors, and philosophy will make the "spirit of the law" box bigger. We will come back to this idea again in Chapter 4 when we discuss how to minimize supervision and maximize performance.

4. Listen, Learn, and Reflect Continuously

The work of leadership involves walking a very fine line. On one hand, the high-speed, open source era requires a significant amount of top-down, autocratic leadership. Leaders must be prepared to push hard on their vision despite initial opposition and resistance. On the other hand, too much autocracy

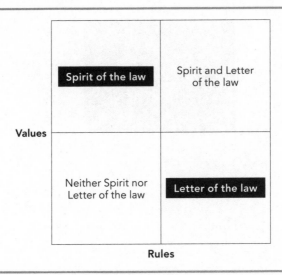

FIGURE 2.6   Rules and Values Framework

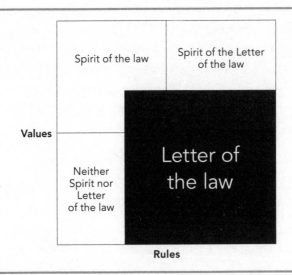

FIGURE 2.7   Restrictive Framework (Boss)

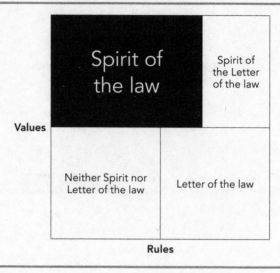

FIGURE 2.8 Freedom Within a Framework (Leader)

can make leaders blind to the changing needs of society and lead to their downfall. So, while they must practice autocratic leadership to drive results, they must make every effort to listen carefully for how things might be changing around them, and question themselves regularly about the efficacy of their values and purpose. Leaders must repeatedly and regularly ask themselves the following questions:

- Are my values still relevant in today's context?
- Will my purpose still create a better future?
- Why should I not pursue my purpose?

If, after careful listening and consideration, they remain convinced about their values and purpose, they must continue along the chosen path. But they must play devil's advocate regularly to ensure that the path is still correct. Listening with an open mind without being defensive is key here, because effective listening leads to learning. Regular effective listening either reaffirms a leader's belief in her vision, or prompts her to change or adjust it. In the open source era, leaders have a heavier onus to continue listening and learning. However, the open source era also places heavy demands on leaders' time. They are bombarded with distractions, and in this busy-ness it is easy to slip into not-listening-and-not-learning mode. To avoid this trap, leaders must make time for regular silent reflection. I know this because I have been coaching C-level executives around the world for over 20 years now. Driving in the heady fast lane of corporate business, they become too busy to take a pause and reflect. In order to keep up with their ever-increasing workload, they begin to multitask, and do with less sleep. They think they are being efficient, but often realize too late that they've made some fatal mistakes. They should talk to themselves regularly to challenge their assumptions about the better future they want to create. In Chapter 3, I will provide a framework on how to do this. The open source era enables followers to disempower leaders with the same ease with which they empower them in the first place. Only if people continue to believe in a leader's values and purpose will they allow him or her the right to top-down, autocratic leadership. To retain the right to top-down leadership, leaders need to retain the trust of their people. Only regular listening and learning combined with honest reflection can enable them to do so.

5. Forgive More Often

Leadership is about creating a better future. Holding grudges and anger creates negative energy, and bogs a leader down from her core work of creating that better future. Forgiveness, on the other hand, frees up the leader to focus on the positive work of leadership. Two quotes sum up why forgiveness is one of the most important (yet perhaps the least understood) leadership tools.

*"To forgive is to set a prisoner free and
discover that the prisoner was you."*
—LEWIS B. SMEDES

*"Forgiveness does not change the past,
but it does enlarge the future."*
—PAUL BOESE

Many examples of forgiveness abound in history, but two of the three names we've been discussing throughout this chapter stand out as those who conducted greatest acts of leadership in the twentieth century—Gandhi and Mandela. In fact, I believe they will remain evergreen examples of powerful leadership for centuries to come. While punishment and revenge have been part of the natural human condition ever since the dawn of humanity, these two men rocked the history of the world by doing the exact opposite. It takes huge courage to forgive. It is far easier to nurture anger and continue to seek revenge. Forgiveness requires one to rise above the hurt and focus on a better future. In the words of Gandhi, forgiveness is not for the weak. Only the strong can forgive. Abraham Lincoln was another leader who understood this idea very well. One of his many examples of forgiveness was appointing Edward Stanton as his Secretary of War, even though a few years earlier Stanton had insulted and humiliated Lincoln publicly. On unexpectedly seeing Lincoln in an Ohio courtroom in 1855, Stanton asked "Where did the long-armed baboon come from?" and described Lincoln as "a long, lank creature from Illinois, wearing a dirty linen duster for a coat and the back of which perspiration had splotched wide stains that resembled a map of the continent." Lincoln was then ignored and required to sit in the spectator's section of the courtroom. According to one of the Ohio lawyers, Lincoln was "pushed aside, humiliated and mortified." Yet, having been impressed by Stanton's courtroom performance, when he needed a really able Secretary of War, Lincoln had no hesitation in approaching Stanton. When criticized about his unwillingness to fight his enemies, Lincoln would say, "I destroy my enemies when I make them my friends."

In the open source era, forgiveness is more important than ever. As I've said before, in this age of speed only those who take risks and try new things will succeed. If business leaders create an environment where it is not safe to take risks, no one will try anything new, and eventually the business will suffer because of a lack of innovation. In a forgiving culture, mistakes and failures are seen as learning steps rather than acts that deserve punishment.

The five keys to positive autocratic leadership allow leaders to respond to market conditions with lightning speed to create breakthrough success. Failure to practice the five keys can easily turn autocratic leadership into a toxic dictatorship. Fortunately, the open source era has a built-in check and balance system for leaders today. Because followers and ordinary people are so connected and empowered today, leaders have no choice but to stay acutely focused on the five keys. This is why we call them *naked* autocrats rather than just autocrats. The nakedness reminds leaders of their vulnerability and keeps them honest to the ideas discussed in this chapter. This is not to suggest that bosses today don't ever cross the line toward dictatorship. They do. But the open source era will not allow them to get away with it for too long. Only real leaders (as against bosses) understand the delicate naked autocrat dance of leadership. Only real leaders succeed in creating a better future.

Dr. Sanduk Ruit—Nepal

Sushma Limbu was only eight years old when she hurt her eye while playing on the fields in the village near Panchthar district, Nepal. Her parents dismissed her injury as a simple scratch; even if they had wanted to do more, the nearest hospital was several days walk away and there were no health clinics nearby. But soon little Sushma was unable to see through her left eye. No longer able to ignore the condition, her parents frantically took the little girl from one hospital to another across eastern Nepal seeking treatment, only to be told repeatedly that there was no cure.

Fifty-year-old Thuli Maya Thing has struggled with life and caring for the needs of her family since losing her eyesight. She is no longer able to fetch firewood, collect water, or cook. In numerous attempts to continue with her regular routine, Thuli has suffered painful falls and repeatedly burnt herself on the stove. Life has become unbearable with the loss of income coupled with days having to go hungry, due to her inability to work. She longs to see her children and husband and participate fully in her home life again.

Sudip recently married Kamala, but he has never truly seen his wife's face. Sudip's eyes are clouded with the milky color of cataract, and all he has been able to see in the last seven years are shapes and shadows. Both husband and wife have walked for two days through the foothills of the Himalayas, carrying only a blanket for warmth, in search of treatment and a life beyond blurry outlines and hazy silhouettes.

Blindness in poor and remote regions of the world such as the Nepal Himalayas is not just a medical condition but a problem with dire consequences for sufferers. Basic survival can be seriously compromised without strong feet and sharp sight. In the Himalayas, prolonged exposure to the sun renders those who live in higher altitudes vulnerable to damage from its ultraviolet rays. By the early 1990s, limited access to medical care, malnutrition, low water quality, and a lack of sanitation had already left more than 100,000 in the Himalayan region suffering from cataract, a preventable blindness. The poor and elderly bore the most of its cruel effects, and without hope of a cure, most had accepted it as part of their unfortunate fate.

This devastating situation would have continued and worsened but for one man who decided not to accept it as fate. Unlike many in Asia and Africa who have become desensitized to the abject poverty around them, he felt deeply about the situation and decided to do something about it. A leader was born! He is Dr. Sanduk Ruit, an ophthalmologist dubbed the "God of Sight" and regarded as a hero in his home country of Nepal. I met Ruit in 2016 and was mesmerized by his story. Among other things, I particularly appreciated how well he has blended social cause with business. He has gained worldwide recognition for his pioneering form of cataract surgery that requires no stitches and can be performed at a fraction of the cost of the normal procedure. Known as the Nepali technique, this viable method of removing cataracts has restored vision to scores of people living in poverty not only in Nepal, but across the world. And Ruit did not wait to strike it rich or secure his own future before dedicating his life to helping the poor. Today, he runs a profitable global business that restores sight to thousands each year and exports low-cost lenses to 30 countries. I am often asked if one has to choose between high pay and higher purpose. The answer is no, not always. There is nothing wrong with desiring prosperity. If one can find a purpose bigger than oneself, and still create wealth, prosperity, and fame for oneself, what's wrong with that? Sanduk's story is a perfect example of blending both needs. Besides combining high pay and higher purpose so successfully, all along his journey he has had to practice the five keys of positive autocracy described in this chapter.

Early Life and Education

Sanduk was born in 1955 to uneducated parents in Olanchungola, northeast Nepal, a poor and remote mountain area. His father, a salt trader, prioritized his children's education. Sanduk vaguely recalls holding his weeping mother's hands at age seven, when he and his father started on a long journey to the nearest school more than a week away. Having walked for days over the mountains to Darjeeling, India, he was left to study at St. Robert's, a missionary school. "It was very tough, very lonely. Between the ages of 7 and 13, I think I went home only twice," he says. Sanduk understood from an early age that he was perceived as a "backward lad" from the remote mountains, and was determined to work extremely hard to prove himself, spending long hours bent over his books and working on homework by the light of a candle. Sanduk's drive to work hard was greatly driven by the devastating loss of his sister. He channeled his grief into his studies. With memories of his late sister on his mind, he sat for the most important entrance examination of his life. This son of a salt trader, from a poor distant village in Nepal, scored so highly that he earned a scholarship to one of India's most prestigious medical colleges, King George's Medical College in Lucknow.

The Trigger Toward a Path of Service

Sanduk's firm resolve to pursue a career in medicine was based on a simple but heartfelt idea. He believed that people should not be blinded, maimed, or sickened because of poverty. From a family of six children he had lost three siblings to what are considered treatable conditions, including, most devastatingly, the painful death of his 15-year-old sister Ying La to tuberculosis. Her passing had such a deep impact on him that he struggled with the loss for a long time. "Unacceptable, unacceptable, unacceptable," Sanduk said to himself repeatedly as he reflected on his siblings' deaths. "Why?" he kept asking, because he knew they didn't have to die. If they had had access to the medical resources available so easily in the rest of the world, they might still be alive today. "We ran door-to-door like refugees trying to find a doctor who could cure her. I didn't want anyone to suffer the same fate as my sister," he has said, when describing his commitment to medical studies.

That painful experience shed immediate light on the path ahead. After graduating with a general medical degree, Ruit was called to study ophthalmology while working as a medical officer on Nepal's northern borders. "In every village, I'd find people blinded by cataracts living like animals, actually worse than animals," he says. Thousands and thousands of people lived in dark huts, resigned to their fate. It was here that Ruit knew cataract surgery would restore their humanity, and made eradicating curable blindness caused by cataracts, regardless of one's ability to pay, his mission in life. Establishing Tilganga Institute of Ophthalmology in 1994, he provides cheap, efficient, and, more important, world-class eye care to the people of Nepal—half for a fee, half gratis. Tilganga also manufactures tiny lenses used in cataract surgery for $3 compared to $200 in the West, trains countless eye surgeons, and implements eye health programs in many parts of the world. For those unable to access the hospital, Ruit and his team run mobile eye camps, trekking through remote and mountainous areas for days, helping the poor, weak, and isolated to see again. All this is possible due to his groundbreaking, stitch-free surgical "Ruitectomy" cataract technique.

Swimming Against the Tide

"Slicing through someone's eyeball with steady hands was hard not to watch, as much as you wanted to look away," said the *101 East* team from broadcaster Al Jazeera, who observed the "God of Sight" in action in 2014. The team watched intently as Ruit removed a cataract and inserted an artificial lens, restoring sight in minutes. It was like a miracle unfolding. This revolutionary technique came about in 1986 when Ruit worked alongside his longtime friend and mentor Fred Hollows, the renowned Australian ophthalmologist acclaimed for his efforts to provide quality healthcare to the underprivileged. Ruit studied with Dr. Hollows for 14 months in Australia. After the study program, and until his death in 1993, Hollows was instrumental in supporting the Nepalese surgeon's fearless goal to provide world-class healthcare in his home country.

Hollows was also a pillar of support in battling resistance from the international medical fraternity over Ruit's new cataract surgery technique. While they were together at a conference, Ruit was met with a rude awakening as he presented his findings and argued for a radical change in the way the world medical community fought cataract disease. "You're wasting our time, this is nonsense" and "It's only logical to work with techniques that have been proven in the field" were some of the many harsh comments that were hurled against him on the podium. These reactions came from the world's most respected authorities in eye care. He recalls his blood pounding in his temples as he responded, "Would you let your own mother or father be operated on with a technique twenty years out of date? Are you saying the millions of poor deserve less than you or I? Are you saying they are children of a lesser God?" as he walked off the podium and out the door.

Nothing could break his spirit. The *Sydney Morning Herald* has described him as the maverick who refused to allow a sceptical medical establishment to get in the way of his dream in providing high-quality affordable eye surgery to the developing world. This was no matter of compromise, nor was it an agenda for consensus. With the clock ticking, Ruit understood that the stakes were too high in view of the number of lives affected by this leading cause of blindness. With boldness, he forged ahead with his new method of treating cataract amidst huge criticism. Being autocratic to his values and purpose, he remained humble and empathetic with people, thereby skilfully mastering the dance of the naked autocrat. An unshakeable spirit is only possible when you know unreservedly that you are on to something larger than yourself, something that would make a huge and lasting difference to humanity—that was the clarity of vision Sanduk Ruit possessed. Nearly two decades forward, the technique once condemned by the international medical community has not only transformed the lives of millions, most of whom live in the developing world, it has now spread worldwide with thousands of doctors being trained in the technique, including U.S. military surgeons who were sent to Nepal to learn under Ruit's tutelage.

The Road Less Traveled

Truth be told, Ruit was always aware of the many lucrative alternatives available to him. With his talent and skills, the world was at his feet. Early in his career, he was offered the opportunity to serve as physician to the Sultan of Oman. It was an offer laced with tempting rewards including a home, driver, and cook of his own. A path of less resistance would also have been to stay on in Australia where he had trained as a specialist, or to move to the United States or India. Despite the many powerful incentives in that direction, Ruit remained committed to his sole mission and driving purpose, grounded on his values of compassion and love.

He is the recipient of many awards, and the subject of several books and films. But his fame is not what makes him great. The recognition is a by-product of his leadership energy, not the purpose of it. His real motivation comes from the inner joy he experiences each time he restores a patient's sight. "Magnificent, highly emotional and energizing," is how Ruit describes the moment when surgical patches are peeled away from once-blinded eyes and patients see the world again. "I am a mortal being after all. I have to do what I do best to give people a better shot at life. I have to do it before my time comes," says the radiant, down to earth, world-renowned eye surgeon, Dr. Sanduk Ruit.

As you can imagine, being a positive autocrat is risky, lonely, and often unpopular. Another challenge is to make sure the positive autocracy does not inadvertently slip into blind or brutal dictatorship, which is why key 4 (listen, learn, and reflect continuously) is critically important. But in today's open source era, it might be the only way to lead effectively. Howard Schultz of Starbucks, John Mackey of Whole Foods, Steve Jobs of Apple, and Jeff Bezos of Amazon are just some examples of corporate leaders that have skillfully practiced positive autocracy. The question is, how to develop enough inner strength to weather the loneliness, unpopularity, and inherent risks of leading in this way? The answer lies in discovering true and authentic leadership energy—a concept we will explore in great detail in the next chapter.

CHAPTER SUMMARY

- Speed is everything in the open source era.
- Contrary to conventional wisdom, a top-down, autocratic style of leadership might be more suited in current times.
- A large proportion of leaders through history have in fact been autocratic.
- While autocratic leadership is required in today's age of speed, thanks to 24/7 connectivity and social media, leaders stand completely exposed and naked.
- The only way to use autocratic leadership is to practice the five keys:
  1. Earn the right to use autocratic leadership.
  2. Be autocratic about values and purpose while remaining humble, respectful, and considerate with people.
  3. Provide "freedom within a framework."
  4. Listen, learn, and reflect continuously.
  5. Forgive more often.

Questions for Reflection

1. What is your style of leadership? Is it working?

2. What do you need to do in order to make your leadership more effective?

3. Do you agree with the need for top-down, autocratic leadership? If so, how can you practice all or some of the five keys of positive autocracy?

CHAPTER 3

Leadership Energy, Not Competencies

The human race has made tremendous progress in the last 200 years in almost every endeavor. Engineers today are significantly more knowledgeable and capable as compared with only a few decades ago. The same is true for scientists, doctors, lawyers, and almost every other profession. Our knowledge, experience, and application has steadily improved over time. But in this era of rapid progression, are we producing more great leaders? Sadly, the answer is no. In recent years, I've seen many CEO surveys (PwC, Harvard, DDI, and the Conference Board to name just a few) that report a shortage of great leadership talent as one of their top challenges. Despite so much progress in other fields and the billions spent every year on leadership development, why are we not getting better at leadership?

In fact, the dearth of leadership talent was reported throughout the 1980s and even earlier—an era that could be considered steadier times. If the state of leadership was not enough then, how can we hope to face the challenges of today's uber-connectivity and uber-population? As we saw in Chapter 1, in the twenty-first century exciting opportunities and daunting challenges exist side by side. Be it finance, healthcare, food production, energy, or water, we need new rules for the new reality that is unfolding as we speak. Now more than ever before, traditional models of leadership will not be enough.

So, what has been and remains the problem with leadership? It begins with the way we define and understand the word itself. We've created several myths around it that need to be busted, the first of which (democratic leadership style is best) we discussed at length in the last chapter. Here are a few more:

Myth 2: Followership = Leadership

For far too long, we've been confusing followership with leadership. What we've been calling leadership is nothing of the sort. Let me explain.

Confusing leadership with followership begins early. Parents love children who listen and obey. Kids learn quickly that the way to be rewarded is to comply with their parents' wishes. From an early age, we learn to follow—and are rewarded for our followership behavior.

In school and college, teachers love students who do what they are told. Anyone who asks too many questions or wants to do something out-of-the-box is generally frowned upon. Even Thomas Edison, the inventor of the phonograph and the light bulb, was thrown out of school for asking too many questions. I will never forget an elective course I took during my MBA program on International Relations. It was about U.S.-Russia (then U.S.S.R) relations during the Cold War. Our professor had a very unique take on the relationship and balance of power between the two countries, and most of the class did not agree with him. When it came to writing term papers (on which the course grade would largely depend), the professor assured us that he did not expect us to agree with him. "I've given you my deductive reasoning as to why I believe what I do, and I need you to do the same. You don't have to agree with me. I will not penalize you for your political opinion. All I want to see is good reasoning and basis for your opinion. So please feel free to think independently and write what you really want to," he assured us repeatedly. Luckily, a senior student who had taken the same course in the previous year told me to ignore the professor's assurances and write exactly what I had heard in class. I did, and I earned an A grade. However, I was one of only a handful of students who received an A in that class. All those who "thought independently" and "wrote what they really wanted to" received B's and C's.

In large companies, when you ask employees what they want from their boss, they usually list hygiene factors such as caring, listening, kindness, and flexibility. In other words, employees state what they "want," which is not necessarily what they "need." So, bosses quickly become pleasers (another form of following), particularly if their leadership performance is measured by employee surveys. I have seen far too many bosses in my career who over time became masters of pleasing their subordinates and "gaming" the surveys. One senior executive I know of at a large international bank was on the verge of getting fired because of consistent low scores on his employee surveys. Sensing that he had to turn the situation around to save his job, he devised a six-month plan of engaging with his team in a way that convinced them he was really turning the corner for the better. To no one's surprise, his scores showed a remarkable improvement in the next survey and he kept his job. Yet amongst the casualties of this exercise was the abandonment of a sorely needed delayering exercise, and rescoping a key project that would have involved some disruption in the normal working pattern of the group. Both of these had a negative impact on the organization as a whole. And the worst part is, this executive abandoned the two initiatives while being fully aware of the fact that he was acting against the larger interest of his bank.

Even in boardrooms followership is rewarded in the name of leadership. When a CEO presents a bold new idea or vision, the first question the board typically asks is, "Where's the McKinsey report showing that others have done this successfully?" Very few projects are approved without best-practice benchmarking and proof.

Wherever you look, leadership is confused with followership. There was a time when best practice replication was enough to lead. If you could be the first to transfer best practice from one part of the world to another, you would be a successful leader because information moved slowly. Today, with the democratization of knowledge and the instant spread of information in the open source era, best practice replication is no longer enough. Winners need to invent "next practices," and do so faster than others.

Myth 3: A Position of Authority = Leadership

Confusing authority for leadership is perhaps the biggest myth of leadership, and the real culprit is the dictionary. If you look up the word *leader* and compare the definition with the word *boss* in the same dictionary, you will find that the two definitions are remarkably similar, if not identical. We automatically assume that the president or prime minister is the leader of his or her country, or that the CEO is the leader of his or her company. We also assume that in order to lead effectively, one needs to be empowered with the right amount of authority. Position and title go hand in hand with how we currently define and understand leadership.

Yet in more than two decades of studying leadership I have found nothing further from the truth. Another quick look at three of the most powerful twentieth-century leaders—Mahatma Gandhi, Nelson Mandela, and Martin Luther King Jr.—should put to rest all notions about the connection between authority and leadership. Coming from Asia, Africa, and the United States respectively, they were all powerful leaders whose lives will continue to inspire generations to come, but none consistently held any officially recognized position. Gandhi never held political office, and had no title or authority given to him by law throughout his lifetime. Mandela was president of South Africa for a few years toward the end of his life, but spent the majority of his younger years in prison. King too did not enjoy a big position or title, yet he occupies a place of pride in the history of humankind. What does that say about great leadership and the need for authority? What made them powerful leaders was certainly not their title, position, or authority given to them through public office. East or West, what made them leaders was who they were, what they stood for, and most important, what they chose to do or not do. In this sense, everyone can be a leader well before they are given formal authority. Authority is *given*, but leadership must be *taken*.

In my seminars, I often ask participants if they think being a boss and a leader is the same thing. Wherever I ask in the world, the answer is always a unanimous "No." I then ask whether every boss is a leader, and again I hear a big "No." Finally, I ask if one needs to be a boss in order to be a leader, and again I get a unanimous "No." Yet outside the classroom, many of these same people complain bitterly about how helpless they are, and why they cannot be good leaders without adequate empowerment and authority. I cannot tell you how many senior people I've met—and by "senior" I mean people in supposedly powerful positions—who've expressed helplessness because of what they consider to be inadequate formal authority and power. A few years ago, this phenomenon prompted me to write a piece called "Powerful Victims" for Forbes.com in which I described how some people feel helpless despite holding powerful positions. Think about it. Do you know of someone who became a leader *because of* the power and authority bestowed upon him or her? And do you know a great leader who failed *because of* inadequate authority? If anything, you will instead find plenty of examples where power corrupted people, absolutely!

"But this is in total contradiction to the case we made for top-down autocratic leadership in the last chapter," you might think. But if you look carefully, you will find no contradiction whatsoever because when you practice positive autocracy, you don't need to use formal power and authority. As we will see later in this chapter, real leadership depends on self-empowerment. Stay tuned.

Myth 4: Leaders Are Born, Not Made

Another of my favorite things to do in my seminars is to ask participants why there are so few great leaders as compared to great scientists, engineers, or accountants. Invariably, someone in the audience always brings up the issues of genetics and heredity. I hear things like:

- Great leaders have something inborn in them that others don't.
- Great leaders are blessed with certain traits, personality, or charisma that makes them more suitable for leadership.

How I wish this were true, and how I wish I could prove it. Why? Because if I could prove that leaders are born, not made, we could pretty much shut down the multibillion dollar a year (estimates range from $30 billion to $80 billion) leadership development industry. Imagine how many hungry people we could feed with the money saved. Alas, no matter how much I tried, I could find no such proof. What I found instead is that leaders are self-made. I also found that great leadership has nothing to do with shallow external symbols of personality and charisma. Instead it has everything to do with character, which is deep and internal.

Consider just one example. It is commonly believed that good salespeople are either "rather extraverted" or "very extraverted," yet there is barely any research evidence supporting that belief. While there is research that explains why extraverts might have an advantage in sales, studies that try to prove a relationship between extraverted personalities and sales success have shown conflicting results. A meta-analysis of 35 studies of more than 3,800 salespeople found that the correlation between extraversion and sales performance was essentially zero (0.07, to be exact). Far more intriguing is research by Professor Adam Grant of the Wharton School of Business. Grant's findings (see

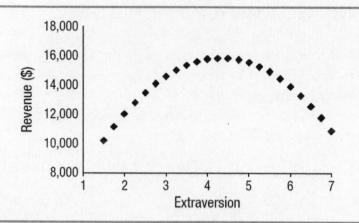

FIGURE 3.1   Sales Revenue by Levels of Extraversion.
Grant's findings: The strong introverts (the people represented on the left of the chart's horizontal axis, around 1 and 2) weren't very effective salespeople. No surprise there. But the strong extraverts (those over to the right, around 6 and 7) weren't much better. The chart denotes that those who fared the best—by a wide margin—were in the modulated middle.

Figure 3.1) reveal that contrary to popular belief, sales performance is highest not among extraverts but "ambiverts," or individuals that exhibit features of both an extravert and an introvert (the term was coined by Kimball Young in his book *Source Book for Social Psychology* in 1927). Ambiverts achieve greater sales productivity because they can express sufficient assertiveness and enthusiasm to persuade and close a sale, but are more inclined to listen to customers' interests and less likely to appear too excited or overconfident. So, in simple terms and contrary to conventional dogma, extreme extraverts don't make the most successful salespeople, and it's the same in leadership. Good leaders and bad leaders come in all personality types. There is no ideal personality profile in determining leadership potential.

If you make a list of your top 10 most admired leaders in history, you will find that they had very different personalities.

No one personality type can be associated with good or bad leadership. You will also find that not all of them had charisma. In other words, leadership is personality and charisma agnostic. Yet the leadership development industry has a subindustry of psychometric personality testing within it, which is built upon that misinformed belief. Our potential clients frequently ask which assessments we include in our programs before awarding leadership development work to us. The look on their faces when we say none is worth a million bucks. They can hardly believe what they hear!

To finish the argument about whether leaders are born or made, I tend to play with words and tell my audiences, "Yes, a leader in you *is* born, but not at the time of your biological birth. The leader in you is born when two things happen to you simultaneously. First, you feel deeply about the inadequacies of current reality, and second, you decide to do something about it." Both must occur together for leadership to surface. And they usually happen at a point in time much later than one's biological birth date. As I will explain shortly, in order to find one's leadership potential, one has to live life awake.

Myth 5: Leadership Can Be Learned Through Case Studies, Role Plays, and Competency Models

Much of the $30 billion to $80 billion global spend on leadership development is spent on developing competency models, writing and discussing case studies, and doing copycat role plays in training programs. The competency modeling approach came into vogue during the 1980s and has been popular ever since. The basis of the approach is that the best predictor of future success is past successful behavior. So, senior successful leaders are interviewed and quizzed to make a list of competencies that made them successful within the context of their company. The competencies are further broken down into specific behaviors. A model (diagram) is typically drawn up, and much of leadership training and performance measurement systems are designed to encourage future leaders to exhibit the same behaviors that made yesterday's leaders successful. Many HR consulting firms offer services to design leadership competency models "customized for your unique context and strategy." But in a world where business models become obsolete within months, how can this rearview mirror–gazing approach create tomorrow's leaders?

Similarly, business schools boast of their great invention of the case study method and claim that the best way to learn leadership is to read and discuss other people's mistakes. Some schools rely solely on the case method for teaching just about anything. I have been to several of these courses, and all you do day after day is read and discuss cases. It is a teaching method that is great for professors and students alike. Professors do not need to prepare much before a class, and can often delegate class discussions to teaching assistants. Participants of executive education programs, who typically want to get away with minimal work, like them because all they have to do in class is participate in a discussion. But does true learning really take place? For those of you who've attended leadership courses at prestigious business schools, I have a question. How many of those cases do you remember? And what were the learnings? When I ask people what they loved the most about such business school courses, they almost always say the same thing—the networking opportunity with other participants! You don't learn leadership by reading other people's mistakes. You learn leadership through your own defining moments, making your own mistakes, and sometimes by falling down multiple times and learning how to stand up again.

Another of my pet peeves with leadership training is role plays. Most people like formulas, because formulas make life easier. So, the leadership development industry has created formulas of its own. The teaching method goes something like this. You get a lesson on greatness from, say, Jack Welch. No doubt it will involve reading and discussing cases on how he led GE during his time as CEO. After the case discussion, the teacher will typically offer a three-or-four-step formula summarizing Jack Welch's approach to handling people or situations. Once the formula is unfolded, the teacher breaks the group into triads and asks two people to role-play the formula, receiving feedback from the third person who acts as observer. The goal is to make you practice copycat formulas so that you too can become a great leader like Jack Welch. But the last time I checked the dictionary, copying somebody else's behavior was followership, not leadership!

It amazes me why even after so many decades of low ROI, no one questions these methods of leadership development. Why don't the smart people who sign off on the annual $30 billion to $80 billion collective global spend question the efficacy of such methods? As Barbara Kellerman of Harvard and Jeffrey Pfeffer of Stanford agree, if they haven't produced leaders in all these years, how in the world will they do so in the open source era where the need for leadership is greater than ever? It is time to reject these myths and develop a new way of thinking about leadership. To begin doing that, consider the following three stories.

Norma Bastidas—Canada

Imagine being an 11-year-old who is raped by the disabled family member you are caring for, and then being routinely sexually assaulted for years afterward. Imagine being desperately poor at 19 and promised a lucrative career in a foreign land only to realize on arrival you have been sold to sex slavery. Imagine being thousands of miles away from home, constantly drugged and raped with no one to come to your aid because you were marked as a prostitute. And years later, imagine finding out that your little son was going blind. What would you do?

This is the story of Norma Bastidas, whom I first saw on CNN and finally met in November 2016. What I learned listening to her is an unparalleled example of the power of the human spirit.

Born to a desperately poor family in Mazatlán, western Mexico in 1967, Norma's father passed away when she was 11 and left her mother alone with a family of five children. Each member of the impoverished family had to work to support the family, including Norma. Her nightmare began when the family moved away from their gang-ridden neighborhood to be closer to extended relatives for support. Some family members took advantage of Norma's vulnerability. Her blind grandfather, whom she was providing care to, raped her. Deep down she knew that what had happened was terribly wrong, but, young and afraid, she kept silent for two years. "The first time I was raped, I was 11 years old. It continued until my midtwenties by different perpetrators," she says. Nobody ever did anything to stop it or to help her, and feeling alone and helpless, Norma turned to alcohol for solace.

Despite the trauma, she managed to finish high school and joined the workforce to support her family despite her dreams of going to university. Several years later, the 19-year-old was noticed and offered a job as a model in Japan. "I remember my mom saying, 'I'm afraid, but I can't stop you,'" she recalls. Despite her fears of sending her daughter across the world, her mother felt this was the only chance for Norma to have a better life. Norma saw this as a golden opportunity, her only chance of getting out from a life of poverty and years of abuse and a way to provide for her family and see her university dreams fulfilled.

Only her second time on a plane, she arrived in Tokyo with great excitement, convinced that this would be the moment her life would change.

On arrival, she was housed in luxury hotels with the other "models." From the best hotels to moving around in expensive cars, the parade of luxury blinded her from the early signals of deception and danger. Finally, one night at the club, forced to display herself in a Playboy bunny costume, she realized she had been sold to the club. Trapped with no money and no passport, she was told that she owed the agency a huge sum of money and would have to repay the large debt by providing escort services to men. Here was a hopeful 19-year-old girl, dreaming of a life she never had, eager to break away from the dark years of growing up in Mexico but instead confronted with the reality of being tricked and forced into a life of sex slavery. "You become a child with no control of anything," she says. Once again, she turned to alcohol to suppress her pain.

After enduring several years of hell in Japan and with help from a nearby school, Norma managed to escape. She later moved to Vancouver, Canada, where she married and had two beautiful sons, Hans and Karl. However, her marriage broke up and she became a single mom. In 2006, Norma was once again stuck in a nightmare. Her 11-year-old son Karl received shattering news that he had an incurable eye condition that would see his vision slowly deteriorate to blindness. He was diagnosed with cone-rod dystrophy, a progressive condition with no cure. The news was unbearable for 38-year-old Norma, then a struggling single parent in Calgary, Canada. Just when she thought things could not get any worse as she was trying to juggle work and staying home with Karl, she lost her job. Lying in bed, at breaking point and not knowing what to do, she put on an old pair of trainers and decided to go for a walk. On that cold September night, that walk became a run and marked the beginning of her journey of release.

Adversity has been a recurring theme in Norma's life, and she is no stranger to struggle. Karl's condition was only one of the many tragedies she had endured, but it was the single event that triggered her running. This time, while dealing with the devastating news of Karl's eye disease and having lost her job, she decided to break the cycle of pain by turning to running instead of alcohol. Running became a form of release and a symbolic sign of her inner strength and endurance. "I just became an incredible runner because of the incredible amount of stress that I had to manage. It gave me something that I could control. I started running at night because I didn't want my family to hear me crying," she told me.

"I couldn't control the rate of progression of my son. I couldn't control whether they were going to fire me again. But I could lace up and train," she says. She was determined to do something that advocated publicly for victims of sexual abuse and human trafficking, and pushed past her limits of endurance. In 2014, she crushed the world record for the longest triathlon in history. She covered 3,762 miles in only 65 days following a route known for human trafficking from Mexico to Washington, DC. Like the journey of her life, the triathlon was plagued with roadside accidents, punishing waves, attacks from sea creatures, and rough weather. She never gave up and pushed forward to send a message. "I have a son who's losing his sight . . . I'm an example to him when I tell him it's hard, but it gets better if you continue." Norma's reason for pushing through her physical limits is also fueled by the desire to send a message to other survivors of human trafficking. "I can't undo what has been done. But by living large, I'm empowering every single victim. Somebody who was once living in a nightmare is now living out her dreams. That's what a world record is—it's a dream." That has become Norma's underlying purpose as she continues to dedicate her athletic feats and life toward raising funds and awareness for the causes close to her heart—eradicating avoidable blindness and putting an end to human trafficking worldwide.

When I met Norma in November 2016 and interviewed her for our website, I asked her why she decided to take destiny in her own hands and do something about it when her son was losing his sight. I probed, "Why not earlier when you were going through so much yourself? Why didn't you decide to do something big then?" Here's what she said. "You know, to pursue something big, and not be scared doing it, you have to have a purpose larger than yourself." Clearly, the power of purpose propelled her to keep going. Even the fact that she did not know how to swim was not enough to deter her from the world record target. She learned to swim just months before she attempted the triathlon.

In business and profession, the same applies. If you're trying to create change, you will encounter resistance. One sure way to keep going in the face of stiff resistance is to have a purpose greater than yourself. Belief in a greater purpose strengthens leaders to keep going. For instance, Jeff Bezos's objective of retailing books online (on Kindle) was not just to make money. He wanted to promote the habit of long-form reading by making every book ever published available to readers anywhere in the world within 60 seconds.

Muhammad Yunus and Grameen Bank—Bangladesh

It was the 1970s. Muhammad Yunus had just returned home to Bangladesh to teach economics at Chittagong University, after completing his PhD at Vanderbilt University in Tennessee. Bangladesh, a country still recovering from a vicious war of independence that had destroyed much of its infrastructure and productivity, had been hit with a terrible famine, and people were dying of hunger. When he saw the extent of the devastation caused by the famine, Yunus realized, "When people are dying of hunger, and you are a young economics teacher teaching economic theory in the classroom, it does not make you feel good. Because all your brilliant and elegant theories don't seem to help the people who are dying. And it's death you cannot explain because it's not caused by disease, it's just not having food to eat."

While questioning the relevance of the grand economic theories he had been teaching, he came face-to-face with the immediate needs of the hungry and the desperation of the poor. He learned that the impoverished villagers had become soft targets for loan sharks and money lenders, who charged exorbitant rates of interest (usually over 10 percent per week) on their loans, which were usually less than one U.S. dollar.

Yunus was deeply disturbed. He felt he couldn't go on simply teaching economic theories in the classroom while people outside campus were starving to death, being cruelly harassed and controlled by loan sharks. He knew he had to do something to make life a little better for the villagers in Jobra—it was time to act!

Working with a student, Yunus took to the streets and traced everyone in Jobra who was borrowing money from loan sharks. From a list of 42 names, the total amount owing was around 856 Bangladeshi Taka. He lent 856 Taka (roughly US$27) to the 42 villagers from his own pocket to help them pay back their loans. It was the defining moment for Yunus— he felt happy about having been able to help a few people in distress, but knew that his personal resources were woefully inadequate to address the endemic problem of poverty. He realized, "People were poor not because they were stupid or lazy. They worked all day long, doing complex physical tasks. They were poor because the financial institutions in the country did not help them widen their economic base." There had to be a financially viable way to meet the credit needs of the poor in a way that helped alleviate poverty, he thought.

He knew that charity was not the answer. "When we want to help the poor, we usually offer them charity. Most often we use charity to avoid recognizing the problem and finding the solution for it. Charity becomes a way to shrug off our responsibility. But charity is no solution to poverty. Charity only perpetuates poverty by taking the initiative away from the poor. Charity allows us to go ahead with our own lives without worrying about the lives of the poor. Charity appeases our consciences."

Having experimented through an action research project at his university, he learned and proved that lending small amounts to the poor could be a profitable business for a bank. So, in 1976 Yunus approached the local branch of Janata Bank, one of the largest government banks in Bangladesh, and pitched the idea of small loans to the very poor. The bank manager rejected the idea at first, saying, "The poor are illiterate and they can't fill out the necessary forms. Plus, they have no collateral." After much effort and negotiation, Yunus finally succeeded in securing a credit line from Janata Bank offering himself as guarantor. He also acted as intermediary, filling out the necessary paperwork for each loan. Against the advice of banks and government, he continued to give "microloans" to villagers, eventually converting his project into the now well-known, full-fledged microfinance bank named Grameen Bank in 1983.

Muhammad Yunus is often referred to as "the world's banker to the poor." His life's work has been to prove that the poor are also creditworthy, and in 2006 he received the Nobel Peace Prize. His revolutionary for-profit microcredit system is estimated to have extended credit to more than seven million of the world's poor, most of them in Bangladesh, which remains one of the poorest nations in the world. The vast majority of

Grameen Bank beneficiaries are women, and today Grameen has a presence all over the world. Amidst all the critique and opposition that surrounds him, Yunus has remained firm in the pursuit of his vision. He believes, "Poverty is the absence of all human rights. The frustrations, hostility, and anger generated by abject poverty cannot sustain peace in any society. To build stable peace we must find ways to provide opportunities for people to live decent lives, fully equipped not only to take care of him- or herself, but also to contribute to enlarging the well-being of the world as a whole."

Sheikh Mohammed Bin Rashid Al Maktoum—Dubai

To the amazement of the world, in 2016 the United Arab Emirates established two new ministries of Happiness and Tolerance, and appointed two young women to head each of them. They also expanded the remit of the existing Ministry of Cabinet Affairs and rechristened it the Ministry of Cabinet Affairs and the Future.

A Ministry of Tolerance in the Middle East? Who would have thought? While it sounds a little New Age, it is in fact a monumental milestone in a region known for turmoil, gender disparity, devotion to rulers, and minimal tolerance for dissent. It is also a deliberate reaction by the UAE government to the recent upheaval across the Middle East that was rooted in frustration about high-level corruption and the lack of opportunity for average citizens, and spread across the region through social media and mobile technology. The new ministries are tasked with transforming information hierarchies and the power balance, and creating open channels of communication, engagement, and empowerment—especially between the government and hard-to-reach segments of society. His Highness Sheikh

Mohammed bin Rashid Al Maktoum, vice president and prime minister of the UAE and ruler of Dubai, tweeted about the new appointments, "I am writing to send a message that governments in our region and elsewhere need to revise their roles. The point is to empower people, not hold power over them. Government, in short, should nurture an environment in which people create and enjoy their own happiness."

The announcements should not be surprising at all if you consider Sheikh Mohammed's track record in recent decades. The picture in Figure 3.2 says it all.

FIGURE 3.2 Dubai 1984 and 2014 *(@GulfNews, Dubai)*

Sheikh Mohammed is the visionary behind the conversion of Dubai from a tiny fishing village to the bustling world city it is today, with ultramodern facilities for transportation, healthcare, education, and entertainment. Both the speed and extent of the transformation are breathtaking. The Sheikh's Dubai dream was conceived atop the Empire State Building in the 1960s when he visited the United States as a young boy with his father. While his father had already laid the foundations, it was Sheikh Moham-med who significantly accelerated the execution after becoming the ruler of Dubai in 2006. When *60 Minutes* reporter Steve Kroft asked him a few years ago why he was in such a hurry to build in five years what most people build in a lifetime, he said, "Why not! When you can have it in Europe, why can't you have it here? I want the highest standard of living for my people not just in the region but in the world. I want them to have a better life *now*. I want them to go to better schools *now*. I want them to have access to good healthcare *now*—not after 20 years!"

Compare the overall development of Dubai and the UAE with other countries in the region (like Saudi Arabia), and it is easy to see that Sheikh Mohammed is not just another mon-arch. As someone born into a royal family and one of the richest people on earth, he really doesn't need to do much. Yet he is a workaholic, personally driving the evolution of Dubai. When asked about Dubai's problems during the 2008 economic crisis, he said, "It is a challenge, and we will come through it. Anybody can lead when everything is all right. A good leader comes about when there are challenges." With the crisis now behind him, Sheikh Mohammed continues to make his city bigger and bet-ter. The October 2016 groundbreaking of what will be known as the Tower at Dubai Creek Harbour is just one example. When completed in 2020, the Tower will be the tallest building in the world, dwarfing Dubai's own Burj Khalifa (the current tallest building) by about 100 meters, and will boast rotating balco-nies, hanging gardens, and other architectural wonders.

So, What Is Leadership After All?

To answer the question of what is leadership, let's reflect on the stories above and ask what these people were trying to do. In essence, they were each trying to create something bigger and better than what already existed. They were so moved by the inadequacies of current reality that they developed a burning desire to create a better future against all odds. Rather than a position or title, *leadership is this burning desire to create a better future.* Leadership does not begin when one is promoted to a big position or when one wins an election. Instead, it begins when one closes one's eyes and clearly visualizes the better future one wants to create. As Stephen Covey, Robin Sharma, and others have said in different ways, all great things are created twice, first in the mind of the leader and then in reality. Leadership is all about dreaming up a better future and then simply getting started. It wasn't Sheikh Mohammed's oil wealth, Mohammad Yunus's privileged position, or Norma Bastidas's charisma or personality type that made them leaders. They are all leaders because they dared to dream and got started. But doing so is not easy. While this is where leadership begins, this is also the point where the leader's troubles begin.

The moment you share your goal to create a different future with people around you, you will begin to get resistance. As anyone who has tried knows only too well, any attempts to change or create something new are met with resistance. No matter how beautiful and strong the promise of a better future, most people prize today's certainty more than tomorrow's uncertainty. Right from the start of a leader's journey to create a better future, her constant companion is resistance. Active resistance, passive resistance, all kinds of resistance. This then raises a critical question. What is the main ingredient of leadership?

Leadership Energy

The main ingredient in leadership is *leadership energy*—the force within that prevents real leaders from caving in when faced with even the most formidable resistance. One must have a deep reservoir of intrinsic, almost spiritual kind of inner energy in order to keep going in spite of the environment. The problem is we humans are social beings, and most of us value society's approval more than anything else. So, when the resistance gets difficult, we give up. Sadly, as we give up, we also give up the right to be called leaders. Real leaders find the energy required to stay true to their dreams, just like the people you met in the stories earlier. As I explained in Chapter 1, in today's open source era, the need to create a better future is greater than ever before.

So where does such leadership energy come from? What prevented Mandela from giving up even during 27 years of imprisonment? In *Too Many Bosses, Too Few Leaders* I explained that leadership energy is a function of two things: clarity of values and clarity of purpose. When she gets crystal clear about a set of deeply held values that move her, and develops an equally clear sense of purpose, she discovers leadership energy. Now, whenever she feels like giving up, she simply closes her eyes and visualizes the better future (purpose) she has in mind, and that visualization energizes her again. Whenever she faces a difficult crisis she asks herself, what would I do if I were to act in accordance with my values? And the answer becomes clear.

Unfortunately, very few people have real clarity of values and purpose. Over the years, I have asked hundreds of very senior and powerful people, what is your purpose? With a few exceptions, most people struggle to answer the question crisply. The usual response I get is something like, "Hmmm! That's a very deep question, I haven't thought about it. No one has ever asked me this before." When I follow up with the values question, they usually walk up and down the room a few times to buy time, then make up a list as they speak. To be fair, these are difficult questions, and finding the answers takes a long time. But there is still no reason why someone who calls himself a leader would not have clarity of values and purpose. Unlike popular notions, leadership is not just a set of skills that one learns in a classroom or by experience. Leadership is also not what one does to other people. Leadership involves finding one's leadership energy—which is the values that drive an individual toward a clearly defined purpose. Without leadership energy, there can be no leadership. People without such clarity usually blame the environment for their lack of leadership.

So, the essence of real leadership can be summarized in five simple points:

1. Leadership is a burning desire to create a better future.
2. Creating or changing something usually meets with stiff resistance.
3. The difference between a leader and a nonleader is that the latter gives up when faced with resistance.
4. In order to stay the course, the leader needs to uncover her long-lasting leadership energy.
5. Leadership energy is made up of deep clarity of values and purpose.

As I will explain a bit later, it is only on the strength of such leadership energy that a leader can master the naked autocrat dance we discussed in the last chapter. It is time the leadership development industry moved away from look-back competency models, case studies, personality assessments, and role plays and instead started focusing on helping people find their leadership energy. It is also time to clearly differentiate between leadership and *boss*-ship and to redefine leadership along the lines we've discussed in this chapter.

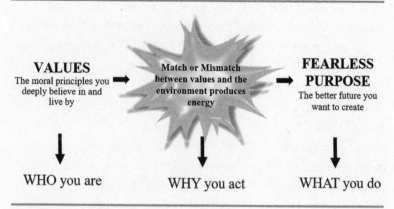

VALUES
The moral principles you
deeply believe in and
live by
➡

**Match or Mismatch
between values and the
environment produces
energy**
➡

**FEARLESS
PURPOSE**
The better future you
want to create

⬇   ⬇   ⬇

WHO you are   WHY you act   WHAT you do

FIGURE 3.3   Sources of Leadership Energy

So, what does this all mean for you and me? The first step
is to get clear on your values. As Figure 3.3 shows, one's values form the basis of one's identity. They also are the reason
why one acts or doesn't. Energy, or the will to do something,
is produced at the intersection of values and day-to-day situations. Any situation in life is either a match or a mismatch with
one's values. A mismatch between values and the situation or
environment produces negative energy in the form of anger or
sadness. A match produces positive energy in the form of joy
and happiness. As one's awareness and clarity about deeply held
values increases, one begins to recognize one's energy. As one
begins to recognize what one has more or less energy for, one
can start looking for purpose. If the energy produced in certain situations is so big that it does not allow the person to stay
still, it can lead to purpose. But for this to happen, deep and
honest reflection is required. For Mohammad Yunus, seeing so
many poor people suffering was a mismatch between his value
of equality and the situation at hand. He was angered and sad-
dened by what he saw. The mismatch produced enough energy
for him to eventually start and run a successful microfinance
business. Sheikh Muhammad's idea of creating a ministry of

tolerance and happiness, on the other hand, was driven by the positive energy he derived from seeing his emirate prosper.

Deeply Held Values

I will come back to finding your purpose a bit later, but let's look at values first. I often ask my audiences for a show of hands if they are totally clear about their top five deeply held values. Typically, a few hands go up each time I ask. I then follow up with a trick question. Under what circumstances is it OK to compromise one of your deeply held values? Most people easily fall into the trap and give very creative answers like, "If it is good for my family, I'll be willing to compromise one of my values," or "For the greater good of my country . . . ." I call this a trick question because if you are willing to compromise your values for a variety of reasons, then they are not deeply held values at all. True leadership requires courage. Only unwavering conviction in your values gives you courage needed to lead against resistance. As Mahatma Gandhi said, "Strength does not come from physical capacity. It comes from an indomitable will."

So how can one identify one's core values? Again, the short answer is deep and honest reflection. But if it helps, let me share what I do to help people who attend my leadership courses. I first ask them to list anything and everything that is important to them. "There is no limit to your desires. List everything you value and would like to have in your life," I tell them. After giving them some time to think and complete their lists, I pose an imaginary dilemma by telling them that they can only have five values if they want to avoid spending the rest of their lives in jail. So, they will need to give up everything in their list except five things in order to remain free. Many people struggle at this stage. Let's say your initial list includes:

- Personal achievement/accomplishment
- Advancement

- Autonomy
- Balance
- Challenge
- Creating something new
- Fame
- Family happiness
- Financial security
- Health
- Independence
- Integrity
- Leisure
- Mastering a field/technique
- Recognition
- Respect
- Teamwork
- Helping others

How would you prioritize your top five? What would you give up? Remember, in this imaginary dilemma, you need to give up the others for good in order to remain free. Which five will you keep?

When they've finally boiled it down to the top five, I give them the final step, which is to rank them in order of importance. Steps two and three get really tough for some people, particularly if they haven't thought along these lines ever before. While doing the exercise, I remind them that the only way this exercise will help them is if they are 100 percent honest with themselves. I ask them to make their choices based on what they want for themselves, not based on what they think looks good to others.

Emotional Integrity

You have no doubt heard and read about emotional intelligence. There is a whole industry around the concept. Countless books, CDs, videos, assessments, and training programs are available—take your pick. But you probably haven't heard the term emotional *integrity*, which I argue is much more important for leadership than emotional intelligence, and must come first. Just like the myths about leadership I discussed earlier, emotional intelligence is seen today as the be-all and end-all of career success. According to generic literature, emotional intelligence consists of two parts:

1. One must recognize and understand one's own emotions, and regulate them intelligently.
2. One must recognize and understand others' emotions, and handle them intelligently.

While this sounds perfectly logical, and not doing these two things can certainly be highly detrimental, emotional intelligence is like personality or charisma, a superficial skill. True leadership instead requires intrinsic strength of character, and this is where emotional integrity comes in. Emotional integrity is the courage to look into the mirror and acknowledge one's deepest wants and desires without using a societal lens. In essence, it is about 100 percent self-honesty. If you value your own personal success above everything else, there is nothing wrong with it. Just before takeoff, most commercial flights make security announcements. In case of a drop in air pressure when wearing oxygen masks becomes necessary, they tell passengers to secure their own mask before helping others. Emotional integrity is a bit like that too. If you cannot make yourself happy, you most likely cannot make others happy either. So, the reflection on selecting one's values must happen with full emotional integrity. As I've emphasized before, leadership (creating a better future) involves facing significant resistance, and being a naked autocrat is hard, lonely, and unpopular. Only if one is totally clear about one's values will one find the strength to make tough decisions and keep going. And the best part is this: leaders who pursue a better future amidst the stiffest of resistance actually derive a lot of personal satisfaction and happiness while doing so. The very fact that they are fighting the good fight and that they are working on something meaningful makes them happy.

Again, as rare as clarity of values and purpose are, emotional integrity is even more uncommon. We literally lie to ourselves even without realizing it. Here's a classic example. For over 10 years now, I've been asking people to identify what's most important to them. "What do you care about the most in your life?" I ask. Can you guess the most common answer all across the globe? Yes, that's right—it is family. The majority of people say "family" regardless of where this question is asked. But I know from experience that it is not true for a lot of people. Sometimes when people say "family," I ask them to show me their diary for the last six months. Flipping through their calendar on their phones for a few minutes, I return the phone saying they failed the diary test. Indeed, every so often there is *no* proof in their calendars that family is the most important thing in their lives. "But I work so hard just for the sake of my family. . . ." comes the protest soon after I tell them that they failed the diary test. I tell them they may be right, but urge them to go away and think deeply about the question overnight with full emotional integrity and to see me the next morning. Many have tears in their eyes when we meet again the next day.

In my own experience, as my awareness about my values and purpose deepened, I realized that my work purpose— which is to wake up as many individuals and organizations as possible to their full potential—is the most important thing for me. Because of this clarity, I work long hours, travel extensively, and often prioritize work over everything else. Strangely enough, even though I am and will always be a long way from being perfect, this realization has made me a better father, husband, and person than before. It has also made me happier and comfortable in my own skin despite all my weaknesses.

So, if it is not true for them, why do so many people say family is the most important thing in their lives? Because it is the societally correct answer. I am not saying family should not be first. All I am saying is that emotional integrity must come *before* emotional intelligence if you want to find long-lasting leadership energy. This values-finding exercise I just explained is a good starting point, but don't expect to find values clarity in one day. Getting clear about values takes time. And even after you clarify your values, living them every day without compromise is the real deal. Living one's values creates conflict. But real leaders embrace such conflict. They don't run away from it.

From Values to Purpose

Once clear about a set of deeply held values, leaders must look to find their purpose to complete the leadership energy equation. Again, finding that purpose requires deep and honest reflection, but sadly, thanks to today's 24/7 connectivity, we've become too busy to take pause. We have become too busy in the business of *busy*ness. Whenever we have a free moment, we fill it up with browsing or messaging. For example, when you step into an elevator to go up a few floors, if you didn't enter the elevator with your eyes and hands on your connectivity device, chances are you will switch it on the moment you take your place amongst the strangers that ride up with you. Think about it: What's the first thing you do when you wake up? What's the last thing you do before you finally shut your eyes? If your answer is something other than browsing or messaging on your phone, congratulations, you're an original!

Nipun Mehta, founder of the Silicon Valley incubator ServiceSpace, likes to say, "We are more connected to our devices than to other people. . . . We may have thousands of friends on Facebook, but how many real friends do we have?" He goes on to say, "Technology was supposed to bring us together, but we are in the midst of a profound crisis of disconnection." It is true. As we get more and more attached to our devices and technology, we are getting increasingly disconnected from people and even more disconnected from our inner selves. When was the last time you spent 20 minutes silently gazing out of the window reflecting upon your own life? When was the last time you took a pause to think about who you are and what your purpose is? Even when we go for holidays, we stress ourselves out with overplanning and the urge to pack in as much as possible.

Fortunately, there is growing realization today that we need to take a pause. Mindfulness is fast becoming a movement in the West. Unfortunately, even though it was invented in the East thousands of years ago, most people there have forgotten it in the business of *busy*ness. East or West, to find our true purpose and with that our leadership energy, we have to make time for reflection. There are no shortcuts. To help you get started, I will now describe a powerful reflection process about how you can move from values to purpose.

Discovering Your Leadership Energy by Living Life Awake

Converting one's deeply held values into fearless purpose is a process of continuous reflection. You literally need to keep asking a set of questions until your own authentic answers become fully clear. Before you start, let me warn you that this will be frustrating and difficult, but if you get through to the end you will empower yourself to live a life more satisfying and fulfilling than words can ever describe. The process involves six bases of honest questioning and self-reflection (Figure 3.4). The first base requires answering questions like what makes me happy, what makes me sad, and what makes me angry.

Answers to questions on the first base may seem obvious at first glance, but most people do not know them beyond the surface level. As you will recall from the earlier section about

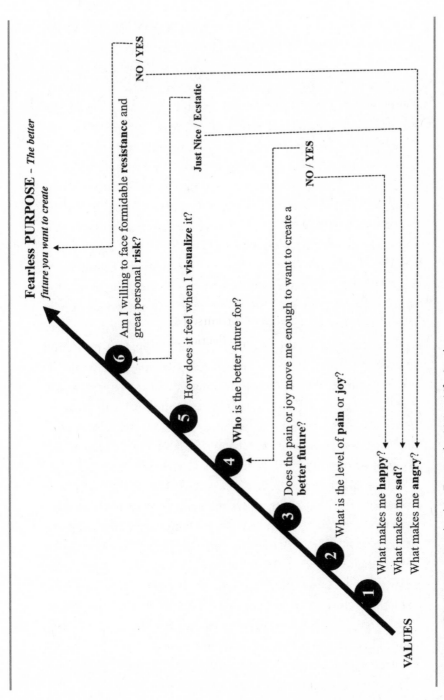

Fearless PURPOSE – *The better future you want to create*

Am I willing to face formidable **resistance** and great personal **risk**?

NO / YES

How does it feel when I **visualize** it?

Just Nice / Ecstatic

Who is the better future for?

Does the pain or joy move me enough to want to create a **better future**?

NO / YES

What is the level of **pain** or **joy**?

What makes me **happy**?
What makes me **sad**?
What makes me **angry**?

VALUES

FIGURE 3.4 Discovering Leadership Energy by Living Life Awake

113

values, energy is produced at the intersection of one's values and life situations. To recognize the extent of energy produced from different stimuli or situations, you will need to be crystal clear about base two, and quantify the level of pain or joy. Until they gain clarity about values and purpose, most people associate happiness with material success and social status. Unfortunately, even as they become immensely successful in the material and social sense, happiness continues to elude many. As Bronnie Ware, a palliative care nurse in Australia, found out after talking to dying patients over several years, unless one reflects early in life about what is really important, one might regret it later. In her global bestseller *The Top Five Regrets of the Dying*, she lists the number one regret of the dying as, "I wish I had the courage to live a life true to myself, not a life others expected of me." Without reflection on what's really important, one gets trapped into a lifetime of chasing power and products, with no guarantee of real happiness or feeling of true success. This is not to suggest that material wealth is not a worthy goal. I am not preaching nonprofit work or social volunteering here. What I am trying to emphasize is the need to be clear about what one really cares about. If material wealth and success it is, so be it. But it should not be the default answer without having reflected on the questions deeply enough.

As you get clear about bases one and two, the third base asks, does the pain or joy move me enough to want to create a better future? Here, one needs to further analyse one's sources of happiness, sadness, or anger, and ask: Do I really want to do something about it? If the answer is not a strong yes, it means answers to base one and two are not fully clear or are not strong enough to convert energy into purpose. Only if the answer to base three is a very convincing yes can one move on to base four. This process of going back to bases one and two needs to be repeated until base three becomes a strong yes. When it does, you move on to base four.

Base four now asks, who is the better future for? Here, emotional integrity is really important. If the better future is just for yourself, so be it. If it is to serve others, so be it. There are no right or wrong answers, there are only honest or dishonest answers. Creating a better future just for yourself is also leadership—self-leadership. You still have to develop a strong set of values and a values-based purpose, and work hard until you achieve your goals. There is absolutely nothing wrong with wanting to become the biggest rock star or tennis player in the world. It requires a huge amount of discipline and leadership energy to keep going even when the going gets really tough.

Whatever your answer to base four, base five asks you to close your eyes and visualize the better future you want to create, and pretend that it is already here. How does it feel? If it feels just nice but not ecstatic, again it means that you still have room for greater clarity about bases one and two, and need to go back there. Basically, what we are trying to do here is find out what you would really want to spend the rest of your life doing, if there were no constraints to pursuing such a path. If the feeling of excitement is so powerful that you cannot wait to get started, you've probably earned the right to move to the sixth and final base.

Base six asks one last time if you are willing to face formidable resistance, great uncertainty, and personal risk while pursuing the better future you have in mind. Again, if the answer is not a resounding yes, you need to go back to bases one and two and start over. Only when your perception of the reward of a better future is greater than the pain and risks associated with getting there can you move forward. Only then will you have found fearless purpose. Again, you will need emotional integrity more than emotional intelligence to do so.

I am often asked how long this journey takes, and what is a good "better future" to pursue. These are impossible questions to answer because it takes different people very different lengths of time to find their values and purpose, if they find them at all. As for what's the right purpose, again it depends on what moves you when you open your eyes. For Norma Bastidas, it was doing something about her son's impending blindness. For Muhammad Yunus, it was the plight of the people in his village, and for Sheikh Mohammed, it was his ambition to make his emirate a world-class city. What do you have your eyes open for? Are you living your life awake? If you are, sooner or later you will find your leadership energy. Meanwhile, here are two stories that might inspire you.

Ben Ripple—USA and Bali, Indonesia

As a college student studying sustainable agriculture and economics, Ben Ripple longed to travel far out of the United States to learn more about agriculture, particularly traditional forms of agriculture and the way they related to modern markets all around the world. Little did he know that inside that restless yearning, he was also in search of purpose, and was soon going to uncover tremendous leadership energy to build a better future for himself and for thousands around him in Bali, Indonesia.

Chancing on the Island of Gods

Landing in the beautiful island of Bali started from a game of chance—poker! Ben and his then-girlfriend Blair won airline coupons and chose the furthest destination flown by United Airlines. They arrived in Australia and traveled on to Bali at the insistence of backpacker friends. In Bali, Ben and Blair (now his wife) were mesmerized by the magic and mystique of the Indonesian archipelago. "This was unlike anything we had ever experienced before," he says when recalling the adventure.

Through several life-changing encounters in that visit, including a surprise gift of a plot of family land and bearing witness to the appalling level of agricultural exploitation in Indonesia, Ben and Blair's lives changed forever and Bali became their home.

"We saw children clothed in nothing but their undergarments, with bare hands deep into pots full of DDT, liquid paraquat (also known as Agent Orange, a defoliant used by the U.S. military during the Vietnam War), and other chemicals, all of which are classified as disastrous chemicals to both human health and the environment," said Ben in his interview with my colleague Adel Jayasuria while describing what he and Blair witnessed. The children were handling chemicals banned internationally since before he was born, yet they were being used across the Indonesian islands by individuals living below the poverty line. "These concoctions were completely inappropriate [to the scale of farming]. It was a horrific economic concept with these individuals using the chemicals without a proper understanding of their ill effects. . . . I saw these communities besieged by the capital markets. . . . There were companies stepping into poor communities, taking complete advantage of them just to make a quick buck. I found that completely unacceptable and distressing."

He realised, "Unless somebody stepped in to show these poor farmers a better way, they would never be ready to deal with the realities of the coming market economy." The realization ultimately became the spark that fueled the establishment and mission of Big Tree Farms. Founded by Ben and Blair in 2000 in the shadow of Bali's sacred Mount Agung, Big Tree Farms had the goal of helping Balinese farmers build sustainable livelihoods while reviving their cultural traditions and natural environment, and changing the balance of power in their interaction with the global market—achieving a healthy balance of economy and ecology.

Defining Moments and Humble Beginnings

Starting with just under an eighth of an acre, Big Tree Farms has grown to become the premier producer of sustainably grown crops in Indonesia, with over 10,000 acres of certified organic land producing well over 50 different crops. "We are now Indonesia's largest certified organic food company, supporting thousands of family farms across five islands," Ben says.

While agriculture has always been a major driving force, Ben's creative spirit also stems from a deep desire to create a positive difference. Upon returning to the United States from Bali to complete his bachelor's in Sustainable Food Production at Evergreen State College in Washington, Ben never lost sight of his original plan of attacking the companies behind the assault on the marginalized Indonesian farmers. He participated in a World Trade Organisation protest in Seattle. "Along with many others in that huge protest, I had myself handcuffed to the door of the hotel where the delegates were." Locked down and teargassed by riot police, he suffered an asthma attack. The individual who held the key to his handcuffs had fled. In that moment of hopelessness and frustration, Ben realized that this was no way of resolving anything. "That kind of activism doesn't create solutions, it only creates more aggression and anxiety in the system." It was a powerful moment in the life of this idealistic activist, who returned to Bali in 1999 upon graduation with the realization that in order to make a difference, he needed to create a financially viable business.

Brace for Impact

Priding themselves on their top-quality, "best in class" food products, an ethos that has taken years to refine, Big Tree Farms endured a journey full of adversity. The first challenge was having a start-up founder lacking business experience. "I wasn't an MBA that came out with a smart packet of how to start a company," he says. "However, Blair and I had made a commitment that no matter what the odds, we were going to find a way to improve the lives of these producers." Big Tree Farms stayed true to its promise, making many mistakes on the journey but not giving up. Taking stock of the numerous lessons, Ben and his team challenged their own idealistic views of sustainability and sustainable supply chains, and reconsidered what volume of risk was acceptable for a market starter like Big Tree Farms. They chose to partner with farmer-producers rather than simply take on all of the risk themselves.

When Adel asked him specifically about a major challenge in getting the business off the ground, he said, "First and foremost, the biggest challenge we faced was profitability. It's been a long and hard road." He explained that Big Tree Farms was born from an emotional ideology of sustainability and social enterprise, but the realities of business meant the fledgling company had to switch to a for-profit model. This required a major change in mindset, vision, and existing company culture. Alongside the new focus on profitability had to come a new way of interacting with their farmer-partners. "We didn't understand how to communicate properly with our [potential farmer-partners], and that contributed to a misconception among farmer groups that Big Tree Farms paid more. Overnight, the company became sort of a celebrity." That was a major obstacle; Big Tree Farms promises to "partner with communities, to co-create production systems and bring about improvement in livelihoods . . . while making viable margin for sustainable growth." Paying top dollar was never their intention, nor what they wanted to achieve. "The real opportunity for change was in the efficiencies [in production and market access]," Ben says. "From that we learned that you really have to know your target market and ensure that the messages sent out are exactly what you mean."

Reaping the Fruits of Labor

Having come a long way, today Big Tree Farms is now Indonesia's largest certified organic food company. It has grown from a small-scale organic farming training venture in 2003, to a profitable integrated social enterprise focused on production and export of food products for retailers and ingredient channels globally. Its products can be found in many global markets such as the United States, European Union, Japan, and Australia on the shelves of major global retailers such as Costco, Whole Foods, and Amazon.

Ben's drive and passion continue despite the many challenges that have come his way. There are many stories on the impact Big Tree Farms has had on the lives of people, the community, and even customers through the production of products that now include coconut sugar and cacao/chocolate products. The most moving stories are ones that describe how poor and destitute farmers have evolved to living decent, more financially sustainable lives. Ben, who has now lived on the island of Bali for 19 years with Blair and their two daughters and speaks fluent Bahasa, shared one particular story that still moves him deeply and reassures him about the positive difference the company has made. Pak Paryono was a farmer well-known in his community as a hard worker. When Ben first met him, he was tapping his own trees and producing his own sugar. He lived in a simple, traditional house with his entire family. As Big Tree Farms started working toward their first organic certificate, a cooperative of farmers was put together and Pak Paryono was voted as the cooperative president. He initially struggled with the new role, having to leave the familiarity of tapping trees and moving to a different style of work. He had to deal with administrative matters, learn how to manage a simple set of finance records, and manage the detailed recording of the organic process. He was given training, and slowly the initial resistance to the new work shifted. Time passed, and one day Pak Paryono came to Ben and expressed his interest in setting up a farmer group cooperative of his own. That move showed Ben the individual Pak Paryono had become. From a simple farmer, he had ambitions to reach out for something more, something he would never have considered without the opportunity and support. And that's exactly what Big Tree Farms provided him. "Menoreh Politan," Pak Paryono's vision of having his own collective of individual farmers, has come to fruition, and he is today one of the top three producers of coconut sugar partnered with Big Tree. He owns a production kitchen as well as a warehouse with production facilities, and has rebuilt his own house and put a down payment on leases for large trucks used in the logistics business he runs to service the demand of Big Tree Farms. But he isn't the only beneficiary. Today, the thousand-plus member farmers in his collective have reaped the benefits of gaining access to a fair economy, making huge strides and living better quality lives.

"I believe that sustainable success relies on believability," says Ben. "Our ideas about business are sometimes radical and our goals aggressive. No doubt, we have countered many obstacles, made plenty of mistakes over the years. But these errors were also wins, because they have served to increase our overall culture, passion, and drive as we continue to build a best-in-class company that produces innovative, high-quality products providing sustainable health, environment, and economy to our customers, farmers, and community."

I visited Big Tree Farms last year with a group of executives who were attending Leading Leaders—a personal and enterprise leadership development program I host a couple of times a year. We could sense strong leadership energy everywhere. Each employee we spoke with, regardless of their title and position, spoke with great passion about their business. They told the same thing in different ways—we are making money, we get paid well, but most importantly, we are changing the world, one farmer and one customer at a time.

Later when the group analysed why Big Tree Farms was so successful, they agreed that Ben's own personal leadership energy—driven by his strong belief in his values and purpose—was infectious. He led by example every day, and inspired his team by being a powerful role model. The group also pointed out that Big Tree Farms has a strong "can do" culture. They don't let obstacles derail them. Rather than blaming and complaining, employees take pride and responsibility in tackling the toughest of challenges head-on. Why? Because they are a purpose-driven company that lives its values everyday.

Dr. William Tan—Singapore

At school, kids constantly teased him, pulled his ears, pinched him, and ran away, knowing he could never chase after them. He spent countless days holed up in a classroom watching from a window while his classmates ran out on the field, leaving him dreaming of the day when he might join them. He routinely had to crawl over dirty floors with his arms and legs covered in open sores. Since his childhood, he had to plan ahead for every single thing, including simple tasks like taking a shower. He almost had to drop out of the prestigious school he had worked so hard to enter because his parents could not afford the costs of transportation. Ultimately, having somehow made it through to university, he had to face the humiliation of being told by his professor that he should not have taken up a precious spot when it could have gone to someone more deserving—more able-bodied. Finally, when he thought he had pulled through it all and soared, he was told at age 51 that he had stage 4 leukemia and only 12 months to live.

How would you feel if you were this person? Devastated, shattered, angry, and defeated? Not if you had the zeal for life and laser-sharp clarity of purpose of Dr. William Tan.

Undaunted, determined, relentless—William has defied all odds, turning adversity into advantage and dreams into reality, allowing nothing and no one to stand in his way. "Physical disability is visible, but there are those who are limited by disabilities which are not visible . . . in the mind and spirit. I believe the human spirit is indomitable and that has helped me stay the course," he says in his book *No Journey Too Tough*.

A Tough Childhood

William was born in Singapore in 1957, and a month before he turned three he contracted polio, which left him paralyzed below the waist. Though poor, William's parents knew that the only way for their son to grow up independently was to have him placed in a mainstream school among the able-bodied. "You may not have legs, but you still have your arms and your brain. You simply have to learn to win with less," his parents told him. "My parents taught me never to worry and complain about what I don't have. Most people make comparisons with others and feel sorry about what they don't have. That makes them give up in despair. Instead, if you focus on what you have, you are filled with hope," said William to a 500-strong audience at the 2016 Leadership Energy Summit Asia—a conference my company hosts every year to spread awareness about leadership energy. That resolve (of winning with less) brought with it struggle, sacrifice, and hard work for the family and for William. William's elder sister Lily had to stop school to care for him. She would carry him on her back up the stairs to his classroom and wait for him till school ended. "I became too heavy for my sister to carry at the age of 10, so my parents approached the medical social worker for a pair of leg braces and crutches. I had to learn how to walk again," he says.

After days of bullying in his first month at kindergarten, young William had had enough. He eventually caught hold and bit the bullying hands that had teased, pulled, and pinched, hard enough that they would never touch him again. Expelled from school for his behavior, with great difficulty the following year his parents found him a place in a new primary school. He topped his year and won a copy of *The Tortoise and the Hare*. In that moment, he was determined to excel in his studies, no matter what obstacles stood in his way, and decided to work toward his childhood dream of becoming a medical doctor. "I was so inspired by the doctors who helped me. I also understood suffering, and I realized that if I can become a doctor, I will be in a really good position to help other suffering patients," William told me as we chatted along the sidelines of the summit.

Next, he went to the Raffles Institute for his preuniversity studies. The physical environment there was so challenging that William nearly dropped out, as his parents couldn't afford the taxi fare from their house to the school. His English language teacher volunteered instead to pick him up and drop him off. She noticed something special about this child. "William was an extremely good student, very conscientious and very shy. He was very sensitive to other people's needs even at a very young age," she said. With the help of teachers such as these, and with his resolve to compensate for his disability by excelling in academics, he finished at Raffles with flying colors and joined the prestigious National University of Singapore. Though very disappointed to not be accepted to medical school, he completed a degree in Life Sciences.

For as long as William can remember, he had to work part-time for extra income. His father's earnings as a street hawker were not enough to support a family of nine. While at primary school he sewed and sold fishing nets, and he sold magazines door to door on crutches while at Raffles Institution. "I encountered a lot of barriers growing up," he says. "I would get very frustrated with staircases and inaccessibility, and difficulties in finding employment."

Despite his disability, as a child William never owned a wheelchair simply because his family couldn't afford one. He was 16 before he was gifted a chair, which changed his life. The first time he got on a wheelchair, he wheeled round and round a circular 400-meter running track. "I was flying, I was unbound," he says recalling the day he found movement and freedom. It was the starting point of an illustrious athletic career that took him to the Paralympics, where he made history as part of the first Singapore Paralympics team, who attended the 1988 games in Seoul, South Korea.

Joining the Singapore civil service for three years, he saved enough to further his studies. He moved to Australia, graduating with a first-class honors masters in physiology from Massey University Veterinary School, before completing his PhD in brain science at the University of Auckland Medical School. As a postdoctoral researcher in Auckland, he was offered a position as research fellow at the world-famous Mayo Clinic in Minnesota, United States—the first-time the Mayo Clinic had offered a fellowship to a non-neurosurgeon candidate. While grateful for the opportunity, it wasn't enough for William. He hadn't forgotten his childhood dream of becoming a doctor. Encouraged by classmates, he left Mayo Clinic and completed a five-year medical degree at the University of Newcastle, Australia, thereby realizing his dream to become a doctor 21 years after originally failing to qualify for medical school. Topping the class in his fourth year, he also won two yearlong scholarships: a Fulbright to Harvard University and a Chevening scholarship to Oxford University. William had overcome enormous adversity to achieve outstanding academic success. He became the only wheelchair-bound doctor in Singapore, and now serves as a resident physician at the Singapore National Cancer Centre. His athletic conquests continued side by side. By April 2009, he had completed seven marathons across seven continents in 27 days, as well as an amazing race stretching from Antarctica to Chile to Kenya and the United States to raise funds for childhood cancer. "It was the peak of my life. I had completed the Antarctica marathon, the North Pole marathon, I had set a world record for achieving marathons in the fastest time across seven continents," he said.

William's athletic endeavors weren't purely for self-fulfillment or for the sake of competition alone. In 1986 William completed a 16-hour charity push to raise money for the Singapore National Kidney Foundation. In 1990, he completed a 1,330-kilometer journey across New Zealand in 22 days to help raise NZD 1.2 million for children with physical disabilities. While at Harvard in 2002, he qualified for the Boston Marathon and became the first wheelchair athlete in the 105-year history of the run to have dedicated his race to the Children's Hospital fund-raising program. Singlehandedly over the last 22 years he has raised more than S$18 million for charities and causes around the world by racing in more than 120 marathons and ultramarathons. He holds six marathon and ultramarathon world records, and is the first person in the world to complete a wheelchair marathon to the North Pole in 21 hours and 10 minutes.

Tragedy Strikes Again

Just when he thought that the worst was behind him, while competing in the Paris marathon in October 2009, William's resilience was tested like never before with the diagnosis of end-stage leukemia. "Here I was, in Paris completing another marathon, and ready to tie the knot with my fiancée right after that, and I noticed I was bleeding from my nose. At first I dismissed it as nothing, and continued with the marathon. Determined to finish the race, I pushed along, and finally went through the Arc de Triomphe. It was great to be there, but I also knew something was seriously wrong as by then the bleeding was profuse," says William. "I thought this cannot be. I am a world-renowned athlete. I am a doctor who gives care to patients, how can I be a patient? How can I have just 12 months to live? It was the first time I realized that there is nothing that is 'too big to fail.' I had read in the papers about the subprime mortgage crisis that was in full swing at the time, and I said to myself, this is my own subprime crisis . . . not long ago I was on the cover of Prime Magazine Singapore, and now I have cancer? This is definitely subprime."

"What happened next?" my colleague Muhammad Sabri asked him in a one-on-one interview, and here is how William replied: "Initially I was disappointed. I was angry. Hadn't I had enough? Why this now? They told me I could try six months of chemotherapy followed by a bone marrow transplant. So, I thought to myself, do I bear the pain of chemotherapy or live the next 12 months completing my bucket list? I finally thought about my mom, who had endured so much to make me who I am today, and decided I could not die before her. How would she feel seeing me go before her? I have to make myself fit again. The choice for pursuing treatment was now clear."

In concluding the interview, Sabri asked, "From being a polio-stricken child, you went on to outperform your peers in elementary and secondary school. You then defied the odds and studied at some of the most prestigious universities including Harvard, studied neuroscience, fulfilled your childhood dream of becoming a doctor, fought cancer, and became a world record–setting athlete. May I ask you, what's next for William Tan?" Already 59, this is how he replied: "Well, I'm very grateful for this second chance, this second lease of life. I have been seven years in remission! In return, I want to do more for humanity. I may not be superman, but there is a lot more I want to do for others. I am back to wheelchair racing since last year, I am just back from a race in London—500 kilometers in four days—to raise money for cancer research. The next will be my tenth Boston Marathon. And I will work towards the 2020

Tokyo Paralympics, and then I will retire and become a volunteer sports administrator to nurture young athletes."

No stranger to difficulty, despite the chemotherapy and bone marrow transplant, William returned to action with hours of training every day to regain strength and fitness levels. He achieved his best time at the Berlin Marathon soon after his treatment and completed two full marathons back-to-back, beating the completion times of his preleukemia days. In all my years studying leadership energy, this is probably one of the strongest stories I have come across. When I asked him what his secret was to keep going despite one setback after another he attributed it to positive visualization and the plasticity of the brain. "It is all about the power of the mind," he said, leaving me completely awestruck by the stunning example of the resilience of the human spirit.

What I've tried to explain in this chapter is a journey most great leaders have undertaken at some point in their lives. Having studied numerous leadership development models over the years, I haven't found a more powerful one. It is tough to undertake this journey, but it is the only way to fortify yourself with the strength you will need if you decide to lead. There are no shortcuts or easy answers to developing limitless leadership energy. Only a well-thought-out set of values and a values-based purpose can give you the fearlessness that leadership needs, particularly in today's open source era. Besides all the examples in this book, I can vouch for this approach from personal experience, too. I do not have the talent or tenacity of Norma Bastidas or William Tan, so I asked myself what my purpose could be. And I found it in my work. I decided to challenge status quo in my profession and uncover new insights. Now, my purpose is to wake up individuals and organizations to their true potential. Ever since I discovered this purpose, I have become more energized than ever before. Now, my work was not just a job, it became a passion. I work much harder than before. As you can imagine, writing books while still doing a full-time job as CEO is not easy. But I don't get tired, and I derive a lot of happiness from working really hard because I have found my leadership energy. While I certainly enjoy and value the monetary rewards associated with my work, they are not the main reason why I work so hard. I get my real reward each time I am able to help an individual or organization achieve their potential.

CHAPTER SUMMARY

- Despite the money spent annually on leadership development, it is not working because it is based on five myths:
    1. Democratic leadership is the best way to create breakthrough success.
    2. Followership = Leadership.
    3. A Position of Authority = Leadership.
    4. Leaders are born, not made.
    5. Leadership can be learned through case studies, role plays, and competency models.
- Leadership is the art of harnessing human energy toward the creation of a better future.
- Leadership energy is the main ingredient of powerful leadership, and it emanates from deep clarity of values and a values-based purpose.
- Most people go through life without clarity of values and purpose, and are therefore devoid of leadership energy.
- Strong leadership energy can only be discovered through reflection based on emotional integrity, which is the courage to acknowledge what one really wants for oneself without using a societal lens.
- Leadership energy forms the basis of practicing the five keys of positive autocratic leadership.

Questions for Reflection

1. What are your most deeply held values that you
   will never compromise, no matter what?

2. Are you totally honest with yourself in terms of
   what you want out of life? Or are you trapped in a
   story you don't like or that is untrue?

3. Do you really want to be a leader?

4. Do you have a carefully thought through and
   well-defined purpose? If so, what is it?

PART 3

Open Source Enterprise Leadership

CHAPTER 4

Minimum Supervision, Maximum Performance

CONTEXT

1. The Open Source Era

OPEN SOURCE PERSONAL LEADERSHIP

2. The Naked Autocrat Creates Breakthrough Results
3. Leadership Energy, Not Competencies

OPEN SOURCE ENTERPRISE LEADERSHIP

4. Minimum Supervision, Maximum Performance
5. No More Engagement Surveys
6. Crowdsourced Innovation and Leadership Succession

U p until now I've discussed in detail the sweeping technological and social trends that will change the face of
our business, social, and economic landscapes over the next
decades. I've tried to make the case that this brave new world
will require brave new personal leadership, and more important, brave new *thinking* about personal leadership. From this
chapter onward, let's switch gears toward leading the organization. If everything we've discussed so far wasn't radical enough
already, prepare yourself for the ride to get a little bumpier. In
this chapter I am going to go further and suggest that some of
our most widely loved people-management tenets must be swept
aside if organizations are to survive and flourish in the coming years. Our old models were suitable for a static past where
workers were expected to stay in one company and one industry, and climb the slippery ladder in pursuit of wealth, perks,
and titles. This is no longer relevant, when so many workers
are carving their own career paths, having multiple employers
in multiple industries, and are driven to succeed for reasons far
more intrinsic or complex than purely financial. Specifically,
I'm going to challenge three basic principles that have been
the mainstay of management thinking for about a hundred
years:

1. All employees must be given stretch goals so that they
   remain energized to go "above and beyond" to make
   the organization highly successful.
2. The immediate manager has the maximum influence on
   employee engagement.
3. Employees must be managed and monitored in order to
   drive high performance.

Instead, I will suggest a radical new open source way of
thinking about performance management that is designed to
cater to the myriad talents and motivations of employees.

Minimum Goals, Unlimited Vacation

I will begin by showing how stretch goals ignore the scientific truth that governs employee performance and motivation, then discuss the seemingly absurd idea of allowing employees to take unlimited vacation.

Stretch Goals

Stretch goals are the cornerstone of many performance management systems today. Usually part of yearly goal setting for an individual employee, they require employees to extend themselves significantly past their usual limit to achieve their goals. Instead of asking for small or incremental changes, the stretch goal (sometimes called a BHAG*—big hairy audacious goal) calls on workers to take a leap into the unknown, far past their usual achievements. The practice of goal setting was first popularized in the mid-1960s by professors Edwin Locke and Gary Latham, who found that setting specific and ambitious goals energized employees and focused their attention to positive effect. The practice has taken off since, notably with former GE CEO Jack Welch, but more broadly across the business landscape, where the importance of stretch goals is held up almost as gospel.

Not surprisingly, stretch goals are credited with inspiring employees to achieve astonishing new feats of creativity and innovation. A widely used example is that of U.S. airline Southwest, that challenged its staff to bring the plane turnaround time on the tarmac down to only 10 minutes. Despite widespread disbelief, Southwest staff managed to do just that, calling on techniques used by pit crews in Formula One racing. Likewise, Google—one of the most innovative and

---

* Popularized by Jim Collins in his global bestseller *Good to Great*.

forward-thinking companies of recent years—has stretch goals embedded in its company philosophy. "We set ourselves goals we know we can't reach yet, because we know that by stretching to meet them we can get further than we expected," it says. Google doesn't always expect its employees to reach the individual stretch goals set in their annual performance targets. A score of 60 to 70 percent is considered enough. However, it continues with the practice in the belief that in some cases the goal will be met, and push the company a little bit further than the rest.

Stretch goals have also come in for a share of criticism. A Harvard Business School report, *Goals Gone Wild: The Systematic Side Effects of Over-Prescribing Goal Setting*, argued that the benefits of goal setting have been enormously overstated and have instead led to high levels of employee stress, unethical behavior and distorted risk-perception, corroded organizational culture, and a reduction in intrinsic motivation. Among several quite fascinating case studies, the report cited the very public failure of the Ford Pinto as an example of the potential disaster of goal setting. In the late 1960s the Ford company set a goal of designing and producing a new car weighing under 2,000 pounds and costing less than US$2,000, to be produced by 1970. The resulting Ford Pinto met the goal, but was rushed through safety checks where engineers failed to notice a key design flaw—that the car ignited on impact. When the flaw was discovered, Ford executives elected to pay out the victims rather than recalling and changing the design of the car. Ford may have reached its stretch goal, but it did so at the expense of customer safety, ethical behavior, and the reputation of the company. The reason I bring up this fairly old story is to point out that decades later in 2008, Tata Motors of India tried to do the exact same thing with disastrous results. The resultant Tata Nano was a huge flop. Chairman Ratan Tata laid out an audacious goal to produce a car costing $2,000, and wouldn't take no for an answer. Well, his engineers gave him what he wanted, but the product had so many problems that it was dead on arrival.

Likewise, the downfall of Enron is in part blamed on the company's stretch goals, which caused employees to take unethical and ill-considered risks that eventually brought down the whole company. The authors of *Goals Gone Wild* believe that Enron's downfall was in part because its stretch goals were entirely financial, with no relationship to the values and ethics supposedly espoused by the company. If they have any chance of being effective, stretch goals must be aligned with not only the strategy but the wider values of the company. They must also offer employees a framework to dictate behavior when the stretch goals seem out of reach.

In addition, *Goals Gone Wild* suggests that managers set stretch goals far more frequently than they actually need to "ensure" employee motivation. Excessive goal setting can harm the employee's intrinsic motivation to do the job well for its own sake, while the psychological impact of goal failure or the constant low-lying stress that the goal will not be achieved can drive down performance even further. The authors conclude, and this is an important point, that stretch goals can be additionally problematic when the same goal is set for many individuals. The goal may be too easy for some and far too difficult for others, and the culture of competition that builds as employees stretch to achieve their goal can break down team camaraderie and cooperation.

Interestingly, a study by Sim Sitkin of Duke University also suggests that setting organization-wide stretch goals can also backfire, simply because the wrong companies are setting them. Stretch goals should be set by large companies that have the resources to fund them, and the cushion to fall back on if the goal isn't achieved. A company like Google is an obvious example; it has an existing reputation for innovation and excellence and a very healthy balance sheet to fall back on if one of its goals fails to launch. Instead, stretch goals are more often used by desperate organizations as a last-ditch solution to a much wider problem, when there is little or no room to fail.

Stretch Goals: Yes or No?

So, what is the answer? Stretch goals are embedded in our organizational structures, not only in the vision, mission, and strategies of many companies but in the day-to-day work and performance management of most employees. They are believed to be the main way to motivate employees, and equally of providing a framework for measuring employee performance whether good or bad. Can we truly consider a performance management system that doesn't include stretch goals? After all, organizations still need a way of assessing employees, and there is no doubt that setting achievable or moon-shoot goals can work. Likewise, in the increasingly fractured workplace where many employees lack permanent contracts, a permanent workspace, or may not even be present in the office, city, or country, goals remain a valuable way of tying staff together to reach a common purpose, or individually working toward personal achievement and organizational success.

My argument is this. Stretch goals are inherently neither good nor bad. They work well for some employees and less well for others, depending on the goal, on the job, and where an individual is in his or her personal or professional life. Stretch goals work well for those who want to be stretched, but can be a source of stress, anxiety, or poorly thought out behavior for others.

The problem with stretch goals lies in the way in which they are applied. Employees are far more aware and educated than ever before. They fully understand that if they want to earn a certain standard of living, they need to work accordingly. If they want a higher standard of living, they will willingly embark upon stretch goals, but if they simply want to make enough to pay their bills and pursue other interests in their spare time, stretch goals will not work for them. Today more than ever before, ordinary people are searching for empowerment and meaning in their personal and professional lives, and are no longer interested in traditional carrot and stick measures of motivation and performance. If they don't like the goal or the demand that they reach it, they will simply move on. Creating arbitrary stretch goals and demanding employees reach them for presumed financial or career gain is not enough for many people, especially in jobs that might seem uncertain, temporary, or eventually obsolete.

Likewise, and most critically, the problem with stretch goals is that *they assume not only that each employee wants to be stretched, but that each employee is capable of being stretched.* What do I mean by this? As we saw with leadership in previous chapters, only a small percentage (20 percent if Pareto is to be believed) of individuals have the energy, drive, desire, and resilience to be a truly effective leader. I'll come back to this statistic again and again, because the same goes for stretch goals. Only a small percentage of employees have the creativity, innovation, and drive to truly relish and achieve stretch goals at any one point or time. Assuming that every employee has the ability and drive to achieve these goals will be tantamount to setting them, and the organization, up for failure and disappointment.

The Ubiquitous 80:20 Rule

We've been referring to this rule throughout the book, and will continue to do so in the remaining chapters as well. Before I discuss *how* and *why* stretch goals should be applied, it might be time to take a detour and delve into 80:20 in a bit more detail. The 80:20 rule (also known as the Pareto Principle) is one of the most ubiquitous rules in nature, science, and business and should be the basis for how our management and organizational practices must evolve to have any chance of keeping up in the twenty-first century.

The Pareto Principle posits that *80 percent of output is a direct result of only 20 percent of input.* It's a principle as old as time, yet the theory as we know it was first developed by Italian economist Vilfredo Pareto in 1906, the result of his survey of land ownership in Italy. Pareto discovered that 80 percent of land was owned by only 20 percent of the population, a statistic he discovered was repeated throughout the Western world. Likewise, Pareto quickly realized the rule's wider relevance when he noted that 80 percent of the peas in his garden came from only 20 percent of the pods, a discovery that is repeated time and again in our natural world. It's interesting to note, also, that the 80:20 rule *also applies within its own rule,* for example in the Richter scale, which measures the impact of earthquakes on a 10-point scale. Each one point increase on the 10-point scale in fact represents a tenfold increase in impact, so the top 20 percent of the top 20 percent has almost unimaginable scale. In fact, once you start looking for the Pareto Principle, also called the "law of the vital few," and the "principle of factor sparsity," you see it everywhere. It has been recognized across the natural, social, and economic landscapes, in areas as diverse as criminology, drug abuse, earthquakes and volcanos, healthcare, and biology.

Obviously, the Pareto Principle has widespread relevance in business as well and is recognizable across sales, marketing, project management, software applications, and customer service. A few examples that might seem familiar: 80 percent of complaints come from 20 percent of customers; 80 percent of profits come from 20 percent of time allocated; 80 percent of sales come from 20 percent of clients; 80 percent of sales come from 20 percent of sales staff. Microsoft, in fact, discovered Pareto applied to both product features (Windows consumers used only 20 percent of features, 80 percent of the time) and software bugs. After discovering that 80 percent of system crashes were caused by 20 percent of the most complex bugs, the company was able to speed up product fixes by focusing on the most mission critical areas. Similar to the Richter scale, Microsoft also discovered that over 50 percent of system problems were caused by a mere 1 percent of bugs.

The Pareto Principle has been used before as a basis for performance management, most notably and notoriously under Jack Welch's leadership at GE. Welch took over GE in 1981, and instituted a "rank and yank" performance management system. Managers were asked to rank employees along the bell curve; the top 20 percent of employees were given praise and generous financial rewards, while the bottom 10 percent were fired. The middle 70 percent were given coaching, training, and goal-setting, based around the opportunity to move into the vaunted top 20 percent. Welch believed that rigorous differentiation between employees was critical, saying that "it's all about being extreme, rewarding the best and weeding out the ineffective. Rigorous differentiation delivers real stars—and stars build great businesses." A feature of Welch's policy was what he called "candor," letting employees know where they stood in the organization, so that, according to him, those who were fired were already expecting it.

Welch's enthusiasm (and spectacular results) at GE were at least part of the reason why the 20:70:10 model became so widespread across the 1980s and 1990s. The argument for Welch's version of the bell curve is obvious—it's important to identify, reward, and incentivize employees who have achieved top results, and equally critical to "trim" employees who are failing to deliver. Done well, the bell curve should also give midrange employees the opportunity to assess their performance and receive support and training. The system is particularly useful in service-driven organizations where impact can be measured quantitatively or through customer results, or when individual performance is considered more important than group work or teamwork. It also gives a useful framework for managers tasked with giving bonuses, and theoretically can increase performance by sparking healthy internal competition.

The downsides to the bell curve model are equally obvious. Critics point out that employee performance does not necessarily follow the model as precisely as it demands. The system lacks the flexibility to reward a greater number of high-performing employees, running the risk of losing some who don't make the cut. Managers are forced to push employees into rankings that might not represent the true nature of their work, nor reflect the increasingly team-driven, cross–business unit workplace. Likewise, the ranking system can promote unhealthy and demotivating internal competition, which distracts staff from focusing on the greater challenge of their external competitors. The bell curve, in addition, has been accused of a lack of transparency in which managerial subjectivity, favoritism, and even discrimination preclude a fair result. It's interesting here again to point out that Enron, the epitome of corrupt practices that I mentioned when discussing the problems with stretch goals, also utilized the forced ranking model, with only 5 percent of employees awarded the top ranking while the bottom 15 percent were fired.

Given that the bell curve is a derivative of the 80:20 rule, I believe Welch was right in using it. In the open source era, the only difference I suggest is to refrain from force ranking and predeciding which of your employees form the top 20 percent, the middle 60 percent, and the bottom 20 percent. In Enron's case, they were playing with the proven statistic itself (5 percent instead of 20 percent), and performance was measured on all the wrong parameters. We will discuss this more in the next chapter, but in today's dynamic environment, it is impossible to slot people based on assessments and other artificial means. There is no guarantee in today's forever-changing business landscape that someone who is performing well today will also do so in the future.

80:20 and Stretch Goals

So how does the 80:20 rule relate to stretch goals? As I am sure you've guessed by now, expecting all employees to write and achieve stretch goals defies the 80:20 rule. If most management teams agree that only 20 percent of their people perform at "above and beyond" levels, what is the point of assigning stretch goals to everyone? And how can the universal truth of 80:20 be effectively applied to performance management without creating the negativity associated with Welch's model? The answer lies in a complete change of mindset, and speaks directly to the empowerment, flexibility, and independence demanded by the workers of today and tomorrow.

I propose that every employee be given the minimum standards required to perform his or her role adequately, and everything beyond that, including stretch goals, be left up to the individual worker to choose.

Radical? Yes. Requiring an enormous change of mindset? Definitely. Unworkable? Not at all. This solution speaks directly to the opportunities and problems presented by stretch goals, and also acknowledges the universal truth that is the 80:20 rule. It also better meets the needs of today's empowered and free workforce. And as I will explain later in the chapter, if applied correctly, this new philosophy will radically change the role of the manager as well.

Consider this. The 80:20 rule (or 20:60:20, if we apply the standard bell curve model rather than Welch's version) dictates that only 20 percent of your employees will be highly motivated achievers. They will contribute the lion's share of the innovation, drive, and performance that a company needs to achieve breakthrough success. Irrespective of what goals are or are not set for them, these workers will always overdeliver and will consistently score in the top percentile of any performance curve. The middle 60 percent of employees play a critical role; they are the supporters, the followers, and the solid citizens who keep the daily operational needs of an organization ticking over. They will deliver or sometimes overdeliver to a greater or lesser extent depending on various factors and motivations, but they will not be pressured to go beyond what they are comfortable achieving. Then there will be the bottom 20 percent. Most of these will likely achieve the minimum standards required of the job, but no more. A small proportion of the bottom 20 percent might not make the minimum standard no matter how much external motivation is applied, and will need to be moved on or retrained.

According to the Pareto Principle and the numerous examples we see every day in organizations, performance will always fall along the certain bell curve no matter what measures or metrics are in place, and even if no metrics are in place. So why not just acknowledge this truth and accept that not every employee can, should, and would be an overachiever, and dispense with the annual stress for managers and employees of setting stretch goals?

This approach differs in a significant way from the approach taken in many companies that believe in the "rank and yank" philosophy. In rank and yank, management acknowledges that performance will roughly fall across the bell curve, but rather than let employees naturally fall within the model depending on their own inclination, it artificially and harshly imposes from above. This leads to dissatisfaction and disempowerment, particularly for those employees forced to reach for stretch goals they don't want. In contrast, allowing employees to choose their level of performance gives empowerment and flexibility to workers, and lets them decide how much or how little they want to go above the minimum requirements for the role. As most business leaders agree, not all roles within their companies require superstars. Some roles simply require a certain standard of performance and no more. So why not let people choose where they want to be on the bell curve?

Another way of looking at this is to go back to Chapter 3 and look at purpose. For some employees, their professional work, or making money, is their main purpose. They may choose to go for stretch goals and exhibit the strongest leadership energy. For some, work might still be an important part of their lives but not their main purpose. They may choose to be in the middle 60 percent so that they have time and energy to pursue other interests. For some people, work may just be a means to pay bills. They may choose to work only to the minimum standards required so that they get paid accordingly, and can devote a majority of their energy to other interests. I will talk about this in a bit more detail in the next chapter. The point I want to make here is this: in the open source economy, people have a lot of choice and a lot of freedom. Thanks to the democratization of knowledge, they are also more aware and knowledgeable than ever before. Giving them stretch goals when they don't want them will not work. Management must rethink the old approach of standing above the workforce with sticks to make sure they don't slack off. As with succession planning and innovation,* in this new era, they need to let the cream rise to the top naturally.

Consider who might be positively affected by this model. One example that springs to mind very quickly is that of young parents, who are juggling the pressures of child-rearing alongside the demands of the busy twenty-first-century workplace. Many women in particular feel they must choose between having children and having a career, and fear that taking their foot off the accelerator while they have young children will have a longstanding and negative impact on their career. My solution

---

* We will discuss natural innovation and succession planning in Chapter 6.

is tailor-made for parents in this position: they can choose to "take a break" from the fast lane and decide how much they can commit to their work beyond the minimum, in the knowledge that this will not impact negatively on their long-term career. Once their children have grown or their life circumstances change, they can choose to press down on the accelerator again. If companies don't allow such flexibility, today's workers will choose to opt out of the company toward the more flexible model of free agency. Rather than lose your best employees, why not change your thinking along with the times, and give them the opportunity to decide?

This model also has the flexibility to work in the changing workforce. We saw in Chapter 1 that the key trait of twenty-first-century employees is diversity—of culture, age, background, and gender—all of whom will have different reasons for working and motivations for working hard. Take for example the baby boomers and the millennials, two widely divergent generational groups who will be playing key roles in the workforce over the next few decades. Many baby boomers will choose to remain at work past their retirement age, either to earn additional money for retirement, to fill gaps in the workforce, to maintain social connections, or to continue deriving the fulfilment they experience from working, while using the skills they have gained over a lifetime. They may be motivated to do a good and effective job that uses their skills, without having the desire to stretch past the minimum. They no longer feel the need to reach upward on the career ladder. Does that mean that they are any less valuable workers? Not at all. Within the generation lies a wealth of knowledge, ability, and skills that should be appreciated by an organization. What this means is that the workers are freed from the pretense of reaching for goals that no longer relate to them, and the organization from the frustration of feeling that every employee should be overachieving. On the other end, some millennials might be looking to maximize their earnings and career acceleration. They may be much more inclined to pursue stretch goals to be one of the top 20 percent.

How Will This Work in Practice?

I can imagine at this point you are thinking, there is no way that this model can work! There is no way that organizations can function without the frameworks and structures that force employees to work a certain number of hours, or work toward certain goals and standards. Without them, there will be nothing to hold an organization together.

Stretch Goals

I'm going to speak to the realities rather than the myths of employee performance and motivation later in this chapter, but first I want to address the claim that organizational performance overall will suffer. Consider Uber, an example I've discussed several times in this book. The strength of organizations like Uber is that they offer drivers the opportunity to choose how much or how little they work, to fit in with personal circumstances, professional goals, or motivations. An Uber driver is not required to work a certain amount of hours, but is instead asked to behave according to the organization's frameworks, mission, and values. Because of this, Uber has a flexible and effective workforce, and has quickly become the largest taxi company in the world. A 2015 study into Uber drivers' motivations for driving with the company revealed that 62 percent of drivers had full- or part-time jobs and used Uber as a supplementary income, while 38 percent used Uber as their primary source of income. Yet Uber is flourishing, because it has accepted the reality of "employee" performance. In that same survey, 78 percent of drivers said they were satisfied with their work, and 73 percent said they would prefer a job where "they are their own boss" rather than the traditional 9-to-5 job, with salary and benefits. Notably, Uber is not simply a career option for those who may feel they have no other options. Forty-eight percent of Uber drivers have tertiary degrees, compared with 19 percent of taxi drivers in traditionally structured companies.

In comparison, the authors in *Goals Gone Wild* cite New York taxi drivers as an example of when daily uniform targets designed to keep employees on track actually demotivate staff and cause a reduction in earnings; when employees see the goal as the "ceiling rather than the floor." Rainy days in New York significantly increase demand for taxis, yet the number of taxis on the street actually drops, particularly at night. The reason is that taxi drivers are given a daily target, which they tend to achieve quicker on rainy days, and then knock off work. There is no incentive (financial or otherwise) for them to work longer hours, as exceeding their daily target one day does not mean a decrease in target for the next. If the drivers were given financial targets that took a longer time horizon and given the flexibility to work longer hours on busier days and shorter hours on less busy days, paradoxically earnings overall would be likely to increase. It involves the organization ceding elements of control and choice to the drivers, yet with a better mutual outcome.

Another relevant precedent for setting minimum rather than stretch goals is the contract grading system used in many U.S. universities. Initially used by professor of history Gerald Herman at Northeastern University in the 1970s, contract grading comes in several different formats. At its heart are a clear and detailed set of guidelines agreed between lecturer and student, which stipulate what assignments a student must complete to receive a certain grade. Within the terms of the contract, students are given the flexibility to choose how many assignments they complete depending on which grade or achievement standard they wish to meet. Each assignment must meet a minimum set of standards but is otherwise ungraded—the raw number of requirements is what determines a student's final grade. Proponents of contract grading argue that the process rewards students who are hard workers and highly motivated, while giving other students the flexibility to devote their time to other courses or priorities depending on their circumstances. Herman particularly believed that a key benefit of contract grading was it allowed for a course to be tailored to a student's individual motivations (a point I'll come back to later in this chapter). By allowing students to pick and choose which assignments they complete, they are also able to tailor their learning experience to align with their particular passions, interests, motivations, and goals.

Other tertiary teachers have subsequently put their own stamp on contract grading, with successful outcomes. Professors Jane Danielewicz and Peter Elbow at the University of Massachusetts sign a contract with their students at the beginning of the course, which gives them an immediate base B grade provided they complete a certain amount of assignments and coursework. Seeking anything above a B involves individual evaluation and assessment by both lecturers. The way Danielewicz and Elbow see it, this version of contract grading gives students the flexibility to accept a B grade if that is all they wish to achieve, but also gives more motivated students the opportunity to stretch themselves further. Danielewicz and Elbow specifically make the distinction between personally evaluated and nonevaluated work, arguing that an assessor is subject to personal opinion, subjectivity, and circumstance like everyone else. Students searching for something more than a B do so in the knowledge that no assessment can be wholly impersonal or objective; the system acknowledges that we are complex beings who bring a series of biases, motivations, and beliefs to our judgement of others. This method directly confronts the accusations of subjectivity and bias that frequently dog both tertiary assessment and workplace performance reviews. The argument, too, is that contract grading attempts to reduce the passivity of students in the learning and grading process. Instead of simply going along with whatever is dictated by the teacher, students take an active decision-making role in their own learning and their own outcomes, leading to greater empowerment, choice, and motivation.

Of course, contract grading is not without its critics. As I would anticipate with my own proposal to let employees choose their achievement levels in the workplace, critics of contract grading fear that without the traditional grading process students won't work as hard, do homework, or study for exams. It also disrupts the traditional power balance between teacher and student by giving more power into student hands to take what they choose from their courses, a concept that can be profoundly threatening to traditional power structures. It is for this reason in particular that I think contract grading, and my own model of performance evaluation, are tailored to the workplace reality of the twenty-first century.

The days of using power and authority to drive people toward desired performance are over. As we exhaustively discussed in the first half of this book, one of the chief outcomes of the technological and population revolutions is the democratization of knowledge and information. The availability of knowledge on the Internet has undermined many of the old tenets that universities held dear; the "sage on the stage" model where a lecturer held knowledge and parceled it out to students is no longer relevant. I recently met Michio Kaku, physicist, futurist, author, television host, and professor of theoretical physics at the City College of New York. We were discussing future trends, and he described a coming near-future in which powerful computing power and vast information will be available at the blink of an eye. He meant it literally, because he was talking about an Internet-enabled device implanted within an ordinary contact lens. From soldiers to surgeons, everyone will have access to instant knowledge and computing power through wearable and implanted devices.

I asked Professor Kaku to talk a bit about the future of education. Much of education today depends upon learning from professors before reproducing that knowledge in exam papers to receive a grade. If all knowledge will be available at "the blink of an eye," what will happen to traditional education? He smiled and told me that my question reminded him of a time when professors debated if calculators should be allowed in class and during exams. "Some professors wanted to ban calculators in class simply because they felt that they had suffered with manual calculations in their time, so why should their students not suffer?" The fact of the matter is that knowledge is going to be even more freely available in the future as compared to today's Internet. It is an irreversible trend. Education therefore will need to be about what the student wants to learn rather than what the professor wants to teach. Grades will depend upon how students process existing knowledge to create new knowledge or ideas, not on how much a student can memorize existing knowledge and formulas. The education industry will need to adapt to the new reality.

Contract grading directly addresses this shift, and instead acknowledges a more egalitarian playing field by giving students an active role in designing their own courses and assessments, and choosing where and how to channel their individual motivations. In a way, this speaks directly to the wider search for meaning that grips our modern society. Instead of being forced to buy into a prefabricated, one-size-fits-all degree, students are given the chance to shape, mold, customize, and make individual meaning from their educational experience. If universities cannot provide this, students will go elsewhere, including to the myriad online courses that are now offered by the most elite institutions. While education is not the subject of this book, universities are another example of organizations that must adapt or die in the coming decades. Just as contract grading is a way that universities can choose to offer a more customized, meaningful, and empowering experience to their key stake-holders, their students, so too organizations must embrace new ways of empowering and adjusting to fit the changing needs of their staff.

What is curious about contract grading, and as yet unexplored in the literature I have read on the subject, is whether students who participate in it fall under the 80:20 rule. My guess is that they probably do! The prevalence of 80:20 is such that university students and their grades are highly likely to fit within that framework. What is key to the success of the method and to the framework is that the teachers involved acknowledge that students will have other commitments, and do not penalize them for choosing to do only the minimum. It doesn't after all mean that students are unmotivated or underperforming; it's that they are making a conscious choice to devote as much or as little of their energy to the task at hand and are aware of and prepared for the outcomes. As Professor Kaku told me, "The early 1900s was an age of mass standardization. Today, we have entered the age of mass customization."

Unlimited Vacation

I will never forget the reaction of an old-fashioned manager in my audience a while back when I first presented the idea of minimum goals. To say that he was furious would be a gross understatement. Without the slightest attempt at listening to understand, he relentlessly shunned the idea as baseless and impractical. No matter what I tried, he kept saying it would not work, and that if we set minimum goals, employees won't even show up to work, thereby disrupting critical services the business offers. "Can you imagine a bus driver having this flexibility? If he doesn't show up, commuters will be stranded." he argued. Clearly, my friend here did not understand the meaning of "minimum performance goals," and what the consequences of not meeting them would be. But the point of raising this incident is not to offer an explanation, because that I think is very clear if you've read the rationale above carefully enough. The reason I bring it up is this: can you imagine what his reaction would have been if I had suggested what I am about to suggest now—that in addition to the flexibility of choosing minimum goals instead of stretch goals, employees should also be allowed to take as much vacation as they want to? I think he would have simply imploded.

I can empathize with such people because what we are talking about is radical compared to conventional practice. But so was the idea of flying airplanes before they were invented, and so was the idea of working from home before it became accepted practice. In the past, new ideas took a long time before going mainstream. My argument now is that in the open source era there is no time to be lost. Speed is everything, and those that don't adapt to the changing reality quickly risk being left behind.

So is the idea of unlimited vacation totally absurd and unworkable? Well, not if you consider what's already going on. Per Thomas Frohlich in *USA Today*, General Electric, Grant Thornton, Grubhub, Netflix, LinkedIn, Virgin Group, and HubSpot are already allowing unlimited vacation. Yes, you read that right—a 124-year-old company like GE is in that list too. This is not a list of funky Silicon Valley start-ups alone. And a quick search on Google revealed that these were not the only companies doing so. It is a small but growing trend. Why? Because in today's economy you cannot force anyone to work more than they want to. More so than ever before, in the open source era we need to let employees be their own entrepreneurs and manage their time and input as they see fit. Of course, they (employees) also need to be prepared to accept the fact that they will reap only what they sow.

Another reason companies are doing this is to manage output, not input. By putting the output onus on employees and turning them free, organizations can free up considerable management time and allow employees to self-manage. Again, the 80:20 rule will apply. Twenty percent of employees will be highly motivated to perform and excel at work, and they will probably take the least vacation. The middle 60 percent will probably take as much as the unspoken norm the organization's culture allows. Perhaps a very small percentage of employees will try to maximize on vacation, with some even attempting to misuse the privilege. In the open source era, such behavior will be totally transparent and visible to all. And the open source performance management system can easily address such misuse by giving (or not giving) people what they deserve based on what they put in as effort and energy, and more important, based on their performance and results. The fact of the matter is, in today's digitally connected world, we wear our reputation "rating" on our forehead—everyone knows who we are and what we are made up of. There is nowhere to hide, and each one of us will need to manage our own reputation in this open, transparent, and naked world, and face consequences accordingly. The best part of the open source era is that it is a self-governing system where undesirable behavior cannot be hidden and becomes a liability for those choosing to practice it. Only genuine and sincere people will survive and thrive in the long run. Coming back to our favorite example of Uber again, would you accept a driver with a 2.5 rating, or would you cancel immediately and request another car?

To summarize, 80:20 is a fact of life. In organizations, it's derivative—the 20:60:20 applies to performance distribution whether we like it or not. So, both with setting goals and vacation time, instead of "managing" performance, we need to free up people to work (or not) as they best see fit, and reward accordingly.

Employee Motivation and the Role of the Manager

So, now that you've read about this new philosophy for performance management, and considered some of the arguments I have put forward, I'll guarantee you have two main objections! First, you are wondering why any employee will be motivated to achieve beyond the bare minimum, and secondly, if we are leaving it up to employees to drive their own performance, where does this leave their immediate manager? Am I right? Well, let's take these one at a time because they are both important points, and critical to understanding the success of the framework. They are also deeply intertwined.

First of all, let's talk about motivation. Motivation at heart is both very complex and very simple. We are all, as workers and as humans, motivated by a complex mix of emotions and drivers based on millions of years of evolution, as well as our personalities, our personal histories, our goals, and our past, present, or future circumstances. We are all uniquely individual and yet frequently quite similar. So complex is motivation that thousands, if not hundreds of thousands of books and articles have been written, attempting to explore the reasons why employees are motivated to perform well or badly. Yet there has never been a clear outcome that has caused every organization to think, *Yes! We know how to motivate our employees to achieve their stretch goals!*

A study by professor of psychology and psychiatry at Ohio State University Stephen Reiss was the result of five years of intensive research into human motivation, and I think sheds interesting light on the problem. Reiss and his graduate students conducted studies of more than 6,000 people and from that identified 16 basic desires that guide our behavior, drive our everyday actions, and make us who we are. Of the 16 desires,* at least 14 (idealism and acceptance are the outliers) may have a genetic component. What makes us all unique is the combination and ranking of these desires. We all prioritize each desire differently, and what drives one person may have no meaning for another.

There are two outcomes that Reiss has found from this study that I think have relevance to our discussion. First, we often tend to assume that we all have very similar motivations and what is best for one person is best for another. Professor Reiss uses "workaholism" as an example of this. Some people may be driven to work long hard hours, not necessarily because they are trying to fill a void or lack in their lives, but because their main drivers are power and status. Working long hours might be considered the best way to achieve their desires, yet those who are not motivated by the same drivers can consider this unhealthy or "wrong." In fact, it's just a manifestation of a different desire profile. Secondly, Reiss makes clear that no one motivation is better or worse than the other, but there are structures and systems built into our society that penalize individuals who might be driven by different desires. He cites the modern education system as an example, arguing that the system assumes that all children are driven by curiosity, and penalizes those children who are naturally not-curious. Instead, he argues, "It's OK to be non-curious. As long as the child is not failing, and *is meeting the minimum standards*, parents need to ease up on expectations . . . all they are doing is ruining their relationship." (Italics mine.)

Ring any bells? As we unpack motivation and understand how this new framework of performance management with minimum goals and unlimited vacation might work, it's critical

---

* The 16 desires identified by Professor Reiss are, in no particular order: power, independence, curiosity, acceptance, order, saving, honor, idealism, social contact, family, status, vengeance, romance, eating, physical exercise, tranquility.

to keep in mind that each employee will be driven by a complex and individual web of motivation. Neither is good or bad, and neither will be exactly the same. To apply a "one-size-fits-all" method of stretch goals to a diverse group of people and to expect them to be motivated and perform equally is an exercise in disappointment. As with the schoolchildren and their parents, so too will organizations need to "ease up on expectations" and realize that their employees can and will not be motivated the same or in fact perform the same, simply because of who we are as diverse individuals.

I'm going to come back to this point later when I discuss the role of the manager, but it's important to keep in mind that Reiss clearly states that no one motivation is more meaningful or "legitimate" than any other. I say this because his 16 drivers include both intrinsic and extrinsic motivations. There is a hierarchy in certain parts of our culture that suggests intrinsic motivation (doing things for the good of others, or doing things for abstractions like honor or idealism) is somehow more "worthy" than doing things for extrinsic motivations (money, power, or status). While there are clear caveats (the disaster at Enron pops to mind), I will argue that both sources of motivation are equally valid, and it is the changing role of the manager that will need to identify, validate, and utilize those motivation drivers.

Are Managers a Dying Breed?

I discussed the role of a manager back in Chapter 1, and discovered that the key tenets of management have remained unchanged since the first half of the twentieth century. Management guru Peter Drucker, working in the 1950s, established the five priorities of managers that still define the role more than 60 years later. They were: objective setting, organizing the group, motivating and communicating, measuring performance, and developing people. Under Drucker's theories, and most theories since, managers have taken on responsibility for their employees' performance, assuming that it is their role to set stretch goals, motivate their staff to achieve them, and then measure and reward their supposedly successful performance.

Let's consider this model and what it might mean. According to Gallup, managers are doing such a poor job in motivating and measuring their workers that at least 50 percent of employees in the United States have left a job to get away from a manager at some point in their career. This finding, and the model, suggests that managers play the core role in employee motivation and performance and are entirely failing. Added to this, organizations and employees are constantly decrying the lack of good managers (if we apply 20:60:20 to this, only 20 percent of managers could be said to be doing a truly inspirational job), with Gallup again finding that companies fail to choose the right manager for the job 82 percent of the time.

Given that the management model was created in the 1950s, it's not surprising that it is no longer working in the open source era. In the mid-twentieth-century landscape, work tended to be more manual or repetitive, and managers tended to play a much more significant role in motivating employees. Furthermore, in the absence of the Internet, they were accessible gurus who provided an example of where an employee could be if he or she worked hard enough. But this is no longer the case. Similar to what we saw in contract grading, the "sage on the stage" model of management is no longer relevant. Workers no longer look to their managers as gurus from whom they can learn, and have resources far beyond their workplace from which to gain knowledge, expertise, or inspiration. *The guru is dead, long live Google!*

So, what do we make of Gallup's "people leave managers, not companies" research? As I said above, the manager was probably the key driver of engagement prior to the advent of the open source era. Both Drucker and Gallup were right—the manager had to shoulder the burden of motivating her employees until then. But is it still true in today's economy? To find out, we asked approximately 16,000 people in 28 countries to tell us on what their motivation to excel at their job most depended. We gave them 100 points and asked them to distribute them into three sources of on-the-job motivation: Boss, Self, or Both. We wanted to test if the manager was still as important in driving motivation, and were curious about how many of our respondents would give more than 50 points to the Self category—in other words, how many would say that the biggest driver of their motivation was within themselves. Guess what percentage of our respondents ended up reporting Self as the main driver? Sixty-nine percent (Figure 4.1). Only 14 percent of respondents nominated their manager as their primary source of motivation, while 17 percent indicated it was a combination of both.

Primary Driver of Motivation: Self or Boss

Breaking down by country, we saw remarkable consistency (Figure 4.2). Even countries where the "self" score was relatively lower, it was still the largest category.

So, while it might still be true that people leave managers, not companies, the reverse is not true. What I mean is that our data shows that managers are not the key drivers of motivation to excel in the job. In other words, having a good manager is no guarantee that the employee will be highly engaged. I agree that managers play a part in an individual's enjoyment of a role—everyone wants to get along with fellow workers, and for many of us the social and team aspects of work contribute to the meaning that we derive from our occupation. But the manager is simply a vessel for individuals' frustrations with their jobs and the failed structure of the performance management system. In some cases, I have no doubt, there are personal issues. This is standard for any enterprise that involves groups of people—we are animals and we clash! So some people might leave because of their relationship with their manager. Yet my research has

Between your Immediate Boss and You, please indicate by way
of percentage on whom your primary motivation to excel at work
most depends.

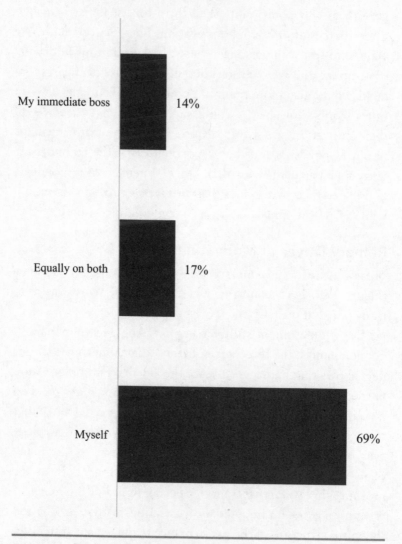

FIGURE 4.1 Primary Driver of Motivation (Aggregate)

Between your Immediate Boss and You, please indicate by way of percentage on whom your primary motivation to excel at work most depends on.

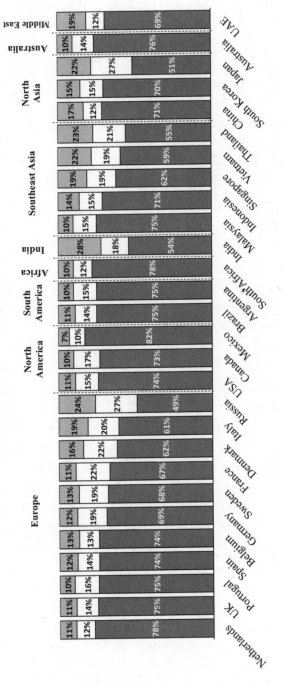

■ Those who allocated more than 50% to Self □ Those who allocated exactly 50% to Both
□ Those who allocated more than 50% to Boss

FIGURE 4.2 Primary Driver of Motivation (by Country)

found that the vast majority of employees are motivated more by themselves and their own individual drivers and desires, rather than by any one thing that a manager does or does not do.

So, what does this say about what a manager's role in the open source era should be? I have two suggestions.

1. Managers Should Stop Bearing the Burden of Motivating Their Employees

No matter how much managers try, they cannot create motivation. Instead, they should get much better at recognizing preexisting motivation, and putting employees to work in areas and on projects that best utilize that preexisting motivation. Speaking of motivation, in our global survey we also asked close to 16,000 respondents to tell us how they are motivated. The first question we asked was: *Are you more intrinsically or extrinsically motivated? Please indicate by way of percentage which you believe is a greater motivator.*

In other words, we asked them to allocate 100 points to three categories of motivation sources: extrinsic, intrinsic, or equally extrinsic and intrinsic. (Figure 4.3). Extrinsic motivation here refers to drivers like money or status, whereas intrinsic motivation refers to self-actualization needs like serving society or a higher purpose. Twenty-seven percent of respondents allocated more than half their points to extrinsic, that is, money and status were the most important motivators for them. Another 27 percent said both were equally important and allocated 50 points to each category. Forty-six percent allocated more than half their points to intrinsic, making it the largest category.

On this question, there were some differences by country, most notably Russia, Malaysia, South Korea, and Japan, where "intrinsic" was not the largest category (Figure 4.4). Overall, however, the data suggests that intrinsic motivation is the bigger of the two drivers of engagement.

Are you more intrinsically motivated or extrinsically motivated?
Please indicate by way of percentage which you believe is a
greater motivator.

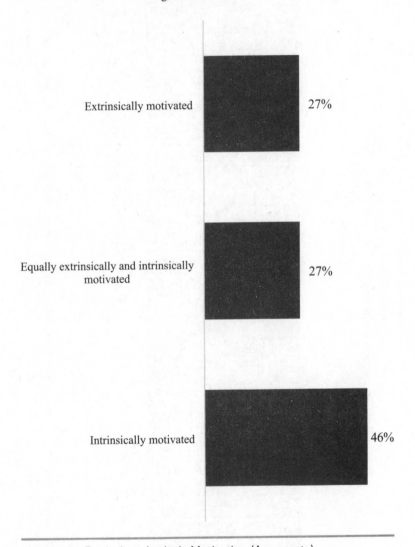

FIGURE 4.3 Extrinsic or Intrinsic Motivation (Aggregate)

Are you more intrinsically motivated or extrinsically motivated? Please indicate by way of percentage which you believe is a greater motivator.

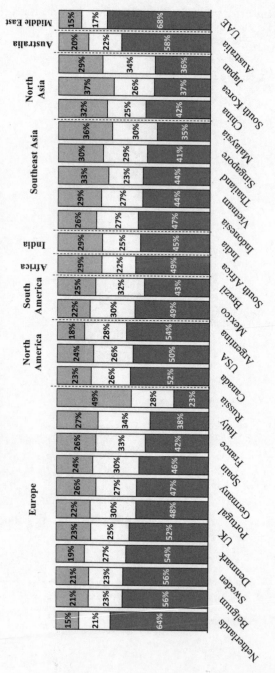

■ Those who allocated more than 50% to Intrinsic ☐ Those who allocated exactly 50% to Both ☐ Those who allocated more than 50% to Extrinsic

FIGURE 4.4 Extrinsic or Intrinsic Motivation (by Country)

What this means for managers is obvious. They need to uncover what exactly motivates each of their people, and align their work accordingly. So, the role of the manager changes, from being "motivators of people" to "motivation aligners." For those respondents who allocated more than 50 percent of their points to the "intrinsic" category, we asked a further question:

Your previous responses indicate your motivation to perform is primarily dependent on yourself, and that you are more intrinsically motivated. Please rank the following drivers of motivation in order of importance to you.

We wanted to find out from those who had chosen "self" as the primary driver in Figure 4.1 *and* "intrinsic" as a motivation source in Figure 4.3, what exactly they need in order to be highly motivated. So, after talking to a large number of such people, we devised a list and asked the "self" and "intrinsic" responders to rank certain drivers in order of their importance to them. The result was Figure 4.5.

To no surprise, the opportunity to work on something that aligned with their passion and strengths ended up at the very top. The opportunity to make a positive difference and to continuously challenge themselves to raise the bar were also seen as very important drivers. In other words, self-motivated people look for meaningful work more than anything else, and are ready to challenge or stretch themselves to make a difference. Perhaps what this data also says is that those who are unclear about their values, purpose, and passions are more dependent upon their environment (boss, working conditions) for their motivation.

It is clear that each person is motivated by different considerations. The primary job of managers should therefore be to find out what they are, and align and assign work accordingly. Additionally, despite this brave new world, organizations will still need structures, still need some administration and performance management, and still need leaders at all levels who can pull together teams with vision and direction. In addition to

Your previous responses indicate your motivation to perform is primarily dependent on yourself, and that you are more intrinsically motivated. Please rank the following drivers of motivation in order of importance to you.
Top 3 Statements

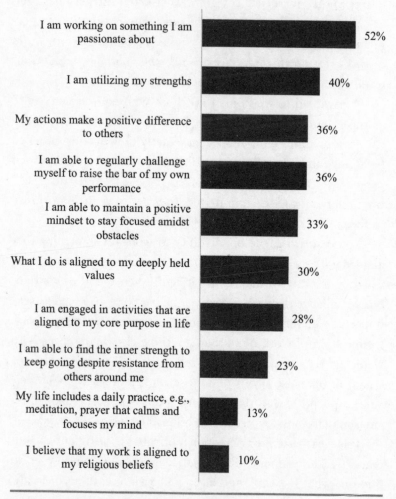

I am working on something I am passionate about	52%
I am utilizing my strengths	40%
My actions make a positive difference to others	36%
I am able to regularly challenge myself to raise the bar of my own performance	36%
I am able to maintain a positive mindset to stay focused amidst obstacles	33%
What I do is aligned to my deeply held values	30%
I am engaged in activities that are aligned to my core purpose in life	28%
I am able to find the inner strength to keep going despite resistance from others around me	23%
My life includes a daily practice, e.g., meditation, prayer that calms and focuses my mind	13%
I believe that my work is aligned to my religious beliefs	10%

FIGURE 4.5   Sources of Intrinsic Motivation

deeply understanding preexisting motivation and aligning staff accordingly, managers must focus on overall vision, mission, and strategy formulation. Therein lies what I believe to be the new role of a manager.

2. Managers Should Accept the 80:20 Rule

Managers must understand that only 20 percent of workers can and want to rise to the challenge of a stretch goal and far exceed expectations. Wholly 60 percent of workers do not find stretch goals motivating, either because they don't align with their intrinsic motivations or because they have other priorities in their life at the time. Twenty percent of workers are never going to be motivated to achieve beyond the minimum, no matter what external motivation or challenge is thrown at them. If managers continue to take on the responsibility of motivating all their employees to the maximum, the exercise can only end in failure and frustration and an allegedly poor performance on the managers' part. Instead, after deeply understanding sources of employees' existing motivation triggers, managers should adopt the philosophy of setting minimum goals, and help those who want to achieve to stretch. In this sense, they should become mentors for those who choose to be in the top 20 percent. It is a mistake to leave your highest performers alone. Many managers do so, to focus instead on their "problem children." This is a double-edged problem because without coaching and mentoring, the high performers don't usually achieve their full potential, and despite all the time and attention, the low performers don't always improve. As I mentioned earlier, a feature of the 80:20 rule is that the top 20 percent of the top 20 percent have a disproportionately higher impact on overall organizational performance. Managers should therefore save enough time to coach and guide them in realizing their true potential. If they adopt the minimum goal methodology, they can free themselves up significantly to do so.

Furthermore, managers must acknowledge that the middle 60 percent and the bottom 20 percent are also essential to the success of a business, and manage them accordingly. It is the remaining 80 percent that support the top 20 percent in creating the magic that they (the top 20 percent) do. If the top 20 percent get bogged down in routine executional work, they will not be as effective. In order to continue innovating, they need the 80 percent to execute their ideas. The top 20 percent are motivated to create excellence through innovation and other means. To do this, they are willing to go above and beyond the normal call of duty. Most of the remaining 80 percent still want to do good work, but not necessarily go above and beyond because they may have other priorities. Just because people do not want to stretch themselves does not mean they are poor workers. The key lies in understanding the needs and desires of all segments of the performance bell curve—a point I will elaborate further in the next chapter. A "one-size-fits-all" stretch goal, and a "one-size-fits-all" way of working does not fit in the empowered open source age, when individuals are looking for meaning both in and outside their work, and have no hesitation in moving on to the next job if the current one doesn't work.

The cornerstone of this new relationship between manager and employee is trust and communication. Employees must be able to trust that they can choose their level of motivation and performance at or above the minimum, and that their choice will not be penalized either in the present or the future. Equally, the manager will have to trust his or her staff member to make the best decision for himself or herself, and not impose his own motivations or career goals onto the employee. For some managers, this will be difficult. We all want what we perceive to be "the best" for ourselves and our staff, but this will involve putting aside our own biases and opinions and accepting that each employee is different, and has different motivations for being at work and deciding what to achieve. It is difficult because the logic is counterintuitive—as I explained earlier, you have to give up control to improve overall performance.

This trust should be based on constant, frequent, and meaningful communication between the two parties, so both are on the same page about motivation, circumstance, goals, and performance. Frequent feedback from both sides will ensure that both parties are clear on expectations. Like contract grading, expectations and rewards must be laid out clearly and concisely, so neither party is caught short come the end of the year.

At first glance, the recommendations of this chapter might seem to contradict Chapter 2, where we argued that leaders need to be autocratic. If we give up control of performance back to our employees, how can we be autocratic? But if you look carefully, there is no contradiction. What this new way of managing implies is that managers remain autocratic about their values and purpose, and at the same time, are sensitive and caring about the needs of their employees. While the values-based behavior should be absolutely nonnegotiable and expected from all employees, how much they choose to contribute (and consequently how much they choose to be rewarded) can be flexible based on each employee's unique motivation triggers. This is completely in line with the "freedom within a framework" concept we discussed in Chapter 2, which Coca-Cola and many other companies use very well in today's context. This philosophy will involve a massive mindset shift, and there are times when it will not be easy. What I am proposing is a move away from almost a century of habit, thought, and practice. It throws away the tropes of motivation and performance that we have held dear for so long. But the fact is that in order to remain relevant in the next decades, organizations must adapt, and those adaptations must be drastic and sweeping. I can understand that organizations and managers will be fearful; what will happen if we stop wielding the big carrot and stick of stretch goals, performance management, and expectation that we have wielded for so long? Yes, this new approach involves giving up control. But giving up control and empowering employees to choose how and how much to contribute will enhance overall organizational performance, and free managers of the burden of "motivating" all employees the same way—something that has always been, and will remain, impossible.

The tectonic shifts that are happening in our organizational, business, and social worlds will continue regardless of whether or not we are ready. The open source era is placing a huge amount of freedom and opportunity at the hands of employees. The command and control style of management, and the one-size-fits-all performance management yardstick, will not work anymore in this age of mass customization. Organizations and leaders which flourish will need to make these bold, brave, unprecedented steps in order to rise to the challenges and opportunities coming our way. Throwing away the old tropes around performance management, stretch goals, and motivation will take a leap of faith, but it is one that is critical to move forward into groundbreaking new territory. Only those managers and leaders who are comfortable and confident in their own skin will be able to do this. To be one of those, you will need to first find your leadership energy from your values and purpose as described in Chapter 3. Once empowered that way, you will not need to worry about loss of control. Your employees will choose to follow you because of your leadership energy, not because of your span of control.

We've discussed some seemingly radical but much needed ideas for open source era performance management in this chapter. In the next chapter let's look at current organizational practices at measuring and managing employee engagement, and see if we need an operating system update there, too.

CHAPTER SUMMARY

- The 80:20 rule is omnipresent and shows that in any group, only 20 percent of the people will excel and work at a stretch level. It is therefore futile to have all employees write stretch goals.
- Organizations should consider setting minimum rather than stretch goals for all employees, and leave it up to employees if they want to do more. Performance will eventually fall into a 20:60:20 bell-shaped distribution. Those that want to excel will come forward and do so.
- Keeping this in mind, some companies have already started allowing unlimited vacations.
- Like leaders, in the open source era, employees are also naked. In this sense, it is a self-governing environment where undesirable players will be exposed and left behind.
- In the open source era, employees must manage themselves like entrepreneurs, and decide how much they want to be rewarded or punished.
- Managers are not the primary source of motivation anymore. Consequently, they should stop "motivating" and start identifying what employees are already motivated by.

Questions for Reflection

1. What is the performance management policy and process at your organization?

2. How can you minimize supervision in order to maximize performance?

3. How must the role of the manager change with changing social and demographic trends?

CHAPTER 5

No More
Engagement Surveys

CONTEXT

1. The Open Source Era

OPEN SOURCE PERSONAL LEADERSHIP

2. The Naked Autocrat Creates Breakthrough Results
3. Leadership Energy, Not Competencies

OPEN SOURCE ENTERPRISE LEADERSHIP

4. Minimum Supervision, Maximum Performance
5. No More Engagement Surveys
6. Crowdsourced Innovation and Leadership Succession

B en Casnocha is a Silicon Valley entrepreneur, angel investor, and coauthor of *The Alliance*, written with LinkedIn founder and chairman Reid Hoffman and fellow Silicon Valley entrepreneur Chris Yeh. Like Dr. William Tan, whom we met in Chapter 3, Ben was invited to speak at the 2016 Leadership Energy Summit Asia (LESA), a conference about leadership energy that my company hosts every year in several Asian cities. The conference has a mix of speakers who discuss either personal or enterprise leadership energy. Having read *The Alliance*, I requested Ben to talk about the latter. Over the two days that he was with us I had several conversations with him, all of which were fascinating.

"The whole foundation of modern employment is based on a dishonest conversation," he said, while describing how companies hire employees these days. Even though both employee and employer know that the company can fire anyone "at will" without any reason whatsoever, and that employees can jump ship anytime they see better opportunities, both parties lie to each other. Employers talk about the possibility of having a long-term career with the company, and employees reciprocate by pretending the company is where they have always wanted to work, and are looking forward to staying for the rest of their career.

Yet we all know that the days of lifetime employment are over. To illustrate his point, Casnocha speaks of General Electric. "In 1963, a GE executive said that *maximizing employee job security is a prime company goal*. In that era, a career was like a marriage. Fast-forward to the 1990s, and Jack Welch, GE's CEO, said that "*loyalty to a company is nonsense, and employees have to prove themselves every day*." Drawing an interesting analogy, he continued, "On one hand, companies hire employees and say, welcome to the family. Yet they fire you the moment things get difficult. In a real family, parents can't fire their children. Imagine disowning a child for poor performance. *We're sorry Suzie, but your mom and I have decided you're just not a good fit for us. Your table setting skills aren't delivering the exceptional customer service experience we're known for. We're going to have to let you go. But don't take it the wrong way; it's just family."*

If loyalty is indeed nonsense in this age of "at will" employment contracts, how can companies ensure high employee engagement? And will traditional methods of measuring and addressing engagement levels work in today's open source era?

Back in 1987, I took up my first full-time corporate job at American Express in India. Since then I have lived in eight countries and worked with many Fortune 100 companies either as an employee or as a consultant. Almost every company I've interacted with so far agrees that employee engagement is one of its top priorities. The logic goes something like this: engaged employees (those willing to go the extra mile in their jobs) make customers happy, and satisfied customers in turn make shareholders happy by giving the company their loyalty and repeat business. So, it makes sense to measure and address employee engagement levels, right? Yes! But the way employee engagement is measured and addressed in most organizations might be causing more problems than it solves. Most organizations rely on an annual employee survey to determine engagement levels and spend significant amounts of time and money each year addressing issues highlighted by the survey. And therein lies the problem.

Problem 1: One-Size-Fits-All Surveys

The biggest problem with employee engagement surveys stems again from ignoring the 80:20 rule. Most HR departments swear by the fact that performance falls on a bell-shaped curve, where 20 percent of employees are exceptional performers, 60 percent are average, and 20 percent are low performers. Even managers who hate the bell curve and strongly oppose any edicts that require them to force-stack their people along the 20-60-20 distribution are unable to deny the fact that everyone in a group cannot perform at the same level. Even in a blue chip company that hires the brightest and the best, employee performance distributes itself in a bell shape. Their bell curve may be on a higher achieving axis than other companies, but the shape doesn't change. Wherever you look in this case, HR is absolutely right.

However, when it comes to sending out the annual employee engagement survey, HR departments send it out to all staff regardless of where their performance falls on the bell curve, then average the data to get scores on each item. The lowest scoring items are then addressed with initiatives led by management, so that overall scores can improve by the following year. But if it is true that 20 percent of the employees produce 80 percent of the results, or only 20 percent of the people perform at a truly exceptional level, what happens when you average out the responses of all employees regardless of performance? Quite simply, the voice of the top 20 percent is drowned under the voices of the remaining 80 percent. Gallup claims to be one of the leading firms when it comes to measuring employee engagement. By its own admission, only 13 percent of the global working population is engaged. In other words, the remaining 87 percent make up the bulk of the voice in employee surveys. If time and money is then spent on addressing employee engagement concerns based on this data, does the company end up encouraging excellence or mediocrity?

This idea of hoping to drive excellence but ending up inadvertently promoting mediocrity is what I call the "Intention Excellence, Outcome Mediocrity" trap. For decades, large organizations around the world have been conducting engagement surveys as described above, and have been victims of the trap. It is time to look for a better way.

The solution is simple. If survey you must, send out the same engagement survey separately (in batches) to your top, average, and low performers, and find out what each segment has to say. This way, the needs of each segment can be better understood, and management can make more informed decisions on where to spend their time and money. As Cy Wakeman says on Forbes .com, "Don't treat every opinion the same. Listen to what your top performers tell you. They've proved their value and earned their credibility, so go ahead, play favorites. Spend less energy on the demands and complaints of your worst employees. You know the ones—resistant, hard to please, full of excuses." Casnocha agrees with this argument and says, "You have to treat your most valuable people differently. Your most valuable people are those with an entrepreneurial mindset."

While I agree with Wakeman and Casnocha to a large extent, I also believe that average performers remain a very important part of any organization. They are the ones who enable the top 20 percent to drive 80 percent of the results. They are generally good workers, but as I highlighted in Chapter 4, they may have interests outside of work as well. They may not be as ambitious about their careers as the top 20 percent, but that does not make them slackers. They simply have different needs and expectations from the workplace that must be understood and addressed. Similarly, the bottom 20 percent may be performing lower than the rest, but if they are doing the minimum required of them, they are needed too.

Let's take another example to illustrate. If we were to plot the earnings of all freelance graphic designers in New York City on a chart, it is probably safe to assume that the earnings data will form a bell-shaped distribution. About 20 percent of the designers will be high revenue earners, about 60 percent will fall in the average earner category, and the remaining 20 percent will be low revenue earners. But can we say that the bottom 20 percent are slackers or bad designers? No. There could be several reasons why people are in the bottom 20 percent. Perhaps they are students who only work on weekends to balance their budgets. Perhaps they are young moms who only work during school hours. Perhaps they do freelance graphics and another job and devote more time to the other job. In other words, they may be in the bottom 20 percent by choice. It does not automatically make them bad graphic designers. The same might be the case with today's full-time employees. As I explained in Chapter 4, they may be performing at the minimum level by choice. In today's free economy, it could mean that they don't want to work any more than the minimum because of other interests and priorities.

At whatever level they choose to perform, every employee needs to be engaged enough to provide a consistent experience to customers. As you will see in the next chapter, even free agents need to be engaged enough to behave in accordance with company values. They must display an "owner mentality" rather than a "renter mentality." So, it is important to understand their voices and needs through a survey or other means, and to address those needs. But treating all employees the same way and averaging engagement scores across the organization distorts the picture, and makes the whole exercise far less effective than it ought to be.

Of course, if performance falls below minimum acceptable standards, or it becomes clear over time that the employee does not have the basic skills needed to perform at a satisfactory level, appropriate action must be taken. But you simply cannot have an entire employee population made up of superstars either. By segmenting the employee engagement survey data and by designing segmented responses, companies can avoid the trap of accidentally promoting mediocrity, and make much better decisions to address the needs of all segments.

Problem 2: Annual Surveys Are a Panacea for All Things Engagement

Are surveys even the best way to address employee engagement in the first place? If a company runs a survey every year, it creates an expectation with employees that something will be done, and that the "something" must be done by management. So, it becomes a one-sided affair. If management responds with a few initiatives, there are many that feel their voice wasn't heard or acted upon. If management does not respond at all, every employee feels cheated. The whole process can very quickly become a lose-lose proposition.

Instead of the annual survey, what if leaders were to use the age-old method of "management by walking around," and actually talk to people throughout the year? And what if companies could leverage social technology to remain in touch with people in real time, all year long? After all, if the aim is to create an environment in which people are happy and flourishing, why wait for the annual survey? Unfortunately, too many HR departments and too many senior management teams get so fixated on improving survey scores that they miss the underlying point—to engage more with their people and improve the wider company culture.

As Bloomberg writer Elizabeth Ryan says, "When you blast out a once-a-year engagement survey, the message it sends your employees is insulting. A reliance on employee surveys in any organization makes it clear that communication isn't what it should be. If you care what your team members think, ask them to talk to you all the time, face-to-face or mediated by technology. If your leadership team has determined through a survey algorithm that you had a problem in some area—say, in the preparedness of your first-line supervisors to lead—what good would that numeric score do you? What would you need to solve the problem? You'd need stories. So why not collect stories from the start, as they unfold?"

Problem 3: Annual Surveys Are Seen as an HR Activity

HR departments love annual surveys because the results get the attention of management. HR analyzes and presents data to management, and management is asked to act upon it. So in this sense it makes HR's life a bit easier—"See, I told you that you need to pay attention to your employees." An external entity usually conducts the survey to ensure anonymity, and it is treated as a stand-alone initiative. In reality most employees also see the survey as an HR issue, and treat it as a check-the-box activity. If results don't improve, the blame is placed squarely on HR's shoulders.

However, if an organization is really serious about employee engagement, the answer instead is to develop a compelling organizational purpose, and a set of values that define its culture. As George Serafeim at Harvard and Claudine Gartenberg at Stern found out in their research study, *purpose-clarity* companies—those companies where employees perceive a higher sense of purpose *and* where management provides clarity of direction—showed better accounting and stock market performance. Purpose-clarity was measured with survey statements like "My work has special meaning, this is not just a job"; "I feel good about the ways we contribute to the community"; "When I look at what we accomplish, I feel a sense of pride"; and "I'm proud to tell others I work here." Management clarity, on the other hand, was measured by statements like "Management makes its expectations clear" and "Management has a clear view of where the organization is going and how to get there."

Problem 4: Survey Scores Are Used to Evaluate Leadership Performance

In some organizations, engagement survey results are linked to leaders' scorecards. This is probably the most inappropriate use of the survey. If leaders and managers know that their performance rating—and therefore their bonus—depends in part on their employee survey results, they quickly learn to game the system and engage in unhealthy behavior just to prop up scores. As I mentioned in Chapter 3, bosses become pleasers—another form of followership—and make decisions based on what their employees want rather than what they need. I have seen many bosses who resort to all sorts of gimmicks during the survey season, like departmental family picnics and office parties. Knowing that employees fill out the survey based on how they feel at a given point in time, bosses are able to manipulate their behavior in the period just leading up to the survey to make sure everyone is in a good mood.

Another fallout of linking leadership performance to employee engagement scores is linked to Problem 1. If a leader is doing what is right for the business, and if that has an adverse effect on the lower half of the bell curve, then lower performing employees can penalize the leader by low-scoring his leadership style. This makes it difficult for the leader to make tough but needed decisions without harming his own interests. To avoid unpopularity and low engagement scores to go with it, bosses at times shy away from doing what is right. By using engagement survey scores to measure leadership performance, we end up promoting followership instead of real leadership.

So, if annual surveys are not the answer to measure and address employee engagement, what should companies do instead? To answer this question, I first want to go back to my conversations with Ben Casnocha to share what he, Reid Hoffman, and Chris Yeh suggest, and then offer my own perspective.

I will in fact offer an alternative to the annual survey that is much more powerful.

Entrepreneurial Employees on Tours of Duty

To maximize employee engagement, Casnocha says the first thing companies need to do is bring honesty back into the employment equation. While acknowledging that the days of lifetime employment are over, his coauthors and he suggest a two-pronged approach: (1) attract people with an entrepreneurial mindset, and (2) offer those people "tours of duty" rather than regular employment contracts. What makes Silicon Valley so successful, they argue, is that it is all about the people. In *The Alliance*, they write, "The most successful Silicon Valley businesses succeed because they use the alliance to recruit, manage, and retain an incredibly talented team of entrepreneurial employees." Instead of trying to treat employees as family, the Valley has honest, limited time alliances with people in the form of tours of duty.

Why entrepreneurial employees? And what kind of employees are they? They are the people who possess a "founder" mindset. To elaborate, *The Alliance* quotes former eBay CEO and PayPal chairman John Donahoe, "People with a founder mindset drive change, motivate people, and just get stuff done." Founders or entrepreneurs are motivated and engaged because it is their own business. In today's gig economy, everyone should be the CEO of his or her own career and have an entrepreneurial or founder mindset, because even if one doesn't start one's own business, most companies still want their employees to behave like entrepreneurs. I argued in Chapter 4 that companies should give employees the maximum freedom possible because in today's economy there is no other option. In return for the freedom, companies have a right to expect responsible entrepreneurial behavior. This is what Silicon Valley is all about. Can this ideology be applied to other industries and in other countries? Absolutely. The gig economy (where short-term temporary positions are common) is a global phenomenon, not just a Silicon Valley anomaly.

Hoffman, Casnocha, and Yeh use the story of John Lasseter at Pixar to describe the entrepreneurial mindset. Lasseter's movies *Toy Story*, *Finding Nemo*, and *Monsters, Inc.* have grossed over $3.5 billion in the United States alone. Lasseter was originally employed at Disney, where he pitched the idea of a fully computer-generated animation film only to be fired for his "crazy ideas." Undeterred, Lasseter took his entrepreneurial mindset and idea to George Lucas, who gave him a job as a computer animator. Lucas eventually sold his company to Steve Jobs, who renamed it Pixar. In 1995, Pixar, in partnership with Disney, released the world's first computer animated film—*Toy Story*. When Disney finally realized its mistake, it brought Lasseter back by buying Pixar from Steve Jobs for $7 billion.

In contrast, the authors talk about Amazon founder Jeff Bezos, who reacted very differently when one of his employees, Benjamin Black, mooted the idea of cloud computing. Bezos recognized the potential and pushed it through, despite opposition from his board about moving away from the company's core business of online retailing. Bezos's decision eventually made Amazon the biggest global player in cloud computing. Clearly, the two stories show how both employees and employers need to maintain an entrepreneurial mindset in today's fast-moving economy.

With entrepreneurial employees, though, companies must have honest alliances in the shape of tours of duty. Instead of offering them false promises of lifetime employment, companies should instead offer *lifetime employability*. In an alliance, an employer and employee agree on a tour of duty of about two to four years in which both parties agree on mutually beneficial outcomes. At the end of a tour of duty, they may either part ways amicably or enter into another mutually beneficial tour of duty. Hoffman and his coauthors describe three types of tours of duty:

- **Rotational.** A structured program of a finite duration, usually aimed at entry-level employees to give them exposure to a number of functions through a structured rotational program.
- **Transformational.** Rather than a finite period, a transformational tour of duty is linked to completing a specific mission that transforms both the company and the employee.
- **Foundational.** In a foundational tour of duty, the employee's personal purpose is the mission of the company itself. There is perfect alignment between the two.

The difference between the three types of tours is the extent of alignment between employee interests and company interests. In a rotational tour, the alignment may be modest; in a transformational tour, it is significant; and in a foundational tour it is almost 100 percent. The key to engaging employees is in having honest, tailor-made agreements based on tours of duty.

Use Culture to Drive Engagement

While I totally agree with Hoffman, Casnocha, and Yeh, I believe leaders can additionally use their culture to drive employee engagement. Instead of using an annual satisfaction or engagement survey, they can use a values-based 360-degree feedback system. Let me explain.

At the end of the day, whether or not an employee is fully engaged depends in large part on the extent of the match or mismatch between an employee's personal values and the culture of the organization he or she works for. Let's understand organizational culture first, then I'll get back to personal values and the 360 idea. What is an organization's culture? It is a word that is often misunderstood or made unnecessarily complicated by many. A quick Google on the words "corporate culture" reveals many confusing or complicated definitions and constructs.

Investopedia defines organizational culture as:

> *the beliefs and behaviors that determine how a company's employees and management interact and handle outside business transactions. Often, corporate culture is implied, not expressly defined, and develops organically over time from the cumulative traits of the people the company hires. A company's culture will be reflected in its dress code, business hours, office setup, employee benefits, turnover, hiring decisions, treatment of clients, client satisfaction and every other aspect of operations.*

The Small Business Encyclopedia defines organizational culture as:

> *a blend of the values, beliefs, taboos, symbols, rituals and myths all companies develop over time. Whether written as a mission statement, spoken or merely understood, corporate culture describes and governs the ways a company's owners and employees think, feel and act.*

These definitions were just on the first search page on Google. In total, there were 14.5 million search results for "corporate culture." So much information, yet culture is so hard to define, shape, and understand. So first things first, let me offer two very simple ways of looking at corporate or organizational culture:

1. Culture is what your people do when no one is looking.
2. Culture is your organizational values in action or inaction.

This might be an oversimplification, but I believe it is required. I have seen too many companies complicating their culture-transformation efforts to such an extent that they amount to absolutely nothing. If we simply look at the culture of an organization in terms of the behaviors and habits of its people, it ought to be enough. Do people do the right thing when the boss is away? Whatever the answer, *that* is the culture of the organization or team. Do people live the stated values of the organization day in and day out, or are the values just posters on the wall? Again, whatever the answer, *that* is the culture of the organization.

So how can an organization ensure that a desired values-based culture takes root? Simple. Make values-based behavior count. If I am measured, rewarded, or punished based on my values-based behavior, I am more likely to pay attention to it. If company values are just pretty posters that management doesn't really do anything with, as an employee I am unlikely to take them seriously. It really does not have to be more complicated than that. Coming back to the question of employee engagement, an employee's engagement to a large extent will depend upon:

1. The extent to which stated values match the employee's personal values
2. The extent to which those values are in action or inaction throughout the organization

Clearly, if the mismatch between personal values and organizational values is too big, or if the values are correct but are not practiced by a majority of the people, the employee will be highly disengaged, and will probably leave. If there is a significant match on those two fronts, the employee is much more likely to be engaged, and will choose to stay.

So how can organizations measure and reward or punish values-based behavior? There are several ways, none of which are perfect. Whichever framework is chosen, management will need to stay on top of it, and tweak it regularly before it becomes ineffective. My favorite framework is to establish a values-based 360-degree feedback process and link it to compensation, rewards, and promotion. To my knowledge, no one does this better than Goldman Sachs, where each year every employee receives 360-degree feedback based on the company's business principles, and employees' compensation is directly linked to the outcome. Goldman partners and employees are often asked why their firm has historically been the most successful on the street, and they all attribute it to their strong culture of team-work, and to their robust 360-degree feedback process.

I believe an annual 360-degree feedback process is far better than the annual employee survey. It measures the extent to which each employee lives the organizational values, and forces them to do so or move on. Since humans are societal beings, nothing shames someone more than getting negative behavioral feedback from peers, subordinates, and seniors. Over time as the system encourages employees to behave in a certain way (or leave), a desired culture takes shape. As the culture takes root, it encourages aligned employees to be highly engaged and stay longer. The 360 process makes engagement a shared responsi-bility between employer and employee, and makes it personal. As I explained in Chapter 4, an annual employee survey is a one-sided affair where employees give feedback but it is the management's responsibility to fix problems.

But don't expect this model to be easily accepted. If you try to implement a compensation-linked 360, expect serious resis-tance. Like any other human system, it has its flaws, but of all the processes I have seen it is the most effective *despite* all the arguments against it. The most common criticism is that it discourages people from making tough decisions that are required for the business. A close second is that it encourages a "you scratch my back and I'll scratch yours" mentality. While both are possible, they can still be better managed as compared to the annual employee survey. If a 360-degree feedback process discourages leaders from making tough decisions, imagine what an all-employee survey does. In the case of 360, only a handful of people provide feedback, and a leader can manage their expectations through honest and regular communication. In an employee survey, everyone provides feedback and makes it much harder for the leader to make tough decisions, particularly if his leadership performance is measured by his survey results. So as far as the first criticism goes, the 360 is much more manageable. As for the second criticism of encouraging the "you scratch my back and I'll scratch yours" mentality, this can be easily mitigated. All you have to do is ensure that employees' rater lists are approved by immediate managers. If someone is making his or her list up with "friends and family," the manager can intervene and ensure only those people the employee works closely and regularly with are included.

When I introduced the annual 360 in my company, many people protested. Some even complained to our board of directors that the practice was unfair, and that too much weight (40 percent in our case) was attached to the 360 scores while measuring overall performance. It has been one of the things that I chose to be autocratic about, and after seven years of doing this annually, I can safely say that we have a great culture of teamwork and excellence. People now know that living the values is nonnegotiable, and that if they don't like the company's values, they can choose to leave. And some did choose to leave. Those that chose to stay have done so because they are comfortable with the company's values and relish the fact that we are a values-based company. We are far more tolerant about employees missing their targets or KPIs as compared to getting repeatedly low scores on their values-based 360. We believe that in a high-ambition company, employees must take risks and try new things. Not all risks and new ideas will work, so KPIs will sometimes not be achieved as imagined. But as long as the employee lives the values of the company, we are not concerned. We quickly put the setback behind us, learn from it, and move on to the next thing. As I explained in Chapter 2, we are autocratic about our values and purpose but compassionate and respectful with our employees. This makes our employees loyal and motivated, which in turn makes us successful as an organization. As consultants, we have helped many of our clients in establishing a robust 360-degree feedback process, and many are really happy with the results.

In summary, much like succession planning (which I will discuss in the next chapter), employee engagement has become a spreadsheet, check-the-box exercise. My purpose behind writing this chapter is to highlight the fact that in today's dynamic free-agency environment of uber-connectivity, only genuine leadership will thrive. The days of check-the-box exercises are over. As Hoffman, Casnocha, and Yeh say, the very foundation of modern employment is based on a dishonest conversation. In the open source era where everyone is naked, there is no place for dishonesty.

Leaders who are genuinely concerned about employee engagement should not need annual engagement surveys. They know how to keep in touch with their people on a human level. If the organization they lead is too large for them to talk to everyone in person, they should devise methods to keep in touch all year round rather than just once a year. For this, many a technology platform is available. Engagement can be much better managed by shaping a winning, values-based culture, and by making each employee a part of the process. Finally, if an annual survey is a must, it is much better done in phases along the bell curve, so that deeper information is uncovered about high, average, and low performing employees.

Having discussed performance management, the role of the manager, and employee engagement in this and the previous chapter, let us now look at two more important responsibilities of organizational leadership—innovation and leadership succession. In Chapter 6, we will look at twenty-first-century ready, open source ways of addressing both.

CHAPTER SUMMARY

- Annual employee engagement surveys remain the main vehicle of measuring and managing employee engagement in large organizations. But there is a big flaw in this process—it goes against the 80:20 rule. The voice of the top 20 percent of performers (who produce 80 percent of the results) is drowned under the voice of the remaining 80 percent. Inadvertently organizations therefore end up promoting mediocrity instead of excellence.
- Organizations should hire employees with an entrepreneurial mindset, and invest in their development through tours of duty. In return, these in-house entrepreneurs will give their best to the organization.
- An annual values-based 360-degree feedback system is perhaps superior to an engagement survey when it comes to building a culture of high engagement.
- If engagement surveys are necessary, doing them in a segmented way along the bell curve might be the way to go.

Questions for Reflection

1. What is the current practice of measuring and addressing employee engagement in your organization?

2. How can the concepts of this chapter (segmented surveys, 360-degree feedback, tours of duty) be applied within your organization?

CHAPTER 6

Crowdsourced Innovation and Leadership Succession

Stephen van Vuuren lives in Greensboro, North Carolina, USA, and has been working for over 10 years to turn his vision into reality. He has spent countless hours weaving together a 40-minute documentary on space. This grand film, *In Saturn's Rings*, is intended for IMAX and Giant Screen Theatres. *In Saturn's Rings* is intended to take viewers on a journey through stunning images of Earth, the Moon, and the Milky Way, culminating in a fly through Saturn's rings. The film uses no computer-generated images. Rather, it relies on over 7.5 million real images captured by the Hubble and other space missions and uses innovative visual techniques developed by Stephen himself. Stephen's purpose in creating the film is to get people excited again about exploring the possibilities that reside in outer space.

Stephen's journey to create this film has taken many twists and turns. When he began the project, his financial condition was less than ideal. He had limited funding, which quickly turned into no funding after he exhausted his own savings. He decided to take an alternative route to resolving his financial dilemma by seeking volunteers to donate funds and help pay for his nonprofit project. Stephen turned to the "crowd," the legions of online amateurs and professionals interested in space and creative films. After making a short video trailer for his film, he posted it online, expecting donations to come rolling in. They did not. In fact, the trailer sat unnoticed for almost a year. In March 2011, an online science fiction magazine asked permission to post the trailer on its site. Stephen says, "The next day my inbox went crazy and donations started rolling in." Things quickly picked up speed from there. NASA posted the video on its website as a photo-of-the-day, and it promptly went viral.

The next step was to translate the enthusiasm into more substantial funding. Using Kickstarter, a platform for crowd-funding whose "mission is to help bring creative projects to life,"

Stephen to date has raised almost $63,500 from more than 500 supporters, almost double his original goal of $37,500. From the online community of space enthusiasts also came volunteers who helped process over seven million photographs to be used in the film. At the time of this writing as of November 2016, Stephen was only months away from completing his film.

What kept Stephen going throughout this long journey? Obviously, he is an example of personal leadership energy in action as discussed in Chapter 3. His clarity of values and purpose has sustained him even when circumstances looked dire, and many others would have given up. What is also remarkable is that Stephen had a vision but no idea of how to make it happen, so he turned to the "crowd," not only to help fund his project but to bring it fully to life. Along the way, he learned a lot about how to work with and leverage the power of the crowd.

Indian Railways is the world's largest employer with over 1.3 million employees, and is notorious for its hierarchical, top-down culture. Once, while talking to some of its executives, I asked how they found out about new assignments, transfers to other locations, or changes in their day-to-day responsibilities. "Surely you must have a conversation with your immediate superior before something like that is expected of you, right?" I asked. To my surprise, they said no. They found out about such things by way of a formal memo. There was hardly any one-on-one communication. All key decisions were made by the Railway Board, and cascaded down for implementation without discussion. For decades, Indian Railways has suffered from declining revenues, bulging costs, low employee morale, and extremely poor service. While the board has tried many new initiatives over the years to improve the overall poor performance, very few have taken off. So, in 2016, they turned over a new leaf. Over a four-month period they organized a massive internal crowdsourcing initiative, covering all 1.3 million employees, to solicit ideas on how to turn around this vast, colonial-era ship. All employees were asked to submit ideas, which were evaluated and patented by zonal teams, and the top 30 ideas were presented to the railway minister and the prime minister at a massive retreat November 18–20, 2016. Ultimately, eight ideas, ranging from converting railway stations into banking and shopping hubs, to creating a one-stop app for all passenger needs, were selected for implementation. Even a government-run organization as old-fashioned as Indian Railways has realized that it needs to bring about transformative change, and that it needed to harness the power of the "crowd" to do so. While results will take some time before they become visible, the quality of ideas collected is already very impressive. Another big benefit is the excitement and pride generated within the rank-and-file. As one linesman exclaimed, "Now, even my voice will reach the prime minister."

From independent filmmakers like Stephen to the world's largest employer, the crowd is now for anyone. It is a powerful tool for individuals and organizations interested in alternative approaches to speed up their innovation and development of products and services. It can also be a source for critical organizational talent in an age where the war for talent, as originally described by McKinsey & Co., has been fought and won by the talents rather than the organization.

But it will take leadership to leverage this power. The Internet has enabled the *democratization* of innovation and talent identification, significantly increasing the chances (and speed) of organizational success and sustainability. Now, anyone can connect with millions of people around the world, any day or any time, to innovate. The Internet is arguably the biggest force shaping the twenty-first century with its power to connect people and things 24/7 and make once closely held knowledge and information available to the masses. The crowd, individuals that virtually congregate based upon shared interests, when engaged correctly and for the right purpose, can be a powerful source of innovation and the talent needed to drive it.

In the first part of this chapter I will describe how crowdsourcing can be, at minimum, an addition to the conventional approach of internal R&D or innovation departments and incubators. I will briefly explore the growing trend by organizations to use crowdsourcing for innovation, discuss advantages and potential disadvantages, and provide examples of successful and unsuccessful uses of crowdsourcing. The chapter is not intended to be a total compendium of knowledge about crowdsourcing. Information available on the various permutations that crowdsourcing takes is exploding and literally fills shelves of books. Consequently, this part of the chapter is presented as a primer on the use of crowdsourcing. It is intended to raise questions and prompt discussion in organizations that have not started to use the crowd for innovation.

The second part of the chapter will examine how the crowd, both in- and outside the organization, can be a source for new talent and revolutionize the traditional approaches to talent searches and succession planning.

Crowdsourcing for Innovation

A quick note on terminology before we begin. There are many ways to refer to leveraging the power of the crowd, including crowd collaboration, crowdfunding, crowd labor, and crowdsourcing. In this chapter I will use the terms *crowd* and *crowdsourcing* interchangeably as a way of simplifying explanations and text.

Why Crowdsourcing for Innovation?

The answer to why we should use crowdsourcing for innovation may well be "survival." Many companies still cling to an outdated model for innovation based upon a bricks-and-mortar structure, where new ideas must be created inside the four walls of their own company. In these organizations, innovation is a top-down driven, internal process. But the results coming from this approach have significantly slowed down in the last decade. In 2013, *The Economist* even questioned whether the global innovation machine had broken down!

To generate new ideas, some organizations have turned to both internal and external stopgap measures, such as promoting greater collaboration within the organization and engaging in acquisitions and strategic alliances externally. But these are just temporary solutions that are probably unsustainable in the long term. In today's uber-connected and uber-populated world, one organization rarely has all the brain trust it needs to remain consistently at the top of its game. Instead, the crowd provides a source of knowledge and ability not found in one location, let alone one company. Consequently, organizations have gradually begun turning to a combination of internal and external sources for innovation generation. One way to think about crowdsourcing from an organizational perspective is to view it as the bridge between traditional internal innovation (R&D departments) and an external solo inventor (individual innovation). As depicted in Figure 6.1, this bridge allows organizations to leverage existing internal innovation structures and enhance and stimulate them by introducing new and different ideas and perspectives.

What Is Crowdsourcing?

The word *crowdsourcing* was coined by Jeff Howe and Mark Robinson, contributing editor and editor at *Wired* magazine. The term was popularized in Howe's 2006 article "The Rise of Crowdsourcing."

According to Howe, crowdsourcing is "the act of taking a job traditionally performed by a designated agent (usually an

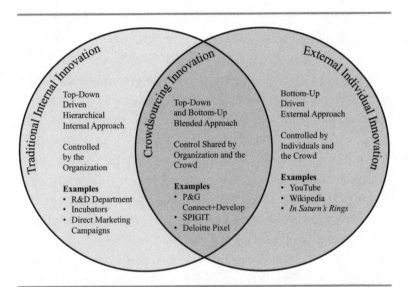

FIGURE 6.1 The Bridge Between Internal and External Innovation
(This graphic is adapted from Daren C. Brabham's article "Using Crowdsourcing in Government," IBM Center for The Business of Government, Collaborating Across Boundaries Series, 2013.)

employee) and outsourcing it to an undefined, generally large group of people in the form of an open call."

The concept of crowdsourcing is not new. In fact, it has been around for centuries under different names. Consider the *Oxford English Dictionary*, which started out in the late eighteenth century as an open appeal by Professor James Murray to collate English idioms and phrases. Over the course of several decades, thousands of volunteers around the English-speaking world sent Murray, who lived in Oxford, England, hundreds of thousands of letters containing the definitions of specific English words. These contributors all strangers to Murray, were unpaid, but worked together as one to collate the definitions and origins of every word in the English language. Murray's project took 70 years to complete, but the *Oxford English Dictionary* was arguably history's first massively crowdsourced collation of English knowledge.

Another example of the use of the crowd that predates the *Oxford English Dictionary* is the Longitude Prize, established in 1714 by a British Act of Parliament to solve the problem of determining a ship's longitude at sea. The prize was established after prominent scientists, including Edmond Halley and Isaac Newton, had tried and failed to come up with a solution. The prize was won by John Harrison, a carpenter and clockmaker, whose highly accurate chronometer enabled the exact triangulation of a ship's location. Harrison was awarded approximately £23,000 for his invention. The Longitude Prize is a unique early example of a crowdsourced contest, an approach that I will discuss in more detail later in this chapter.

Two parallel but contemporary examples of crowdsourcing are the United States' National Air and Space Administration (NASA) and Wikipedia. Accessing the crowd in the form of challenges and prizes is part of NASA's innovation tool kit. In a personal interview, Jason C. Crusan, the director of Advanced Exploration Systems Division at NASA's Human Exploration and Operations Mission Directorate, told my colleague Michael Kossler that many people assume that NASA does all its innovation internally. In fact, NASA spends less than 10 percent of its budget on its civilian workforce. Much of its budget is spent on open innovation, a form of crowdsourcing. "Our use of open innovation is basically a different way to contact and access people outside our organization, in a way that gets to nontraditional players," said Crusan. Instead of setting up its own site for accessing the crowd, NASA approached several existing online communities and asked how to engage them (an important point that will be discussed later in the section on how to work with the crowd). Crusan notes that NASA is keen on using the crowd to help solve a variety of software, engineering, and hardware problems. In fact, he goes so far as to say that he has "not found a project that could not have benefited from the crowd."

Wikipedia is another example of crowdsourcing in the form of collaborative efforts. Wikipedia is one of the top-10 most visited websites in the world. While not as large as Google (the reigning champion), according to Wikipedia's own statistics its English language encyclopedia consists of over 5 million pages of information with almost 30 million registered users. Overall, Wikipedia is available in 295 languages, and its various sites receive close to 500 million visitors per month. What makes Wikipedia unique is the fact that its online encyclopedia has been and continues to be built by volunteers who contribute to one of the world's largest repositories of free information and knowledge. It took James Murray 70 years to compile the *Oxford English Dictionary*, but Wikipedia, founded by Jimmy Wales, has been built in just 15 years. It is a prime example of the power of crowdsourcing for innovation, and of the speed of the open source era.

Crowdsourcing Trends

Use of crowdsourcing by corporations for innovation has increased dramatically in the last decade, and has been pioneered by some of the world's largest tech companies listed on Interbrand's list of Best Global Brands. Organizations such as Apple, Google, Microsoft, and Samsung have been some of the largest users of the crowd for distributed innovation during the last decade. More recently, brands from the fast-moving consumer goods (FMCG) sector have overtaken tech brands in the use of crowdsourcing.

According to eYeka, a large crowdsourcing platform host, the use of crowdsourcing increased by 30 percent among the Best Global Brands that have been using it since 2004. eYeka's report on *The State of Crowdsourcing in 2016* reflects a clear trend (of increased usage of crowdsourcing) across all industries.

Again, according to eYeka, the list of the top-20 brand players incorporating crowdsourcing into their innovation strategies is striking. As Figure 6.2 illustrates, the list of top-20 brands using crowdsourcing in 2015 was led by Coca-Cola, Danone, Nestlé, and PepsiCo with each company showing increased use.

Even more striking is the increase in use of crowdsourcing by the subset of companies that fall into the category of FMCG. As illustrated by Figure 6.3, this group increased their usage of crowdsourcing by 27 percent in 2015 as compared to 2014, outpacing many of the tech companies that originally used the crowd for innovation. Additionally, the same FMCG companies use of the crowd to generate new ideas almost doubled (+95 percent) in 2015!

Perhaps the most intriguing trend impacting the use of the crowd for innovation is mobility. In its annual Mobility Report, Ericsson, the Swedish networking and telecommunications equipment and services company, predicts that by 2020 global smartphone subscriptions will more than double to 6.1 billion, 70 percent of people will use smartphones, and 90 percent will be covered by mobile broadband networks. Even more striking is the fact that almost 80 percent of new smartphone subscriptions by the end of 2020 will come from Africa, the Middle East, and Asia-Pacific. That's a lot of untapped potential. Organizations will be able to take advantage of that mobile saturation by making innovation anytime, anywhere, and from any device.

The Crowd's Potential

The crowd has tremendous potential to transform and disrupt just about any industry. Two of the most recognizable examples are Airbnb and Uber. Airbnb, which started renting out air mattresses, is now valued at over $25 billion without owning any tangible assets such as apartments or hotels. Uber, whose app-based taxi fleet of cars is continuously expanding, is worth more than $50 billion without owning vehicles or employing drivers. These two "sharing economy" companies

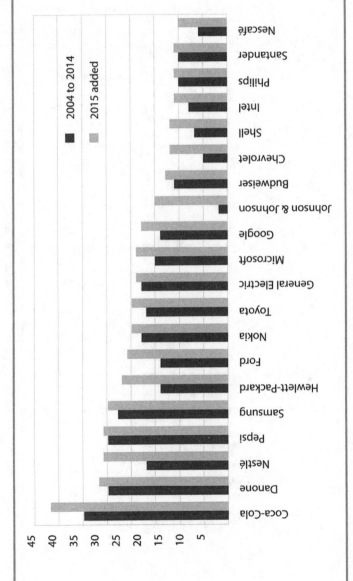

FIGURE 6.2 Increased Use of Crowdsourcing by Top-20 Brands *(Graphic used with permission from eYeka.)*

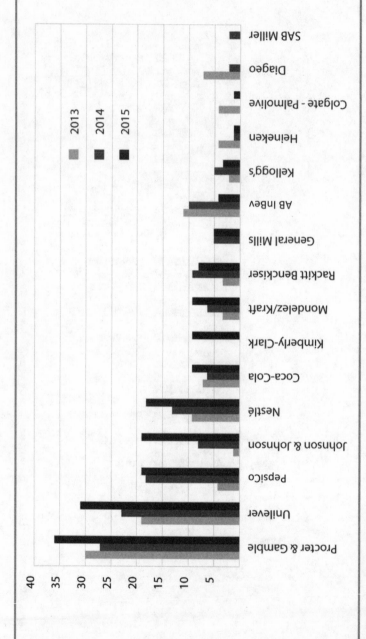

FIGURE 6.3 FMCGs' Increased Use of Crowdsourcing for Innovation (*Graphic used with permission from eYeka.*)

are leveraging the crowd's resources, producing a domino effect not just in their respective markets but also redefining the very concept of consumption, from rides to apartments to private aircraft. In case you are wondering, there are Uber equivalents for air travel. The goal of companies like OpenAirplane, Air-Pooler, and Flytenow is to simplify air travel and cut costs for the consumer. The ability to order a pilot and airplane with a few taps on a mobile device has already begun. Without a doubt, these enterprises are disrupting the traditional airline, hotel, and taxi industries.

But crowdsourcing also has the potential to reshape entire industries. For example, traditional marketing is in transition from a broadcast model dependent upon demographic segmentation and print, radio, and television advertising to a model of individual participation and cocreation. For example, PepsiCo used video games, sweepstakes, and voting to induce the crowd to collaborate on a new flavor for one of its popular beverages, Mountain Dew. As a result, changes are under way in market research, product development, and brand/marketing strategies. Another example is Reflik, a platform that combines referrals and crowdsourcing to match qualified candidates with organizations seeking new talent. Reflik and other similar platforms have the potential to completely revolutionize how organizations source new talent. I'll talk about the implications of using crowdsourcing to identify talent later in this chapter.

Perhaps the one person who understands the potential of the crowd better than most is Sean Parker, who at age 19 hacked his way into the music industry with Napster, his short-lived music file–sharing service. Learning from the experience, he later launched Spotify, which is a fully legal and highly popular music streaming service today. "It's technology, not business or government, that's the real driving force behind large-scale societal shifts," said Parker in 2010. While his focus is on technology, what Parker has been doing is leveraging the crowd.

Napster was a peer-to-peer file sharing platform that enabled people to easily share their music files. Yes, it was technology, but the idea behind it was the need for human connection, which is a powerful aspect of the crowd. Parker was also a key early investor in social media giant Facebook—together, Spotify and Facebook have entirely transformed the way we communicate, collaborate, and consume. Together they have helped to further the potential of the crowd.

Now Parker is using his creativity to accelerate cancer research. Based on his strong belief that one thing holding back the discovery of a cancer cure is the lack of collaboration between leading research institutes and scientists, Parker has pledged $250 million to reshape the field of cancer immunology through the new Parker Institute for Cancer Immunotherapy (PICI). However, his disruptive influence remains intact. Unusually, the Institute *hacks* into the secretive world of cancer research, but in a positive way. It brings together six of the biggest research institutes and entrepreneurial individual scientists to collaborate and share their research. Now, scientists are sharing their research at every milestone, so that they can collectively accelerate overall progress. PICI will own the intellectual property rights of all marketable findings, allowing scientists within the wider consortium to quickly share results with participating colleagues and ultimately bring effective products to market faster and cheaper.

Crowdsourcing also has the potential to have positive impact on corporate innovation. As I mentioned in the Introduction, GE used the crowd to solve a jet engine mounting problem with an investment of just $20,000. Another example of this is the pharmaceutical company Merck. In 2012, Merck used the crowd to streamline its drug discovery process. The traditional industry practice for identifying new molecules that might be effective in targeting specific diseases involves testing hundreds of thousands of compounds. There is no cost-effective way to test all of them against all potential diseases. Working with Kaggle, a predictive data analytics platform that hosts crowdsourcing competitions, Merck set up an eight-week, $40,000 contest in which it released data on chemical compounds it had previously tested and challenged participants to identify which held the most promise for future testing. The contest attracted 238 teams that submitted well over 2,500 proposals. The winning solution came from computer scientists (not professionals in the life sciences) employing machine-learning approaches previously unknown to Merck. The results were dramatic enough that the *New York Times* reported the results in a front-page story. Merck is now implementing the solution.

The Crowd Has Many Faces

The "crowd" takes many shapes and forms. It has been associated with self-organization, creation, contests, design, jams, outsourced labor, collaboration, funding, and wisdom. Other writers (Brabham, Howe, Sloane, and Shellshear, just to name a few) have written about the various permutations taken by the crowd. Since the focus of this chapter is how the crowd can be used by organizations, the number of shapes and forms that can be taken by the crowd has been intentionally restricted to four general approaches, represented in Figure 6.4. The idea for this figure has been influenced by the work of others such as Deloitte Consulting, Daren Brabham, Kevin Boudreau, and Karim Lakhani.

Four general ways of using crowdsourcing for innovation are:

1. **Crowd contests.** As the title suggests, a crowd contest is used to generate an idea or solve a specific problem. Organizations that use contests typically offer some type of cash prize for the winning idea or best solution.

CROWDSOURCE APPROACH	PURPOSE	GOOD FOR	CHALLENGES	EXAMPLES
Crowd Contests	• Generate lots of potential solutions to complex problems on a large scale through individual contributions	• Analytical, design, scientific, technical problems • Gathering diverse and independent ideas	• Problem must be well defined • Engagement of crowd • Intellectual property issues	• Coca-Cola Happiness is in the Air • Doritos' Crash the Super Bowl • Starbucks' White Cup Contest
Crowd Labor	• Efficiently and flexibly matching talent to specific tasks that require human labor	• Well-defined work that is easily described and evaluated • Not hiring full- or part-time employees	• Identify which tasks to outsource • Size of task (micro vs. macro) • Managing the labor pool and quality	• Amazon Mechanical Turk • CloudCrowd • RapidWorkers
Crowd Complementors	• Encourage innovative solutions to user problems with an organization's core products	• Open source products, operations	• Need to provide access to organization information on the core product while still protecting intellectual property	• BASF Future Business • P&G Connect+Develop • Star Alliance Airlines
Crowd Collaboration	• Aggregate a large number of ideas into a unified whole drawing upon the ideas of many	• Drawing upon the collective wisdom of the crowd	• Crowd is harder to manage since it lacks the unifying cohesiveness of an organization • Intellectual property issues	• Wikipedia • In Saturn's Rings

FIGURE 6.4 Different Approaches to Organizational Crowdsourcing

2. **Crowd labor.** Crowd labor is used to match external talent to specific organizational work. A good example of this is Amazon's Mechanical Turk, an "online work marketplace." With crowd labor the workplace has no walls, no national borders, and virtually no limits.

3. **Crowd complementors.** Crowd complementing allows organizations to use external input to expand and evolve existing products or services. Procter & Gamble, for example, uses its Connect+Develop platform to seek out new uses for existing products.

4. **Crowd collaboration.** Crowd collaboration involves partnering with the crowd to advance thinking around specific ideas or problems. Wikipedia is probably the premier example of crowd collaboration.

Any of these approaches can help an organization drive its innovation. However, one of the questions that organization leaders will need to address is which approach best fits their organization. I will discuss this question in more detail a bit later in the chapter.

Advantages of Crowdsourcing

Using the crowd for innovation has some distinct advantages not found within the four walls of the traditional organization, including access to knowledge, resources, and scale.

The amount of knowledge available through the crowd is staggering, and shifting through all that information can be challenging. Consider this. Between 2009 and 2019, global data generation is expected to increase by a factor of 40. Every day, 475 billion content items are shared on Facebook alone, and 90 percent of the world's data has been produced in just the last two years. However, accessing a user group, interest group, or peer-to-peer learning community can frequently help make the process of finding information faster. These communities offer reviews, feedback, guidance, and solutions (charges may apply!). A simple example of this type of group is TripAdvisor, a platform where travelers provide feedback ratings and information about airlines, hotels, and things to do in a particular geographic location, as well as service providers such as restaurants and tour guides. Five bubbles on TripAdvisor has become a coveted rating. The crowd can also put organizations in touch with a wide range of resources for funding and labor. Platforms such as Kickstarter, Indiegogo, and GoFundMe can help individuals and small enterprises raise funding through the crowd.

Outsourcing a variety of work to the crowd is well under way. The type of workers that can be found online ranges from micro-manual labor (organizing and reviewing data, completing surveys, labeling photographs) to highly sophisticated design, engineering, and IT specialists. Skilled work completed in the service economy can literally be re-created in the crowd via online platforms. Organizations that have work to be completed can post it on specific platforms. Individuals who want to work can post their profiles, advertise and sell their services, and receive reviews from users. RapidWorkers is a good example of this type of platform.

Does your organization have a large-scale project to be completed in a short time frame? Is your organization struggling with a complex problem that no one in your internal R&D department has been able to solve? Is your organization looking for the next molecule to beat cancer? The crowd could be your solution. Crowdsourcing can put your organization in touch with millions of people who can potentially complete your project in record time or provide solutions to previously unsolvable problems. The crowd can also provide your organization with fresh perspectives that can lead to new products and services. This is the power of today's uber-connected and uber-populated world.

Another advantage to crowdsourcing is a potential reduction in costs and overheads. Most of today's organizations prefer to hire full- or part-time staff to closely control all aspects of the business. But this approach to staffing can be very costly when salaries and benefits are taken into consideration. Crowdsourcing can give organizations access to millions of professions for significantly less cost.

The Challenges of Crowdsourcing

While crowdsourcing has distinct advantages, it also presents some unique challenges, especially the interface between the organization and the crowd, intellectual property (IP) rights, and quality. As we will see later in this chapter, managing the interface between the organization and the crowd can be a challenge. Defining the problem, selecting the approach to the crowd (contest verses collaboration), handling questions, determining rules for engagement, and determining the most appropriate solutions all takes time and must be carefully managed.

Intellectual property (IP) rights can likewise be a tricky issue. While conditions will vary from one project to the next, the organization sourcing the problem typically retains the IP rights. However, in the case of projects where many users have provided solutions like an IT design contest, the question of who owns the rejected designs must be addressed as part of the contest's terms and conditions.

Unfortunately, whether performing a task or solving a problem, there is no guarantee that crowdsourcing will result in usable solutions or solutions of sufficient quality. Sometimes the results will exceed expectations, while other times the results can be very disappointing. To illustrate these points, here are a couple of humorous examples of how crowdsourcing can backfire:

- **NASA.** Using a crowdsourced contest, NASA invited the public to help name the International Space Station. The public was given the opportunity to vote for suggestions put forward by NASA as well as suggestions coming from the public. When Stephen Colbert, an American comedian and host of *The Colbert Report*, learned about the contest he got his thousands of fans to vote for the space station to be named after him. The turnout was so massive that the name "Colbert" won the contest, not exactly what NASA had in mind. After some negotiations, NASA agreed to name a specially designed treadmill after Colbert (Combined Operational Load Bearing External Resistance Treadmill, or COLBERT).
- **Kraft.** In 2009, Kraft Foods used a crowdsourced contest to introduce a more spreadable version of Vegemite, a popular spread made from yeast extract. While the competition was under way, the nameless product was made available on supermarket shelves with a cleverly designed label that read "Name Me." More than 48,000 people responded to the challenge to come up with a name for the new combination of cream cheese and Vegemite. When the winning product name was revealed to be iSnack2.0, things quickly turned sour for Kraft. The new "Americanized" name did not reflect the product's Australian roots and hit a nerve with the public, annoyed that the iconic spread was now American-owned. Kraft faced a huge backlash. After just four days, Kraft announced that it would dump iSnack2.0 and let the public decide on the new name through a poll, which resulted in the new name "Cheesybite."
- **President Obama.** In 2009, U.S. President Barack Obama tried crowdsourcing to gather questions for a press conference. His website, "Open for Questions," was quickly overtaken by supporters for the legalization of marijuana.

Driving Innovation Through Crowdsourcing

How can the crowd best be used for innovation? As noted previously, it is important to make the distinction between external crowdsource problem solving and traditional internal approaches. Most organizations are good at collecting and organizing specialized knowledge to address problems and innovation challenges. In contrast, the crowd is flexible and decentralized. The crowd exposes an innovation problem to a widely diverse group of individuals who have varied experience, perspectives, and skills. It can operate on a scale that exceeds even the largest multinational corporation by bringing together many more individuals to focus on any given challenge. This means it is possible to use the crowd to solve problems more efficiently (and faster) due to the number of people involved. In the age of breakneck speed that we live in today, product shelf lives are shrinking at an alarming rate. Innovation too needs to be sped up in order to survive and thrive. Enter the crowd!

However, there are a variety of outcome-oriented issues to consider when determining whether to use crowdsourcing for innovation. Issues such as how to approach and keep the crowd engaged, what platform to use, and how much and what kind of information to make available are just a few of the many issues to consider. Here are some successful examples of how organizations are using the crowd.

Corporate Sponsored Platforms Where Ideas Are Submitted Directly to the Sponsor

1. **Dell's IdeaStorm.** Launched in 2007, the purpose of Dell's platform is to gauge which ideas are most important and most relevant to its users. According to Dell's website, IdeaStorm has received over 25,000 submissions and the company has implemented almost 550 of them.

2. **Procter & Gamble's (P&G) Connect+Develop.**
Launched in 2002, the website serves as its "open front door to the world," allowing innovators anywhere to share their ideas with P&G. The website states, "It's a fact: collaboration accelerates innovation. In an increasingly connected world, the biggest business wins come from working together. When we partner externally, inspiration and innovation—and mutual value creation—are at our fingertips." According to the company, Connect+Develop, which includes translations in Chinese, Japanese, Spanish, and Portuguese, receives about 20 submissions every weekday—or more than 4,000 a year—from all over the world.

3. **My Starbucks Idea.** Launched in 2008, in its first year the site generated over 70,000 ideas directly from consumers. Now eight years later, the site has received more than 200,000 ideas, approximately 300 of which have been implemented by Starbucks. Engaged customers can share ideas regarding anything linked to the Starbucks brand in three broad categories: products, in-store experience, and involvement (social responsibility, building a community, etc.).

4. **Unilever Foundry.** Originally launched in 2014, Unilever's Foundry was intended to be a single-entry point platform to harness, nurture, and evolve thousands of innovative ideas from the entrepreneurial community. Its goal was to simplify the way in which small start-ups and entrepreneurs engaged with Unilever. In 2015, Unilever announced its commitment to increase the use of crowdsourcing, with the launch of its Unilever Foundry IDEAS. The new platform is to become Unilever's hub to centrally organize all crowdsourcing, and allow the company to increase its Foundry IDEAS tenfold as an idea-generation mechanism by 2020.

Intermediary Platform Providers

Intermediary platforms make connections between solution seekers and solution providers. These platforms generally bring solution seekers and solution providers together through a challenge or competition that involves a monetary reward. Solution providers are attracted to these sites not just for the financial reward, but also for the notoriety and acknowledgment they receive from the crowd community for their ideas. Solution providers typically register with intermediary platforms that focus on either specific industries or unique challenges. Registered solution providers are usually familiar with the specific type of business the platform supports, making it possible to gain more useful innovative ideas from them. The number of organizations providing these platforms is growing almost daily. Listed below are three examples of these intermediary platforms.

1. **Spigit** is a provider of innovation management software used by diverse industries including financial services, manufacturing, healthcare, and energy. Spigit has worked with brands such as AT&T, Citi, MetLife, Pfizer, and Unilever.

2. **InnoCentive** is also a provider of innovation management software that hosts a wide range of "challenges" with a goal to find solutions to business, social, policy, scientific, or technical problems. InnoCentive has worked with brands such as AstraZeneca, Boehringer-Ingelheim, Ford, and Thomson Reuters.

3. **IdeaConnection** is another provider of innovation management software that offers a variety of crowdsource options. IdeaConnection has worked with brands such as Kraft, Syngenta, Nike, and Kellogg's.

Working with the Crowd

While Stephen van Vuuren is not a corporate executive, his experience and insight derived from working with the crowd is instructive and serves as a good starting point for understanding how to best approach the crowd. He suggests that organizations:

1. Turn to the crowd when you need a lot of help, not because you "think it is cool."
2. Have a clearly defined and compelling problem that will not just attract but also keep the crowd engaged. "The more universal appeal your problem has the more it will attract people."
3. The timing of your approach to the crowd is critical. "If you go to the crowd too far into your own process the door may be closed." You need to find the "right inflection point for engaging and exiting from the crowd."
4. Provide leadership. With the crowd, "leadership is even more important when it is outside of the confines of the traditional organizational hierarchy. The crowd craves vision and leadership for something larger than itself. In fact, when you think about it, a crowd without leadership is a mob."

Based upon my own research, here are several other suggestions for working with the crowd. First, determine the right crowdsourcing strategy for your organization. Are you going to use a single approach, such as crowd contests, or a combination of approaches? Are you going to build your own platform, partner with an existing platform provider, or post your organization's challenge or problem on an intermediary platform? As noted earlier in Figure 6.4, a wide range of approaches to crowdsourcing exists. Before launching any crowdsourcing initiative, it is important to determine your organization's ultimate goal. Do you want to draw upon your customers to provide a new design for a coffee cup, as Starbucks did? Are you trying to find technical solutions to a vexing problem, as GE Aviation did? Or, are you trying to find short-term labor for a large data crunching project, like AOL Inc., when it set out to determine whether it was getting the best use of its video library?

AOL's task required a tool to measure which of the thousands of web pages it publishes daily contained videos. Instead of developing video-detecting software, which would take too long, or hiring temps to accomplish the task, which also would take too long, AOL turned to crowdsourcing. If your challenge is highly technical in nature, it might be best to use an intermediary's platform that attracts engineers, IT specialists, or medical research scientists. For less technical issues, such as naming a product, general platforms are more appropriate.

Next, clearly define the input you seek or the problem you are trying to solve. Have defined targets. Crusan at NASA says, "How you pose problems to an online community is fundamentally different. It takes greater levels of specificity to optimize the composition of the online community. Figuring out how to define a problem for this larger community took us the longest time. In the Advanced Exploration Systems Division, we probably spend 80 percent of our time formulating problem statements for the online community. Working with the crowd has helped us become better problem solvers." If you are looking for new ideas, define what you mean by new ideas. If you have a complex problem to solve, describe the problem, what steps have been taken so far, any attempted solutions that failed, and what issue an ideal solution would resolve. You could potentially be searching through thousands of ideas, which can be complicated and painstaking. Taking time to define the outcomes you seek is important.

Part of the difficulty in bringing a challenge or problem to the crowd is to make sure that it is appropriately "extracted" from your organization. Your challenge or problem needs to be easily understandable to outsiders. If your problem is highly technical in nature, it is best to remove all company jargon from the challenge or problem description unless the crowd you are working with is highly technical. Additionally, trade secrets or patented processes or technologies should be removed. If Coca-Cola wanted to come out with another "new" Coke, it would most likely not make its secret formula available to the crowd.

If this is your organization's first foray into crowdsourcing, it will be best to seek ideas that have some degree of success already. For example, trying to find expanded or new uses for a product that has already proven successful in the marketplace is a good starting point. If soliciting brand new product ideas from the crowd, request working prototypes or proof of consumer interest.

Most important, trust the crowd! If deferring to internal subject matter experts was the answer to your organization's development problems, there would be no need for the crowd. The crowd is powerful because of the myriad perspectives and experiences of the individuals inhabiting it. Do not make the mistake of assuming the crowd is inferior to your internal experts. Polaris Industries, a manufacturer of all-terrain vehicles (ATVs), partnered with Spigit (see above) to address its traditional, top-down innovation process. The company's existing innovation process was entirely manual, making progress fragmented, expensive, time-consuming, and siloed. It had no way to predict the risk, value, or viability of an idea, which made it difficult to get executive sponsorship. Polaris needed a way to access greater idea diversity, streamline processes, and drive implementation of new ideas. When Polaris turned to the crowd using Spigit's platform, it could fully automate its Ideate Innovation program, making the process of ideation to execution 80 percent faster. The result was a bestselling three-wheel motorcycle in the United States.

When you trust the crowd, it will trust you back, and can provide your organization with valuable feedback. Seek out and use the crowd's feedback. The crowd can be an incredible source of innovative ideas, but it can also be a source of critical feedback, which can lead an organization in new directions. Take the pharmaceutical company Pfizer as an example. Pfizer is one of the top 10 pharmaceutical companies in the world. The pharmaceuticals market consists of healthcare experts, doctors, manufacturers, nurses, pharmacists, researcher scientists, and more. This hugely diverse "crowd" can sometimes hinder innovation efforts, since it is often difficult for experts to think outside of conventional patterns and processes. But when Pfizer began using crowdsourcing, everything changed. The company's first innovation challenge (hosted on a platform provided by Imaginatik) was to identify and select ideas from a crowd of employees, customers, and/or partners. It had nearly 6,000 participants and resulted in 660 viable ideas. It also led to a significant increase in employee engagement—330 percent more people submitted and voted on ideas than the company originally anticipated. Pfizer quickly learned that people want to provide feedback and share their ideas, but it needed to give them the right place to do it.

If your organization decides to use the crowd for innovation, you need to consider how to promote your challenge or problem in a way that draws the attention of the crowd. Offering the right incentive is critical. In addition to scale and diversity, crowds offer benefits that organizations find difficult to match. While companies can provide salaries and bonuses, research shows that crowds are energized by intrinsic motivations, such as a desire for meaningful work. This desire comes into play when people decide for themselves what problems to address.

Jeff Howe says that the most important ingredient of a successful crowdsourcing event is a "vibrant, committed community." The obvious incentive is some type of reward for effort like prizes or cash, but there are other incentives worth considering. Identifying what will attract your crowd initially and keep it engaged is critical. Is your crowd interested in learning something new or improving its skills, being a part of an online community of people with similar interests, or looking for notoriety as the one innovator who solved your organization's problem? For some participants, increased stature among peers is an important motivator. Additionally, people can be incentivized simply by the organization they are working with. The crowd willingly gave Stephen van Vuuren money, time, and knowledge, all for free, because it was interested in his project.

Finally, a couple of "don'ts" when using the crowd for innovation. Don't pretend to be seeking input or innovation from the crowd when you have no intention of using the ideas and suggestions you receive. A couple of individuals responsible for maintaining their organization's crowdsource platform told me confidentially that their companies rarely use the ideas they receive from the crowd. Don't use the crowd because it is the new thing to do. The crowd can be very sophisticated and can turn against you quickly. United Airlines learned this the hard way. In 2008, Canadian Dave Carroll and his band the Sons of Maxwell were on a United Airlines flight to Nebraska. While the plane was sitting on the airport tarmac, Dave had a perfect view of the baggage handlers loading bags on the plane. Dave watched as the United employees carelessly loaded the band's instruments into the plane and damaged them. After a year of phone calls and meetings with United which produced no results, Dave and the band wrote, recorded, and uploaded to its website the hit song "United Breaks Guitars." Since the music video was released in 2009 it has been watched over 16 million times on YouTube. The video negatively impacted United's image and is a perfect example of how quickly the crowd can turn against a company.

Special Considerations for Organizational Sponsors and Advocates

In addition to my suggestions for how best to work with the crowd, there are a couple of special considerations to which crowdsourcing sponsors or advocates within an organization need to pay attention.

The first is to make certain your organization is truly committed to using the crowd. While crowdsourcing for innovation can potentially save and generate revenue in both the short and long term, setting up your organization's crowdsourcing strategy takes time. Be clear about why your organization wants to use crowdsourcing, what outcome you expect, and how it fits into your overall innovation strategy. Crowdsourcing is not a replacement for your internal R&D or innovation department. Rather it is an enhancement and supplement. Yes, crowdsourcing may permit you to reduce the size of your R&D or innovation department, but you will still need knowledgeable and skilled internal experts to help manage the process.

The second consideration is that crowdsourcing needs to be built into your organization's innovation culture. This will not be a natural process because many people initially may feel a loss of control when the crowd is used for innovation. But, per NASA's Crusan, this perceived loss of control is artificial and more psychological. He compares crowdsourcing to issuing a traditional contract where you select one winning bid with the expectation that you will receive a specific deliverable. But you never truly know whether the winning bid can actually deliver on expectations. When you use the crowd, you are using multiple sources for input, which the law of statistics says increases your chance of getting the right solution. Ultimately, Crusan believes that working with the crowd in fact gives you more control. Using the crowd for innovation did not catch on at Procter & Gamble until 2000 when then-CEO A. G. Lafley set an organizational goal for 50 percent of its innovations to come from outside the company. Lafley's strategy was not to replace the capability of its innovation team but to better leverage it. Through its crowdsource platform Connect+Develop and other internal improvements, Procter & Gamble's innovation productivity went up 60 percent between 2000 and 2006.

Finally, the issue of intellectual property (IP) rights deserves special consideration. Most organizations are used to controlling all the innovation rights to their products and services. But when an organization turns to the crowd for ideas and input, things can quickly become complicated. Two IP issues in particular stand out: confidentiality and infringement. For example, crowdsourcing usually involves interacting with a crowd of people unknown to your organization. Even when nondisclosure agreements are signed there is only a certain amount of confidence you can anticipate with a large, sometimes anonymous group. How prepared are you to lose control of some information if it were to be hacked or passed on to someone else? Just ask Hillary Clinton's former campaign manager, John Podesta, about his hacked e-mails, which were published by WikiLeaks and revealed the sometimes questionable inner workings of Washington politics and power-broking. The other issue is infringement. With crowdsourcing, your organization can receive anywhere from a few to thousands of ideas and solutions. All of these ideas will have to be reviewed before a final decision is made. But what about the solutions that are rejected? Your organization will need to make sure that none of your future work uses any of the rejected solutions, otherwise you are at risk of an infringement lawsuit.

The Verdict

Crowdsourcing for innovation has and continues to demonstrate tremendous potential. As I have discussed in this part of the chapter, traditional approaches to corporate innovation are increasingly limited when compared to the potential breakthroughs offered by the crowd. Organizations that do not include the crowd as one of the sources of innovation risk being left behind, or worse, becoming irrelevant in today's open source era. So, while it is messy and difficult to manage, the days of corporations living in secrecy and isolation are over. In the open source era, living inside the box is not even an option anymore. Join the crowd!

Crowdsourcing for Talent and Leadership Succession

As noted previously, there are four broad approaches to crowd-sourcing: competition, labor, complementary, and collaborative. In this section, I will focus on using crowdsourcing for talent solutions, including for external hiring and internal succession planning. In addition to being a source for innovation, the crowd has the potential to be a solution for many labor-related issues including: short-, mid-, and long-term staffing issues; attracting talent; and developing the leaders your organization will need for long-term sustainability.

Crowdsourcing Talent

According to IMPACT Hiring Solutions, roughly 56 percent of newly hired executives fail within two years of starting a job. That's less than the probability of correctly guessing the result of a coin toss. Barry Deutsch, founding partner of IMPACT Hiring Solutions, says that "year after year companies experience this syndrome of 56 percent hiring failure, and yet they keep doing the same thing over and over hoping for better results . . . didn't Benjamin Franklin call that the definition of insanity?" I think most of us can relate to Deutsch's comment. The question is, what can we do instead? The answer might lie in crowdsourcing.

Given the uber-connected economy, the first question hiring managers need to ask is whether this position really needs to be a full-time, in-house role. Can the work instead be outsourced to free agents who work on-demand? Websites like *upwork.com* now allow hiring or sourcing managers to outsource work to individuals or teams in a variety of disciplines like code writing, web design, virtual assistants, or copywriting. They simply post their work requirements on the site, which almost immediately starts matching the right freelance workers with the work. As I mentioned in Chapter 1, a significant part of the workforce now prefers free agency as compared to traditional full-time employment, making this a possible win-win arrangement for both employers and workers. Employers need not incur recurring costs of full-time hires, and need not bear the risk of the hiring decision going bad. Even for more senior positions where full-time employment is necessary, why not hire someone on a 6- or 12-month contract initially before giving the person a full-time job? There is no stigma attached to contract work anymore.

Let me make a distinction between on-demand labor and longer-term talent solutions. By on-demand labor I mean contract labor that does work either on an item or project basis for your organization. These are individuals that are not considered employees. Most likely, these individuals are very mobile and will work for you from virtually anywhere in the world. When I refer to crowdsourcing for talent, what I mean is the process of searching for, identifying, and recruiting suitable employees for your organization by soliciting the input of large numbers of people using a variety of online means. These individuals typically will join your company as some type of employee.

On-Demand Workers

On October 24, 2016, a *New York Times International Edition* article described how many skilled and unskilled professionals are starting to move into on-demand roles, in what has become known as the "gig economy." The gig economy is a work arrangement in which temporary positions are common, and organizations contract with independent free agents for short-term engagements. These short-term engagements are filled by individuals who come from diverse backgrounds and professions (accountants, designers, skilled laborers, etc.). The work can involve watching a video and responding to an eight-minute survey or proposing questions that could be used on a survey to complete complex IT or medical tasks. Fees for this work can range from $0.05 to thousands of dollars. According to an Intuit Forecast report, more than 40 percent of the U.S. workforce will be freelancers by 2020. Some of this is driven by the workforce's desire for more flexibility, and some by companies hiring free agents to reduce costs. Either way, the arrangement can benefit both employers and employees.

From the employees' perspective, working on-demand in the gig economy provides the flexibility to work anytime and anywhere on projects they find interesting and engaging. From an organizational perspective, there are several benefits to using an on-demand approach to work. The 2014 State of the Industry report conducted by the International Association of Outsourcing Professionals (IAOP), in collaboration with Accenture, indicates that the advantages to organizations using on-demand workers include business flexibility, cost savings, and access to skills and knowledge currently not available to the company. According to the IAOP's report, 57 percent of its respondents cite increasing business flexibility as the main reason for using on-demand labor.

Online platforms such as Amazon's Mechanical Turk or Allegion's crowdsourcing platform are easy ways to access on-demand talent. However, organizations face some challenges when trying to source work from the crowd. Ironic as it may seem, high-demand talent is not interested in submitting résumés or checking career and job platforms. This type

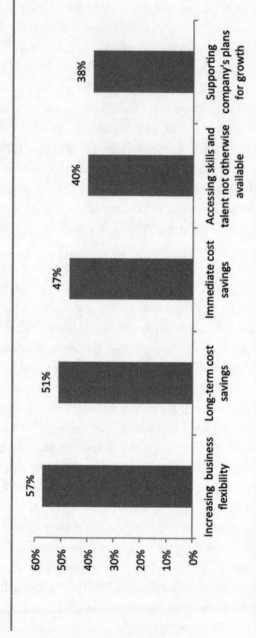

FIGURE 6.5 Main Reasons for IAOP's Respondents' Using On-Demand Outsourcing *(Graph used with permission.)*

of talent works by word-of-mouth through a circle of friends and colleagues, or participation in relevant online forums. For example, most talented free agents tend to have more work than they can easily handle. They are generally not looking to move. But if something more engaging and exciting comes along, this type of talent will move unless something is done to hold their attention.

Additionally, many of these talents also look to build long-term relationships with organizations. They don't want to work for a company, but they do want to collaborate with it on projects that are challenging and interesting. While this talent may want the flexibility to work with any organization when they want to, they are still interested in developing a mutually beneficial, long-term relationship.

Finally, while money is important to these talents, the best way to engage them is to be transparent, provide recognition for good, quality work, and make it easy for them to work with your company. Remember, in the age of Uber, these workers have options and can shift their loyalties quickly.

A Cautionary Note

While there are many benefits to using the crowd for on-demand workers, I offer one cautionary note for consideration. In his book *The Ownership Quotient: Putting the Service Profit Chain to Work for Unbeatable Competitive Advantage*, Harvard Business School Professor James L. Heskett describes two types of worker mentalities: "owners" and "renters." Owner-workers have a mentality that leads them to take responsibility for their organization and its customers. They exhibit this mentality when they "take responsibility for improving relationships, products, and processes as well as referring new employee candidates." Owner-workers notice things that need to be corrected and act on it, even when it is not their area of responsibility. They exhibit a high degree of loyalty to their organizations. Renter-workers, on the other hand, literally come and go. They are on-demand workers who do the work assigned to them and nothing more.

Ultimately ownership is psychological, not financial. Heskett points out that ownership here is not real estate or physical assets, but people and relationships. A key challenge that leaders in the open source era will need to address is how to ensure an adequate amount of "ownership" even within free agents. Whether we like it or not, the gig economy is here to stay. Uber has already paid a heavy price in some countries due to the bad behavior of some of its drivers. Even if workers are free agents, they cannot have a "renter" mentality. They need to adhere to company values and give customers a consistent experience. So how do leaders ensure such consistency with free agents? First, they will need to determine very carefully which jobs are suitable for free agents and which require full-time employees. Second, they will need to take advantage of today's full transparency and do careful screening before hiring free agents. Thankfully, with openly available information this should not be difficult. And finally, after hiring they will need to monitor performance closely through user reviews and other means, and weed out those with a renter mentality.

Hiring Talents Through the Crowd

Two decades ago, to recruit talent most employers relied upon a combination of classified advertisements in newspapers, and trade magazines, and executive search firms. But with the growth of the Internet, organizations have expanded into the online realm by posting job positions on a wide range of recruiting job sites such as Career Builder and Monster.com. The challenge with these sites is how to identify the right, high-quality talents out of thousands of often low-quality applicants. Frequently the best candidate is already employed and not actively seeking a job.

As a result, many organizations are turning to the crowd to identify potential talent, and leveraging professional and social networks to sort through the large volume of job seekers and find the best talent match. Crowdsourcing talent allows an organization to leverage databases, extensive professional and social networks, and the "wisdom" of the crowd to locate and identify the best candidates for any type of position. Using the crowd also has the potential to speed up the recruitment process, starting from the time a position becomes available to when a hire is made. The crowd can help to quickly identify potential applicants and narrow the respondents to a select group of high-quality candidates.

There are two types of crowdsourcing strategies your organization can consider when it comes to identifying potential talent: employee based, when your own employees refer talent to fill open positions; and crowdsourcing, where the public is encouraged to make referrals. Of these two strategies, creating a partnership with your own employees to identify external talent is probably the best starting point. Your own employees know the organization, its culture, and the work required. They are in the best position to assess an external candidate's "fit" in the organization. Start by asking them to participate in an online forum that focuses on topics or areas of interest to your company. Ask them to invite their friends and professional colleagues to participate. If the content of the forum is targeted to the interests of high-demand talent (e.g., auditors, designers, and engineers) they will want to participate and share their expertise, raise questions, and offer solutions. Ask your talented existing employees to rate the various people who participate, and use this information to identify potential candidates. Filling vacant positions through an employee referral program is a proven method that many organizations have used successfully. A study by Undercover Recruiter found that while internal referrals may only account for 7 percent of corporate applications, they turn into 40 percent of all hires. Zappos, the online shoe and clothing company, exclusively hires new talent through an employee referral and social networking system called Zappos Insider. If you decide to engage your employees to identify potential talents, you may need to consider some type of incentive, usually in the form of a cash reward.

Since the majority of today's workforce uses some form of social media, the other option for finding and hiring talent is to turn to the crowd. Facebook and LinkedIn are examples of social media platforms that can be used to help identify potential talent. New recruitment platforms, such as the one hosted by Reflik, are intended to bring together employers, independent recruiters, and individuals to match skilled candidates with positions. Organizations pay a fee to Reflik to list positions. With each job listing, Reflik pays a referral reward if a candidate is hired through a recruiter's referral.

Leadership Succession

Traditional methods of succession planning are quickly becoming outdated in today's economy. With the rate at which change happens today, how can companies forecast who amongst their ranks will make good leaders in a few years? Until the early 1990s, the succession planning process was relatively simple. HR departments usually helped their companies identify a few possible successors for each key job, and developed these potential successors through a combination of classroom training, on-the-job experiences, and coaching. It was easier to predict future success because business was relatively steady. Behaviors that made leaders successful in a particular company in the past could be codified into competency models, and future leaders assessed and developed on the basis thereof. The competencies themselves did not change much from decade to decade, so the best predictor of future success was considered to be the replication of past successful behaviour. Consequently, companies maintained nine-box grids that plotted their talent into boxes based on two axes—current performance and future potential. Those on the top right-hand side of the grid then became the designated future leaders of the company and were given a special development diet of job rotations, training, mentoring, and coaching for their future roles. As and when senior positions became available, HR would simply tap into the pool of anointed successors and fill them.

In comparison, today the rate of obsolescence is faster than ever before. According to some estimates, half of what an engineering student learns in the first year of a four-year degree is outdated by the time he or she is in the third year. In this environment, how can companies correctly predict future performance? Why should they anoint a few successors based on subjective criteria and hope they will work out? After investing in their special development diet, what is the guarantee that these future leaders will even stay with the company, or that the skills and experiences developed will even be relevant? And why risk disenfranchising the rest of the employee population because they were not chosen? What about the late bloomers and early fizzlers? Could there be a better way to identify and develop future leaders? Yes, there is, and the answer again lies in *internal* crowdsourcing. Let me explain with an example from my own career.

Back in the nineties when I was a young currency trader with American Express in Mumbai, India, my colleagues and I became frustrated with our hiring failure rate. One in every two traders we hired turned out to be unfit for trading, even though on average 7 to 10 people interviewed each candidate. Barry Deutsch was right then too! The company had a global program called the Chairman's Award for Quality (CAQ), in which any staff member who had an idea to improve something in the company could form a team and work on the idea. Once the work was completed, teams would submit reports about their projects to a designated committee that would evaluate all projects and select the best. The top projects from each country would qualify for a regional contest, and the best from each region would compete for a global award. Even if your project did not make it to the regional or global stage, you could still compete for a country level award. There was no compulsion for anyone to join the program; it was totally voluntary. There were no barriers to entry either—anyone who wanted to could participate, but employees would need to make time for their projects over and above their normal duty.

I decided to take advantage of the program and formed a team of colleagues from the trading room and operations, and together we created an interactive, real-time trading game that we converted into a weeklong training program. We would bring in participants from around the company to attend the program in batches of 16 to 20, teach them the basics of markets, then have them trade with each other using connected computers that simulated a live forex market environment. Our idea was to see which participants exhibited the skills and aptitude for trading and to hire future traders from amongst the program's alumni, thereby reducing the hiring failure rate.

To cut a long story short, the program became a huge success and won the country level gold award. While it did not get past the country level, our hiring success rates improved considerably. But there was one more unintended positive consequence for me. The head of HR noticed that I seemed to have a natural flair for teaching and offered me a job in HR to head Learning and Development. After getting over my initial hesitation I accepted the job, and it changed my life forever. The program and my subsequent work eventually received broader attention, and I landed a global job in New York. Had it not been for the CHQ program, I would have most likely remained a trader for the rest of my life, would probably never have discovered my true passion, and certainly would not have moved to the

United States. While many of my colleagues and I were always willing to go the extra mile to get recognized, there was no real avenue (before the CHQ program) available to showcase our talents and energy. The CHQ program became a vehicle not only for my career progression, it was also the basis on which I was selected for the global job.

The point I am trying to make is this. Gone are the days when past successful behavior was a reliable predictor of future success. Instead of using subjective criteria to map people on a performance/potential grid, why not crowdsource internally for leadership energy just like the CHQ program did at American Express? Throw out such challenges to the entire employee base and see who comes forward to showcase their talent and energy. Those who raise their hands year after year to solve company problems or exploit revenue opportunities are your natural leaders for tomorrow. Let the cream rise to the top naturally!

Besides natural succession planning, internal crowdsourcing for leadership energy allows companies to solve problems and exploit opportunity at virtually no cost. Remember our definition of leadership from Chapter 3: leadership is the art of harnessing human energy toward the creation of a better future. Internal crowdsourcing as proposed here automatically and organically identifies better future creators.

Whether for driving innovation, attracting talent, or succession planning, crowdsourcing is the way to go in today's uber-connected and uber-populated economy. In 1997, Steven Hankin of McKinsey & Co. coined the term *The War for Talent*, suggesting that there was an acute shortage of great leadership talent and that companies needed to develop exciting employee value propositions (EVPs) to attract and retain the best of the best. While the latter part is still true—that companies need to have excellent EVPs—the scarcity of talent aspect is not. As Raghu Krishnamoorthy, VP Human Resources at GE Healthcare, said in a talk a few years ago, "talent is abundant, not scarce." To illustrate his point, he described the GE Aviation crowdsourcing of innovation experiment I mentioned in the Introduction. Thanks to uber-connectivity and uber-population, we can source talent and innovation from the crowd, both internally and externally, more easily than ever before in history. With this, we can lower the cost and increase the speed and accuracy of both innovation and talent development.

CHAPTER SUMMARY

- Traditional methods of innovation (secretive R&D incubators) are giving way to crowdsourced innovation in the open source era.
- Global companies across industries are increasingly using the crowd for innovation.
- Using the crowd requires leadership, and is not without its challenges. However, the risks are well worth it because it increases and speeds up innovation while keeping costs low.
- Internal crowdsourcing can be used not only for innovation, but also for top talent identification and developing leadership succession.

Questions for Reflection

1. What is the state of innovation in your organization, and how can you use the crowd to increase and speed it up?

2. How does your organization currently plan for leadership succession?

3. How can the idea of internal crowdsourcing be applied within your organization?

FINAL THOUGHTS

Congratulations for reaching here. We've covered a lot of ground, starting with how the fourth industrial revolution is dramatically reshaping our lives, to what it means to lead personally in this brave new world, and to how open source thinking must replace organizational leadership and management dogma. Hopefully you enjoyed the ride. If the book has left you with more questions than answers, then my research team and I have achieved our objective. As I said in the Introduction, this is more of a "think book" rather than a "how-to book." At the end of the day, leadership is more art than science—and art requires judgment rather than formulas. Consequently, in this book I have avoided giving definitive formulas or answers because each situation is different, and only you can judge yours. And here's the thing about judgment ability—it gets better as you engage in more mindful reflection. So the best way to make use of what you've just read is to reflect carefully on how it all applies to you personally, and to the organization or group you lead. If you haven't already done so, pondering over the questions at the end of each chapter might help.

Whether we like it or not, the open source era is upon us. Rather than complaining about how different young people are these days, and trying to resist the megatrends shaping society, we will all be better off accepting the new reality and asking ourselves what we need to change about ourselves and our organizations to survive and thrive. I meet too many people calling themselves experts with "decades of business experience and wisdom" who reject ideas emerging from the unfamiliar open source era. But as Vinod Khosla once said, "Many times experts fail because they are experts in the past version of the world." My hope is that this book has served as a reminder of just how much has changed, and encourages us all—employees, free agents, managers, C-suite leaders, and board directors—to keep an open mind.

Finally, there is a lot of talk these days about technological singularity—a time when computer intelligence will surpass human intelligence, and there will be no jobs left for us mere humans. Personally, I don't think that day will ever come because computers will never have emotions, feelings, and judgment. Some may argue that artificial intelligence and machine learning are making computers smarter by the day, and so computers *are* developing the ability to make judgments. I respectfully disagree because artificial intelligence is only making computers quicker at sifting through data and finding formula-based solutions. The human ability to judge is based on both the left and the right brain. The information-processing, linear left brain must work along with the amygdala (the house of feelings and emotions in our brain) in order to make judgments. So if leadership is all about judgment, which in turn relies heavily on feelings and emotions, then I don't think computers will ever lead humans. But to secure our future as a race, we must continue to *make the choice to lead* as we discussed in Chapter 3. Simply *living* life is not good enough anymore. We must *lead* our lives. Never before in our history has this been more important.

Since we are still in the early stages of the open source era, this book is a work in progress. In the true spirit of open source thinking, I invite you to add to it by sharing your thoughts and ideas on how we can live and lead better in this new era. As my team and I hear from you, we will update this work from time to time. You can also access all the data we've presented from our 28-country research at the open source portal we've created on our website. Here, you can not only take the survey yourself, you will also be able to map your scores by country and other slices. You can connect with me on any of the following:

Email: rajeev@rajeevpeshawaria.com or rajeevp@iclif.org

LinkedIn: Rajeev Peshawaria

Twitter: @rajeevpeshawria

Open Source Portal: www.iclif.org/opensource

So, what better future will you create, and for whom? Good luck on your chosen journey!

APPENDIX

Open Source Leadership—a Global Study

As mentioned in Chapters 3 and 6, the goal of the Open Source Leadership study was to learn how people viewed leadership and motivation for superior performance. We wanted to test some generally accepted "truths" and ascertain if they were still valid in today's uber-connected and uber-populated world.

Through a structured questionnaire we asked approximately 16,000 senior and midlevel executives from 28 countries the following:

Q1. What do Nelson Mandela, Steve Jobs, Mahatma Gandhi, Jack Ma, Abraham Lincoln, Howard Schultz, Aung San Suu Kyi, and Soichiro Honda have in common?

Q2. What do business leaders most need to do in order to drive unprecedented success in today's fast-paced environment?

Q3. On a 1–5 scale where 1 is "strongly disagree," 2 is "disagree," 3 is "neither agree nor disagree," 4 is "agree," and 5 is "strongly agree," please rate your level of agreement with the following statement:

In order to drive unprecedented success for the organization in today's fast paced environment, a significant amount of top-down leadership is required.

Q4. Who does your primary motivation to excel at work
most depend on, yourself or your immediate boss?

Q5. Are you more intrinsically or extrinsically motivated?

For Q1 and Q2, we gave them a list of leadership attributes/behaviors and asked them to rank order them in terms of importance. About half the attributes/behaviors were top-down, even a bit autocratic, and the other half were democratic and all-inclusive. The categories were hidden and statements randomized when shown to respondents. Q3 aimed to quantify the views expressed in Q1 and Q2. With Q4 we wanted to test the popular notion that an employee's primary motivation driver is his or her relationship with the immediate manager. Finally, with Q5, we wanted to ascertain how important intrinsic factors of motivation were as compared to extrinsic ones.

In order to maintain data integrity and total independence, we outsourced the survey to Kadence and SSI. Kadence is a full-service global market research consultancy, and SSI is a premier global provider of data solutions and technology for consumer and business-to-business survey research. Sample sizes for each country were chosen in accordance with generally accepted margin of error guidelines. The project was led by Philip Steggals, managing director of Kadence Singapore.

Our analysis and insights from the study have already been discussed in Chapters 2 and 4. Overall global results and country-specific snapshots are shown in Figures A.1 through A.29.

GLOBAL RESULTS (n=15704)

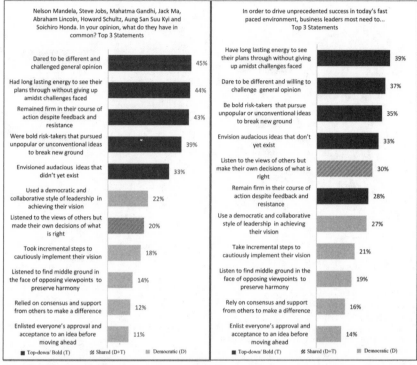

Nelson Mandela, Steve Jobs, Mahatma Gandhi, Jack Ma, Abraham Lincoln, Howard Schultz, Aung San Suu Kyi and Soichiro Honda. In your opinion, what do they have in common? Top 3 Statements

Statement	Value
Dared to be different and challenged general opinion	45%
Had long lasting energy to see their plans through without giving up amidst challenges faced	44%
Remained firm in their course of action despite feedback and resistance	43%
Were bold risk-takers that pursued unpopular or unconventional ideas to break new ground	39%
Envisioned audacious ideas that didn't yet exist	33%
Used a democratic and collaborative style of leadership in achieving their vision	22%
Listened to the views of others but made their own decisions of what is right	20%
Took incremental steps to cautiously implement their vision	18%
Listened to find middle ground in the face of opposing viewpoints to preserve harmony	14%
Relied on consensus and support from others to make a difference	12%
Enlisted everyone's approval and acceptance to an idea before moving ahead	11%

■ Top-down/ Bold (T)   ⧰ Shared (D+T)   ▦ Democratic (D)

In order to drive unprecedented success in today's fast paced environment, business leaders most need to... Top 3 Statements

Statement	Value
Have long lasting energy to see their plans through without giving up amidst challenges faced	39%
Dare to be different and willing to challenge general opinion	37%
Be bold risk-takers that pursue unpopular or unconventional ideas to break new ground	35%
Envision audacious ideas that don't yet exist	33%
Listen to the views of others but make their own decisions of what is right	30%
Remain firm in their course of action despite feedback and resistance	28%
Use a democratic and collaborative style of leadership in achieving their vision	27%
Take incremental steps to cautiously implement their vision	21%
Listen to find middle ground in the face of opposing viewpoints to preserve harmony	19%
Rely on consensus and support from others to make a difference	16%
Enlist everyone's approval and acceptance to an idea before moving ahead	14%

■ Top-down/ Bold (T)   ⧰ Shared (D+T)   ▦ Democratic (D)

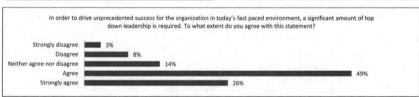

In order to drive unprecedented success for the organization in today's fast paced environment, a significant amount of top down leadership is required. To what extent do you agree with this statement?

Strongly disagree	3%
Disagree	8%
Neither agree nor disagree	14%
Agree	49%
Strongly agree	26%

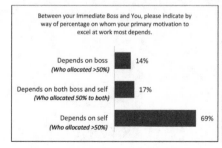

Between your Immediate Boss and You, please indicate by way of percentage on whom your primary motivation to excel at work most depends.

Depends on boss *(Who allocated >50%)*	14%
Depends on both boss and self *(Who allocated 50% to both)*	17%
Depends on self *(Who allocated >50%)*	69%

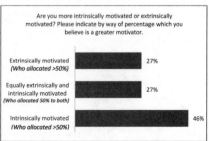

Are you more intrinsically motivated or extrinsically motivated? Please indicate by way of percentage which you believe is a greater motivator.

Extrinsically motivated *(Who allocated >50%)*	27%
Equally extrinsically and intrinsically motivated *(Who allocated 50% to both)*	27%
Intrinsically motivated *(Who allocated >50%)*	46%

FIGURE A.1 Global Results

ARGENTINA (n=324)

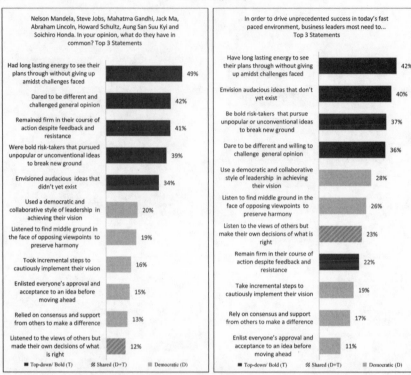

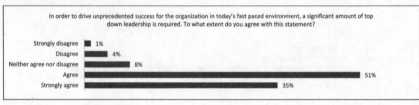

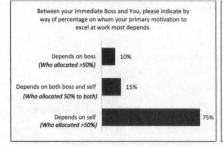

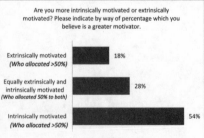

FIGURE A.2 Argentina

AUSTRALIA (n=589)

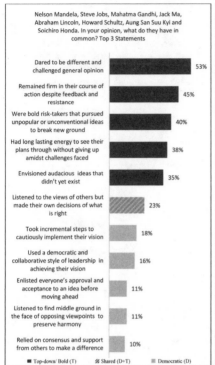

Nelson Mandela, Steve Jobs, Mahatma Gandhi, Jack Ma, Abraham Lincoln, Howard Schultz, Aung San Suu Kyi and Soichiro Honda. In your opinion, what do they have in common? Top 3 Statements

- Dared to be different and challenged general opinion — 53%
- Remained firm in their course of action despite feedback and resistance — 45%
- Were bold risk-takers that pursued unpopular or unconventional ideas to break new ground — 40%
- Had long lasting energy to see their plans through without giving up amidst challenges faced — 38%
- Envisioned audacious ideas that didn't yet exist — 35%
- Listened to the views of others but made their own decisions of what is right — 23%
- Took incremental steps to cautiously implement their vision — 18%
- Used a democratic and collaborative style of leadership in achieving their vision — 16%
- Enlisted everyone's approval and acceptance to an idea before moving ahead — 11%
- Listened to find middle ground in the face of opposing viewpoints to preserve harmony — 11%
- Relied on consensus and support from others to make a difference — 10%

■ Top-down/ Bold (T)　⧅ Shared (D+T)　▨ Democratic (D)

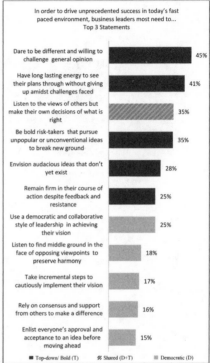

In order to drive unprecedented success in today's fast paced environment, business leaders most need to... Top 3 Statements

- Dare to be different and willing to challenge general opinion — 45%
- Have long lasting energy to see their plans through without giving up amidst challenges faced — 41%
- Listen to the views of others but make their own decisions of what is right — 35%
- Be bold risk-takers that pursue unpopular or unconventional ideas to break new ground — 35%
- Envision audacious ideas that don't yet exist — 28%
- Remain firm in their course of action despite feedback and resistance — 25%
- Use a democratic and collaborative style of leadership in achieving their vision — 25%
- Listen to find middle ground in the face of opposing viewpoints to preserve harmony — 18%
- Take incremental steps to cautiously implement their vision — 17%
- Rely on consensus and support from others to make a difference — 16%
- Enlist everyone's approval and acceptance to an idea before moving ahead — 15%

■ Top-down/ Bold (T)　⧅ Shared (D+T)　▨ Democratic (D)

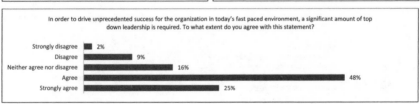

In order to drive unprecedented success for the organization in today's fast paced environment, a significant amount of top down leadership is required. To what extent do you agree with this statement?

- Strongly disagree — 2%
- Disagree — 9%
- Neither agree nor disagree — 16%
- Agree — 48%
- Strongly agree — 25%

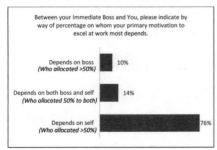

Between your Immediate Boss and You, please indicate by way of percentage on whom your primary motivation to excel at work most depends.

- Depends on boss (Who allocated >50%) — 10%
- Depends on both boss and self (Who allocated 50% to both) — 14%
- Depends on self (Who allocated >50%) — 76%

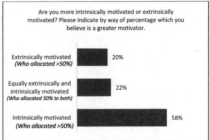

Are you more intrinsically motivated or extrinsically motivated? Please indicate by way of percentage which you believe is a greater motivator.

- Extrinsically motivated (Who allocated >50%) — 20%
- Equally extrinsically and intrinsically motivated (Who allocated 50% to both) — 22%
- Intrinsically motivated (Who allocated >50%) — 58%

FIGURE A.3　Australia

BELGIUM (n=320)

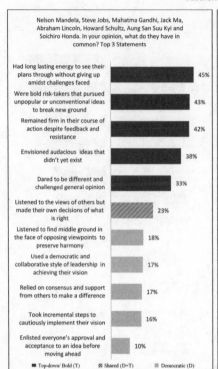

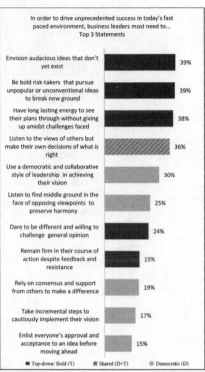

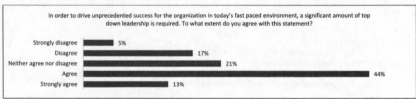

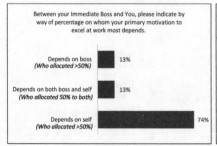

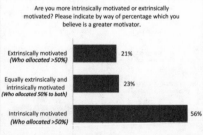

FIGURE A.4 Belgium

BRAZIL (n=321)

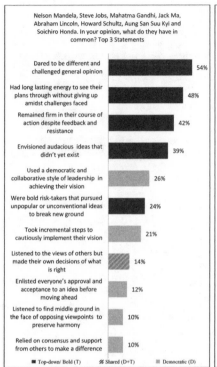

Nelson Mandela, Steve Jobs, Mahatma Gandhi, Jack Ma, Abraham Lincoln, Howard Schultz, Aung San Suu Kyi and Soichiro Honda. In your opinion, what do they have in common? Top 3 Statements

- Dared to be different and challenged general opinion — 54%
- Had long lasting energy to see their plans through without giving up amidst challenges faced — 48%
- Remained firm in their course of action despite feedback and resistance — 42%
- Envisioned audacious ideas that didn't yet exist — 39%
- Used a democratic and collaborative style of leadership in achieving their vision — 26%
- Were bold risk-takers that pursued unpopular or unconventional ideas to break new ground — 24%
- Took incremental steps to cautiously implement their vision — 21%
- Listened to the views of others but made their own decisions of what is right — 14%
- Enlisted everyone's approval and acceptance to an idea before moving ahead — 12%
- Listened to find middle ground in the face of opposing viewpoints to preserve harmony — 10%
- Relied on consensus and support from others to make a difference — 10%

■ Top-down/ Bold (T) ▨ Shared (D+T) ▤ Democratic (D)

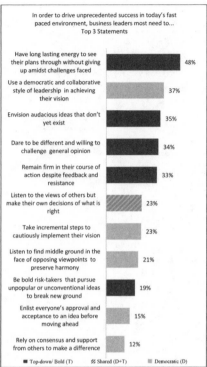

In order to drive unprecedented success in today's fast paced environment, business leaders most need to... Top 3 Statements

- Have long lasting energy to see their plans through without giving up amidst challenges faced — 48%
- Use a democratic and collaborative style of leadership in achieving their vision — 37%
- Envision audacious ideas that don't yet exist — 35%
- Dare to be different and willing to challenge general opinion — 34%
- Remain firm in their course of action despite feedback and resistance — 33%
- Listen to the views of others but make their own decisions of what is right — 23%
- Take incremental steps to cautiously implement their vision — 23%
- Listen to find middle ground in the face of opposing viewpoints to preserve harmony — 21%
- Be bold risk-takers that pursue unpopular or unconventional ideas to break new ground — 19%
- Enlist everyone's approval and acceptance to an idea before moving ahead — 15%
- Rely on consensus and support from others to make a difference — 12%

■ Top-down/ Bold (T) ▨ Shared (D+T) ▤ Democratic (D)

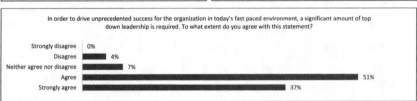

In order to drive unprecedented success for the organization in today's fast paced environment, a significant amount of top down leadership is required. To what extent do you agree with this statement?

- Strongly disagree — 0%
- Disagree — 4%
- Neither agree nor disagree — 7%
- Agree — 51%
- Strongly agree — 37%

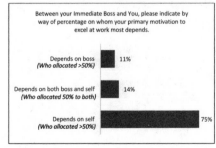

Between your Immediate Boss and You, please indicate by way of percentage on whom your primary motivation to excel at work most depends.

- Depends on boss *(Who allocated >50%)* — 11%
- Depends on both boss and self *(Who allocated 50% to both)* — 14%
- Depends on self *(Who allocated >50%)* — 75%

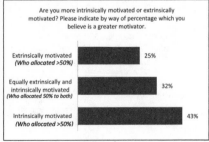

Are you more intrinsically motivated or extrinsically motivated? Please indicate by way of percentage which you believe is a greater motivator.

- Extrinsically motivated *(Who allocated >50%)* — 25%
- Equally extrinsically and intrinsically motivated *(Who allocated 50% to both)* — 32%
- Intrinsically motivated *(Who allocated >50%)* — 43%

FIGURE A.5 Brazil

CANADA (n=586)

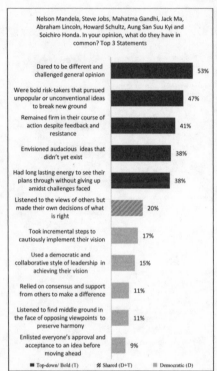

Nelson Mandela, Steve Jobs, Mahatma Gandhi, Jack Ma, Abraham Lincoln, Howard Schultz, Aung San Suu Kyi and Soichiro Honda. In your opinion, what do they have in common? Top 3 Statements

Statement	%
Dared to be different and challenged general opinion	53%
Were bold risk-takers that pursued unpopular or unconventional ideas to break new ground	47%
Remained firm in their course of action despite feedback and resistance	41%
Envisioned audacious ideas that didn't yet exist	38%
Had long lasting energy to see their plans through without giving up amidst challenges faced	38%
Listened to the views of others but made their own decisions of what is right	20%
Took incremental steps to cautiously implement their vision	17%
Used a democratic and collaborative style of leadership in achieving their vision	15%
Relied on consensus and support from others to make a difference	11%
Listened to find middle ground in the face of opposing viewpoints to preserve harmony	11%
Enlisted everyone's approval and acceptance to an idea before moving ahead	9%

■ Top-down/ Bold (T)　▨ Shared (D+T)　▦ Democratic (D)

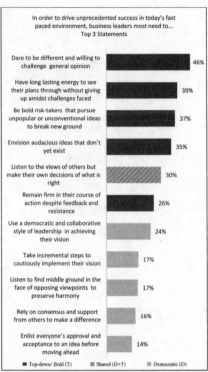

In order to drive unprecedented success in today's fast paced environment, business leaders most need to... Top 3 Statements

Statement	%
Dare to be different and willing to challenge general opinion	46%
Have long lasting energy to see their plans through without giving up amidst challenges faced	39%
Be bold risk-takers that pursue unpopular or unconventional ideas to break new ground	37%
Envision audacious ideas that don't yet exist	35%
Listen to the views of others but make their own decisions of what is right	30%
Remain firm in their course of action despite feedback and resistance	26%
Use a democratic and collaborative style of leadership in achieving their vision	24%
Take incremental steps to cautiously implement their vision	17%
Listen to find middle ground in the face of opposing viewpoints to preserve harmony	17%
Rely on consensus and support from others to make a difference	16%
Enlist everyone's approval and acceptance to an idea before moving ahead	14%

■ Top-down/ Bold (T)　▨ Shared (D+T)　▦ Democratic (D)

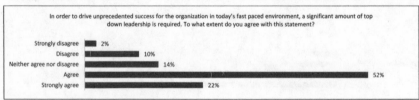

In order to drive unprecedented success for the organization in today's fast paced environment, a significant amount of top down leadership is required. To what extent do you agree with this statement?

	%
Strongly disagree	2%
Disagree	10%
Neither agree nor disagree	14%
Agree	52%
Strongly agree	22%

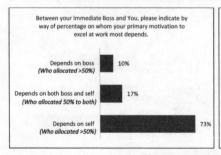

Between your Immediate Boss and You, please indicate by way of percentage on whom your primary motivation to excel at work most depends.

	%
Depends on boss (Who allocated >50%)	10%
Depends on both boss and self (Who allocated 50% to both)	17%
Depends on self (Who allocated >50%)	73%

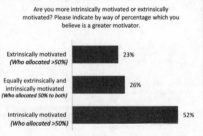

Are you more intrinsically motivated or extrinsically motivated? Please indicate by way of percentage which you believe is a greater motivator.

	%
Extrinsically motivated (Who allocated >50%)	23%
Equally extrinsically and intrinsically motivated (Who allocated 50% to both)	26%
Intrinsically motivated (Who allocated >50%)	52%

FIGURE A.6　Canada

CHINA (n=668)

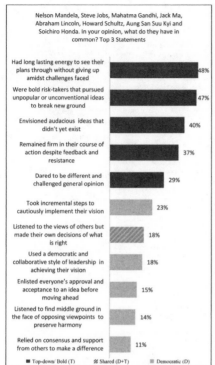

Nelson Mandela, Steve Jobs, Mahatma Gandhi, Jack Ma, Abraham Lincoln, Howard Schultz, Aung San Suu Kyi and Soichiro Honda. In your opinion, what do they have in common? Top 3 Statements

- Had long lasting energy to see their plans through without giving up amidst challenges faced — 48%
- Were bold risk-takers that pursued unpopular or unconventional ideas to break new ground — 47%
- Envisioned audacious ideas that didn't yet exist — 40%
- Remained firm in their course of action despite feedback and resistance — 37%
- Dared to be different and challenged general opinion — 29%
- Took incremental steps to cautiously implement their vision — 23%
- Listened to the views of others but made their own decisions of what is right — 18%
- Used a democratic and collaborative style of leadership in achieving their vision — 18%
- Enlisted everyone's approval and acceptance to an idea before moving ahead — 15%
- Listened to find middle ground in the face of opposing viewpoints to preserve harmony — 14%
- Relied on consensus and support from others to make a difference — 11%

■ Top-down/ Bold (T)   ▨ Shared (D+T)   ▨ Democratic (D)

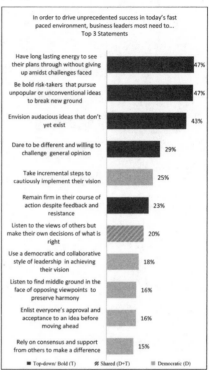

In order to drive unprecedented success in today's fast paced environment, business leaders most need to... Top 3 Statements

- Have long lasting energy to see their plans through without giving up amidst challenges faced — 47%
- Be bold risk-takers that pursue unpopular or unconventional ideas to break new ground — 47%
- Envision audacious ideas that don't yet exist — 43%
- Dare to be different and willing to challenge general opinion — 29%
- Take incremental steps to cautiously implement their vision — 25%
- Remain firm in their course of action despite feedback and resistance — 23%
- Listen to the views of others but make their own decisions of what is right — 20%
- Use a democratic and collaborative style of leadership in achieving their vision — 18%
- Listen to find middle ground in the face of opposing viewpoints to preserve harmony — 16%
- Enlist everyone's approval and acceptance to an idea before moving ahead — 16%
- Rely on consensus and support from others to make a difference — 15%

■ Top-down/ Bold (T)   ▨ Shared (D+T)   ▨ Democratic (D)

In order to drive unprecedented success for the organization in today's fast paced environment, a significant amount of top down leadership is required. To what extent do you agree with this statement?

- Strongly disagree — 1%
- Disagree — 5%
- Neither agree nor disagree — 18%
- Agree — 52%
- Strongly agree — 24%

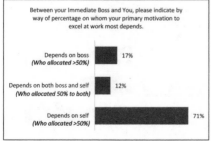

Between your Immediate Boss and You, please indicate by way of percentage on whom your primary motivation to excel at work most depends.

- Depends on boss *(Who allocated >50%)* — 17%
- Depends on both boss and self *(Who allocated 50% to both)* — 12%
- Depends on self *(Who allocated >50%)* — 71%

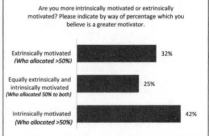

Are you more intrinsically motivated or extrinsically motivated? Please indicate by way of percentage which you believe is a greater motivator.

- Extrinsically motivated *(Who allocated >50%)* — 32%
- Equally extrinsically and intrinsically motivated *(Who allocated 50% to both)* — 25%
- Intrinsically motivated *(Who allocated >50%)* — 42%

FIGURE A.7   China

DENMARK (n=318)

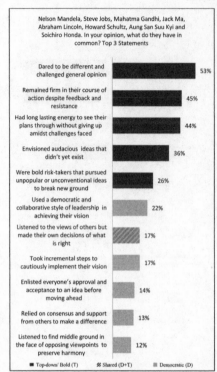

Nelson Mandela, Steve Jobs, Mahatma Gandhi, Jack Ma, Abraham Lincoln, Howard Schultz, Aung San Suu Kyi and Soichiro Honda. In your opinion, what do they have in common? Top 3 Statements

Statement	%
Dared to be different and challenged general opinion	53%
Remained firm in their course of action despite feedback and resistance	45%
Had long lasting energy to see their plans through without giving up amidst challenges faced	44%
Envisioned audacious ideas that didn't yet exist	36%
Were bold risk-takers that pursued unpopular or unconventional ideas to break new ground	26%
Used a democratic and collaborative style of leadership in achieving their vision	22%
Listened to the views of others but made their own decisions of what is right	17%
Took incremental steps to cautiously implement their vision	17%
Enlisted everyone's approval and acceptance to an idea before moving ahead	14%
Relied on consensus and support from others to make a difference	13%
Listened to find middle ground in the face of opposing viewpoints to preserve harmony	12%

■ Top-down/ Bold (T)　▨ Shared (D+T)　▦ Democratic (D)

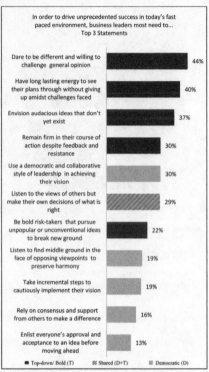

In order to drive unprecedented success in today's fast paced environment, business leaders most need to... Top 3 Statements

Statement	%
Dare to be different and willing to challenge general opinion	44%
Have long lasting energy to see their plans through without giving up amidst challenges faced	40%
Envision audacious ideas that don't yet exist	37%
Remain firm in their course of action despite feedback and resistance	30%
Use a democratic and collaborative style of leadership in achieving their vision	30%
Listen to the views of others but make their own decisions of what is right	29%
Be bold risk-takers that pursue unpopular or unconventional ideas to break new ground	22%
Listen to find middle ground in the face of opposing viewpoints to preserve harmony	19%
Take incremental steps to cautiously implement their vision	19%
Rely on consensus and support from others to make a difference	16%
Enlist everyone's approval and acceptance to an idea before moving ahead	13%

■ Top-down/ Bold (T)　▨ Shared (D+T)　▦ Democratic (D)

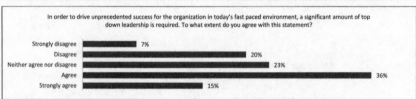

In order to drive unprecedented success for the organization in today's fast paced environment, a significant amount of top down leadership is required. To what extent do you agree with this statement?

	%
Strongly disagree	7%
Disagree	20%
Neither agree nor disagree	23%
Agree	36%
Strongly agree	15%

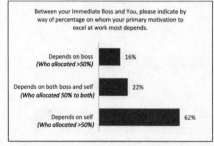

Between your Immediate Boss and You, please indicate by way of percentage on whom your primary motivation to excel at work most depends.

	%
Depends on boss *(Who allocated >50%)*	16%
Depends on both boss and self *(Who allocated 50% to both)*	22%
Depends on self *(Who allocated >50%)*	62%

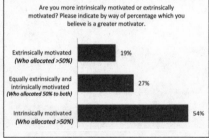

Are you more intrinsically motivated or extrinsically motivated? Please indicate by way of percentage which you believe is a greater motivator.

	%
Extrinsically motivated *(Who allocated >50%)*	19%
Equally extrinsically and intrinsically motivated *(Who allocated 50% to both)*	27%
Intrinsically motivated *(Who allocated >50%)*	54%

FIGURE A.8　Denmark

FRANCE (n=578)

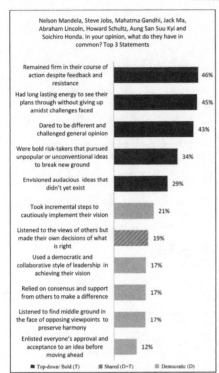

Nelson Mandela, Steve Jobs, Mahatma Gandhi, Jack Ma, Abraham Lincoln, Howard Schultz, Aung San Suu Kyi and Soichiro Honda. In your opinion, what do they have in common? Top 3 Statements

- Remained firm in their course of action despite feedback and resistance — 46%
- Had long lasting energy to see their plans through without giving up amidst challenges faced — 45%
- Dared to be different and challenged general opinion — 43%
- Were bold risk-takers that pursued unpopular or unconventional ideas to break new ground — 34%
- Envisioned audacious ideas that didn't yet exist — 29%
- Took incremental steps to cautiously implement their vision — 21%
- Listened to the views of others but made their own decisions of what is right — 19%
- Used a democratic and collaborative style of leadership in achieving their vision — 17%
- Relied on consensus and support from others to make a difference — 17%
- Listened to find middle ground in the face of opposing viewpoints to preserve harmony — 17%
- Enlisted everyone's approval and acceptance to an idea before moving ahead — 12%

■ Top-down/ Bold (T)   ⧄ Shared (D+T)   ▨ Democratic (D)

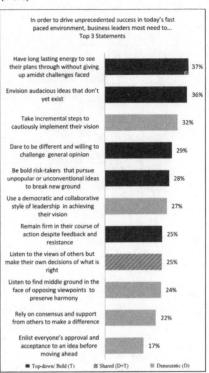

In order to drive unprecedented success in today's fast paced environment, business leaders most need to... Top 3 Statements

- Have long lasting energy to see their plans through without giving up amidst challenges faced — 37%
- Envision audacious ideas that don't yet exist — 36%
- Take incremental steps to cautiously implement their vision — 32%
- Dare to be different and willing to challenge general opinion — 29%
- Be bold risk-takers that pursue unpopular or unconventional ideas to break new ground — 28%
- Use a democratic and collaborative style of leadership in achieving their vision — 27%
- Remain firm in their course of action despite feedback and resistance — 25%
- Listen to the views of others but make their own decisions of what is right — 25%
- Listen to find middle ground in the face of opposing viewpoints to preserve harmony — 24%
- Rely on consensus and support from others to make a difference — 22%
- Enlist everyone's approval and acceptance to an idea before moving ahead — 17%

■ Top-down/ Bold (T)   ⧄ Shared (D+T)   ▨ Democratic (D)

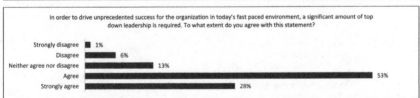

In order to drive unprecedented success for the organization in today's fast paced environment, a significant amount of top down leadership is required. To what extent do you agree with this statement?

- Strongly disagree — 1%
- Disagree — 6%
- Neither agree nor disagree — 13%
- Agree — 53%
- Strongly agree — 28%

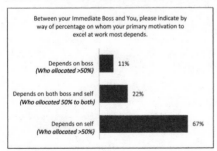

Between your Immediate Boss and You, please indicate by way of percentage on whom your primary motivation to excel at work most depends.

- Depends on boss (Who allocated >50%) — 11%
- Depends on both boss and self (Who allocated 50% to both) — 22%
- Depends on self (Who allocated >50%) — 67%

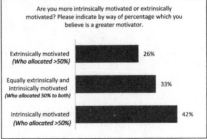

Are you more intrinsically motivated or extrinsically motivated? Please indicate by way of percentage which you believe is a greater motivator.

- Extrinsically motivated (Who allocated >50%) — 26%
- Equally extrinsically and intrinsically motivated (Who allocated 50% to both) — 33%
- Intrinsically motivated (Who allocated >50%) — 42%

FIGURE A.9   France

GERMANY (n=601)

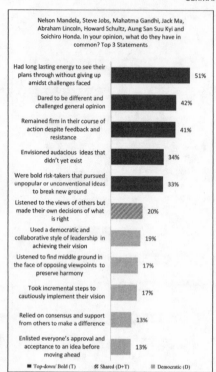

Nelson Mandela, Steve Jobs, Mahatma Gandhi, Jack Ma, Abraham Lincoln, Howard Schultz, Aung San Suu Kyi and Soichiro Honda. In your opinion, what do they have in common? Top 3 Statements

Statement	%
Had long lasting energy to see their plans through without giving up amidst challenges faced	51%
Dared to be different and challenged general opinion	42%
Remained firm in their course of action despite feedback and resistance	41%
Envisioned audacious ideas that didn't yet exist	34%
Were bold risk-takers that pursued unpopular or unconventional ideas to break new ground	33%
Listened to the views of others but made their own decisions of what is right	20%
Used a democratic and collaborative style of leadership in achieving their vision	19%
Listened to find middle ground in the face of opposing viewpoints to preserve harmony	17%
Took incremental steps to cautiously implement their vision	17%
Relied on consensus and support from others to make a difference	13%
Enlisted everyone's approval and acceptance to an idea before moving ahead	13%

■ Top-down/ Bold (T) ▨ Shared (D+T) ▪ Democratic (D)

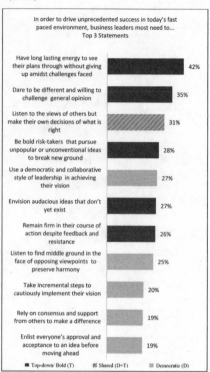

In order to drive unprecedented success in today's fast paced environment, business leaders most need to... Top 3 Statements

Statement	%
Have long lasting energy to see their plans through without giving up amidst challenges faced	42%
Dare to be different and willing to challenge general opinion	35%
Listen to the views of others but make their own decisions of what is right	31%
Be bold risk-takers that pursue unpopular or unconventional ideas to break new ground	28%
Use a democratic and collaborative style of leadership in achieving their vision	27%
Envision audacious ideas that don't yet exist	27%
Remain firm in their course of action despite feedback and resistance	26%
Listen to find middle ground in the face of opposing viewpoints to preserve harmony	25%
Take incremental steps to cautiously implement their vision	20%
Rely on consensus and support from others to make a difference	19%
Enlist everyone's approval and acceptance to an idea before moving ahead	19%

■ Top-down/ Bold (T) ▨ Shared (D+T) ▪ Democratic (D)

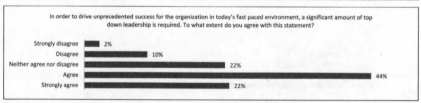

In order to drive unprecedented success for the organization in today's fast paced environment, a significant amount of top down leadership is required. To what extent do you agree with this statement?

Strongly disagree	2%
Disagree	10%
Neither agree nor disagree	22%
Agree	44%
Strongly agree	22%

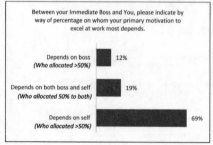

Between your Immediate Boss and You, please indicate by way of percentage on whom your primary motivation to excel at work most depends.

Depends on boss (Who allocated >50%)	12%
Depends on both boss and self (Who allocated 50% to both)	19%
Depends on self (Who allocated >50%)	69%

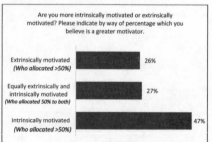

Are you more intrinsically motivated or extrinsically motivated? Please indicate by way of percentage which you believe is a greater motivator.

Extrinsically motivated (Who allocated >50%)	26%
Equally extrinsically and intrinsically motivated (Who allocated 50% to both)	27%
Intrinsically motivated (Who allocated >50%)	47%

FIGURE A.10 Germany

INDIA (n=675)

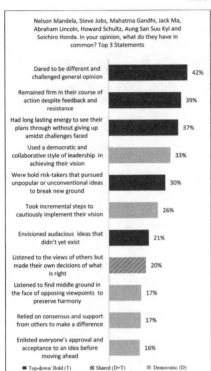

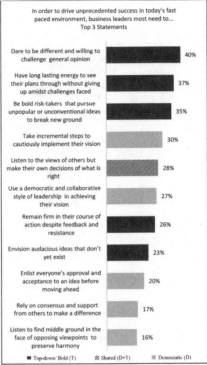

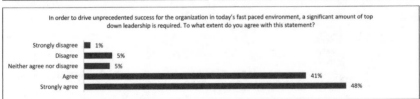

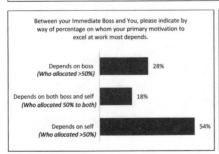

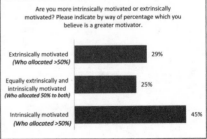

FIGURE A.11 India

INDONESIA (n=396)

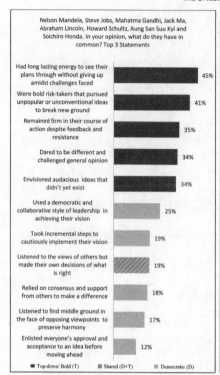

Nelson Mandela, Steve Jobs, Mahatma Gandhi, Jack Ma, Abraham Lincoln, Howard Schultz, Aung San Suu Kyi and Soichiro Honda. In your opinion, what do they have in common? Top 3 Statements

Statement	%
Had long lasting energy to see their plans through without giving up amidst challenges faced	45%
Were bold risk-takers that pursued unpopular or unconventional ideas to break new ground	41%
Remained firm in their course of action despite feedback and resistance	35%
Dared to be different and challenged general opinion	34%
Envisioned audacious ideas that didn't yet exist	34%
Used a democratic and collaborative style of leadership in achieving their vision	25%
Took incremental steps to cautiously implement their vision	19%
Listened to the views of others but made their own decisions of what is right	19%
Relied on consensus and support from others to make a difference	18%
Listened to find middle ground in the face of opposing viewpoints to preserve harmony	17%
Enlisted everyone's approval and acceptance to an idea before moving ahead	12%

■ Top-down/ Bold (T)   ⁄⁄ Shared (D+T)   ▩ Democratic (D)

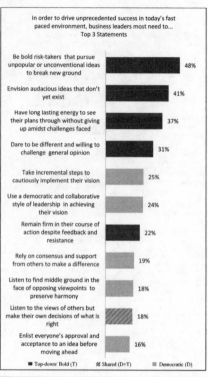

In order to drive unprecedented success in today's fast paced environment, business leaders most need to... Top 3 Statements

Statement	%
Be bold risk-takers that pursue unpopular or unconventional ideas to break new ground	48%
Envision audacious ideas that don't yet exist	41%
Have long lasting energy to see their plans through without giving up amidst challenges faced	37%
Dare to be different and willing to challenge general opinion	31%
Take incremental steps to cautiously implement their vision	25%
Use a democratic and collaborative style of leadership in achieving their vision	24%
Remain firm in their course of action despite feedback and resistance	22%
Rely on consensus and support from others to make a difference	19%
Listen to find middle ground in the face of opposing viewpoints to preserve harmony	18%
Listen to the views of others but make their own decisions of what is right	18%
Enlist everyone's approval and acceptance to an idea before moving ahead	16%

■ Top-down/ Bold (T)   ⁄⁄ Shared (D+T)   ▩ Democratic (D)

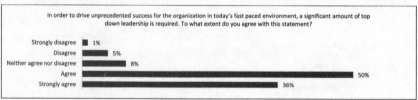

In order to drive unprecedented success for the organization in today's fast paced environment, a significant amount of top down leadership is required. To what extent do you agree with this statement?

	%
Strongly disagree	1%
Disagree	5%
Neither agree nor disagree	8%
Agree	50%
Strongly agree	36%

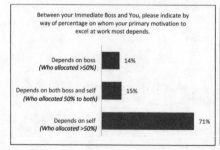

Between your Immediate Boss and You, please indicate by way of percentage on whom your primary motivation to excel at work most depends.

	%
Depends on boss (Who allocated >50%)	14%
Depends on both boss and self (Who allocated 50% to both)	15%
Depends on self (Who allocated >50%)	71%

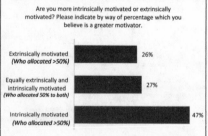

Are you more intrinsically motivated or extrinsically motivated? Please indicate by way of percentage which you believe is a greater motivator.

	%
Extrinsically motivated (Who allocated >50%)	26%
Equally extrinsically and intrinsically motivated (Who allocated 50% to both)	27%
Intrinsically motivated (Who allocated >50%)	47%

FIGURE A.12 Indonesia

ITALY (n=320)

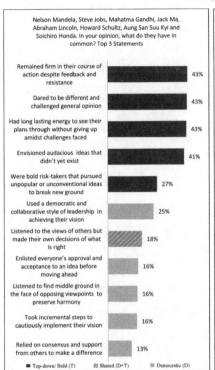

Nelson Mandela, Steve Jobs, Mahatma Gandhi, Jack Ma, Abraham Lincoln, Howard Schultz, Aung San Suu Kyi and Soichiro Honda. In your opinion, what do they have in common? Top 3 Statements

- Remained firm in their course of action despite feedback and resistance — 43%
- Dared to be different and challenged general opinion — 43%
- Had long lasting energy to see their plans through without giving up amidst challenges faced — 43%
- Envisioned audacious ideas that didn't yet exist — 41%
- Were bold risk-takers that pursued unpopular or unconventional ideas to break new ground — 27%
- Used a democratic and collaborative style of leadership in achieving their vision — 25%
- Listened to the views of others but made their own decisions of what is right — 18%
- Enlisted everyone's approval and acceptance to an idea before moving ahead — 16%
- Listened to find middle ground in the face of opposing viewpoints to preserve harmony — 16%
- Took incremental steps to cautiously implement their vision — 16%
- Relied on consensus and support from others to make a difference — 13%

■ Top-down/ Bold (T) ▨ Shared (D+T) ▨ Democratic (D)

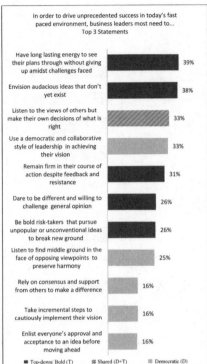

In order to drive unprecedented success in today's fast paced environment, business leaders most need to... Top 3 Statements

- Have long lasting energy to see their plans through without giving up amidst challenges faced — 39%
- Envision audacious ideas that don't yet exist — 38%
- Listen to the views of others but make their own decisions of what is right — 33%
- Use a democratic and collaborative style of leadership in achieving their vision — 33%
- Remain firm in their course of action despite feedback and resistance — 31%
- Dare to be different and willing to challenge general opinion — 26%
- Be bold risk-takers that pursue unpopular or unconventional ideas to break new ground — 26%
- Listen to find middle ground in the face of opposing viewpoints to preserve harmony — 25%
- Rely on consensus and support from others to make a difference — 16%
- Take incremental steps to cautiously implement their vision — 16%
- Enlist everyone's approval and acceptance to an idea before moving ahead — 16%

■ Top-down/ Bold (T) ▨ Shared (D+T) ▨ Democratic (D)

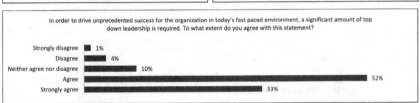

In order to drive unprecedented success for the organization in today's fast paced environment, a significant amount of top down leadership is required. To what extent do you agree with this statement?

- Strongly disagree — 1%
- Disagree — 4%
- Neither agree nor disagree — 10%
- Agree — 52%
- Strongly agree — 33%

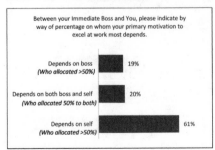

Between your Immediate Boss and You, please indicate by way of percentage on whom your primary motivation to excel at work most depends.

- Depends on boss *(Who allocated >50%)* — 19%
- Depends on both boss and self *(Who allocated 50% to both)* — 20%
- Depends on self *(Who allocated >50%)* — 61%

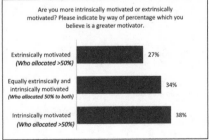

Are you more intrinsically motivated or extrinsically motivated? Please indicate by way of percentage which you believe is a greater motivator.

- Extrinsically motivated *(Who allocated >50%)* — 27%
- Equally extrinsically and intrinsically motivated *(Who allocated 50% to both)* — 34%
- Intrinsically motivated *(Who allocated >50%)* — 38%

FIGURE A.13 Italy

JAPAN (n=601)

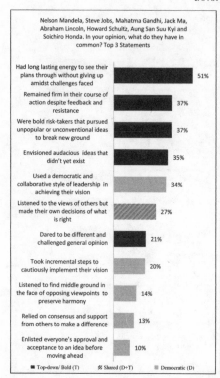

Nelson Mandela, Steve Jobs, Mahatma Gandhi, Jack Ma, Abraham Lincoln, Howard Schultz, Aung San Suu Kyi and Soichiro Honda. In your opinion, what do they have in common? Top 3 Statements

- Had long lasting energy to see their plans through without giving up amidst challenges faced — 51%
- Remained firm in their course of action despite feedback and resistance — 37%
- Were bold risk-takers that pursued unpopular or unconventional ideas to break new ground — 37%
- Envisioned audacious ideas that didn't yet exist — 35%
- Used a democratic and collaborative style of leadership in achieving their vision — 34%
- Listened to the views of others but made their own decisions of what is right — 27%
- Dared to be different and challenged general opinion — 21%
- Took incremental steps to cautiously implement their vision — 20%
- Listened to find middle ground in the face of opposing viewpoints to preserve harmony — 14%
- Relied on consensus and support from others to make a difference — 13%
- Enlisted everyone's approval and acceptance to an idea before moving ahead — 10%

■ Top-down/ Bold (T)   ⁄⁄ Shared (D+T)   ■ Democratic (D)

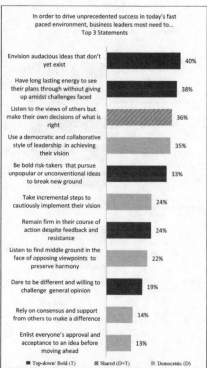

In order to drive unprecedented success in today's fast paced environment, business leaders most need to... Top 3 Statements

- Envision audacious ideas that don't yet exist — 40%
- Have long lasting energy to see their plans through without giving up amidst challenges faced — 38%
- Listen to the views of others but make their own decisions of what is right — 36%
- Use a democratic and collaborative style of leadership in achieving their vision — 35%
- Be bold risk-takers that pursue unpopular or unconventional ideas to break new ground — 33%
- Take incremental steps to cautiously implement their vision — 24%
- Remain firm in their course of action despite feedback and resistance — 24%
- Listen to find middle ground in the face of opposing viewpoints to preserve harmony — 22%
- Dare to be different and willing to challenge general opinion — 19%
- Rely on consensus and support from others to make a difference — 14%
- Enlist everyone's approval and acceptance to an idea before moving ahead — 13%

■ Top-down/ Bold (T)   ⁄⁄ Shared (D+T)   ■ Democratic (D)

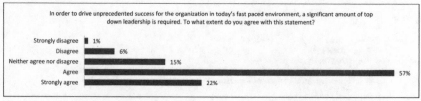

In order to drive unprecedented success for the organization in today's fast paced environment, a significant amount of top down leadership is required. To what extent do you agree with this statement?

- Strongly disagree — 1%
- Disagree — 6%
- Neither agree nor disagree — 15%
- Agree — 57%
- Strongly agree — 22%

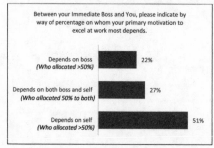

Between your Immediate Boss and You, please indicate by way of percentage on whom your primary motivation to excel at work most depends.

- Depends on boss *(Who allocated >50%)* — 22%
- Depends on both boss and self *(Who allocated 50% to both)* — 27%
- Depends on self *(Who allocated >50%)* — 51%

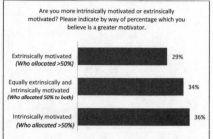

Are you more intrinsically motivated or extrinsically motivated? Please indicate by way of percentage which you believe is a greater motivator.

- Extrinsically motivated *(Who allocated >50%)* — 29%
- Equally extrinsically and intrinsically motivated *(Who allocated 50% to both)* — 34%
- Intrinsically motivated *(Who allocated >50%)* — 36%

FIGURE A.14 Japan

MALAYSIA (n=3368)

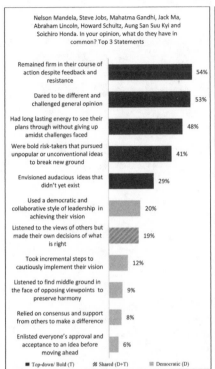

Nelson Mandela, Steve Jobs, Mahatma Gandhi, Jack Ma, Abraham Lincoln, Howard Schultz, Aung San Suu Kyi and Soichiro Honda. In your opinion, what do they have in common? Top 3 Statements

Statement	%
Remained firm in their course of action despite feedback and resistance	54%
Dared to be different and challenged general opinion	53%
Had long lasting energy to see their plans through without giving up amidst challenges faced	48%
Were bold risk-takers that pursued unpopular or unconventional ideas to break new ground	41%
Envisioned audacious ideas that didn't yet exist	29%
Used a democratic and collaborative style of leadership in achieving their vision	20%
Listened to the views of others but made their own decisions of what is right	19%
Took incremental steps to cautiously implement their vision	12%
Listened to find middle ground in the face of opposing viewpoints to preserve harmony	9%
Relied on consensus and support from others to make a difference	8%
Enlisted everyone's approval and acceptance to an idea before moving ahead	6%

■ Top-down/ Bold (T) ▨ Shared (D+T) ▤ Democratic (D)

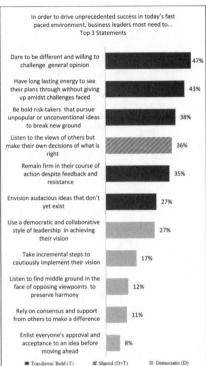

In order to drive unprecedented success in today's fast paced environment, business leaders most need to... Top 3 Statements

Statement	%
Dare to be different and willing to challenge general opinion	47%
Have long lasting energy to see their plans through without giving up amidst challenges faced	43%
Be bold risk-takers that pursue unpopular or unconventional ideas to break new ground	38%
Listen to the views of others but make their own decisions of what is right	36%
Remain firm in their course of action despite feedback and resistance	35%
Envision audacious ideas that don't yet exist	27%
Use a democratic and collaborative style of leadership in achieving their vision	27%
Take incremental steps to cautiously implement their vision	17%
Listen to find middle ground in the face of opposing viewpoints to preserve harmony	12%
Rely on consensus and support from others to make a difference	11%
Enlist everyone's approval and acceptance to an idea before moving ahead	8%

■ Top-down/ Bold (T) ▨ Shared (D+T) ▤ Democratic (D)

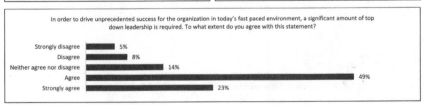

In order to drive unprecedented success for the organization in today's fast paced environment, a significant amount of top down leadership is required. To what extent do you agree with this statement?

	%
Strongly disagree	5%
Disagree	8%
Neither agree nor disagree	14%
Agree	49%
Strongly agree	23%

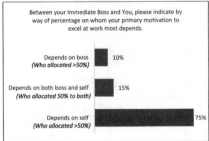

Between your Immediate Boss and You, please indicate by way of percentage on whom your primary motivation to excel at work most depends.

	%
Depends on boss (Who allocated >50%)	10%
Depends on both boss and self (Who allocated 50% to both)	15%
Depends on self (Who allocated >50%)	75%

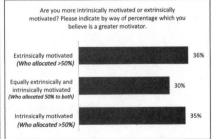

Are you more intrinsically motivated or extrinsically motivated? Please indicate by way of percentage which you believe is a greater motivator.

	%
Extrinsically motivated (Who allocated >50%)	36%
Equally extrinsically and intrinsically motivated (Who allocated 50% to both)	30%
Intrinsically motivated (Who allocated >50%)	35%

FIGURE A.15 Malaysia

MEXICO (n=324)

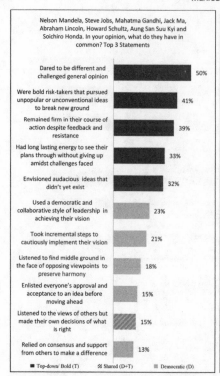

Nelson Mandela, Steve Jobs, Mahatma Gandhi, Jack Ma, Abraham Lincoln, Howard Schultz, Aung San Suu Kyi and Soichiro Honda. In your opinion, what do they have in common? Top 3 Statements

Statement	%
Dared to be different and challenged general opinion	50%
Were bold risk-takers that pursued unpopular or unconventional ideas to break new ground	41%
Remained firm in their course of action despite feedback and resistance	39%
Had long lasting energy to see their plans through without giving up amidst challenges faced	33%
Envisioned audacious ideas that didn't yet exist	32%
Used a democratic and collaborative style of leadership in achieving their vision	23%
Took incremental steps to cautiously implement their vision	21%
Listened to find middle ground in the face of opposing viewpoints to preserve harmony	18%
Enlisted everyone's approval and acceptance to an idea before moving ahead	15%
Listened to the views of others but made their own decisions of what is right	15%
Relied on consensus and support from others to make a difference	13%

■ Top-down/ Bold (T)   ⚹ Shared (D+T)   ▨ Democratic (D)

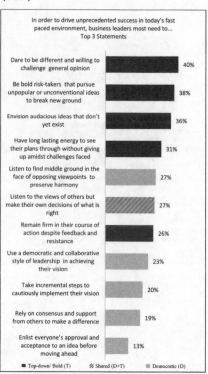

In order to drive unprecedented success in today's fast paced environment, business leaders most need to... Top 3 Statements

Statement	%
Dare to be different and willing to challenge general opinion	40%
Be bold risk-takers that pursue unpopular or unconventional ideas to break new ground	38%
Envision audacious ideas that don't yet exist	36%
Have long lasting energy to see their plans through without giving up amidst challenges faced	31%
Listen to find middle ground in the face of opposing viewpoints to preserve harmony	27%
Listen to the views of others but make their own decisions of what is right	27%
Remain firm in their course of action despite feedback and resistance	26%
Use a democratic and collaborative style of leadership in achieving their vision	23%
Take incremental steps to cautiously implement their vision	20%
Rely on consensus and support from others to make a difference	19%
Enlist everyone's approval and acceptance to an idea before moving ahead	13%

■ Top-down/ Bold (T)   ⚹ Shared (D+T)   ▨ Democratic (D)

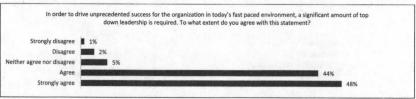

In order to drive unprecedented success for the organization in today's fast paced environment, a significant amount of top down leadership is required. To what extent do you agree with this statement?

	%
Strongly disagree	1%
Disagree	2%
Neither agree nor disagree	5%
Agree	44%
Strongly agree	48%

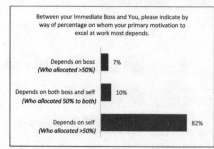

Between your Immediate Boss and You, please indicate by way of percentage on whom your primary motivation to excel at work most depends.

	%
Depends on boss (Who allocated >50%)	7%
Depends on both boss and self (Who allocated 50% to both)	10%
Depends on self (Who allocated >50%)	82%

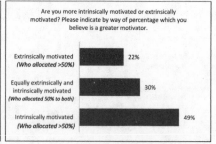

Are you more intrinsically motivated or extrinsically motivated? Please indicate by way of percentage which you believe is a greater motivator.

	%
Extrinsically motivated (Who allocated >50%)	22%
Equally extrinsically and intrinsically motivated (Who allocated 50% to both)	30%
Intrinsically motivated (Who allocated >50%)	49%

FIGURE A.16   Mexico

NETHERLANDS (n=588)

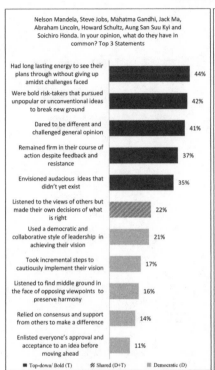

Nelson Mandela, Steve Jobs, Mahatma Gandhi, Jack Ma, Abraham Lincoln, Howard Schultz, Aung San Suu Kyi and Soichiro Honda. In your opinion, what do they have in common? Top 3 Statements

Had long lasting energy to see their plans through without giving up amidst challenges faced — 44%
Were bold risk-takers that pursued unpopular or unconventional ideas to break new ground — 42%
Dared to be different and challenged general opinion — 41%
Remained firm in their course of action despite feedback and resistance — 37%
Envisioned audacious ideas that didn't yet exist — 35%
Listened to the views of others but made their own decisions of what is right — 22%
Used a democratic and collaborative style of leadership in achieving their vision — 21%
Took incremental steps to cautiously implement their vision — 17%
Listened to find middle ground in the face of opposing viewpoints to preserve harmony — 16%
Relied on consensus and support from others to make a difference — 14%
Enlisted everyone's approval and acceptance to an idea before moving ahead — 11%

■ Top-down/ Bold (T)   ▨ Shared (D+T)   ▩ Democratic (D)

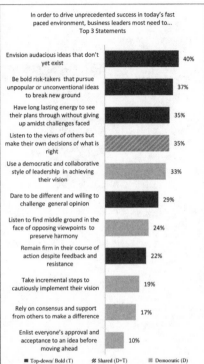

In order to drive unprecedented success in today's fast paced environment, business leaders most need to... Top 3 Statements

Envision audacious ideas that don't yet exist — 40%
Be bold risk-takers that pursue unpopular or unconventional ideas to break new ground — 37%
Have long lasting energy to see their plans through without giving up amidst challenges faced — 35%
Listen to the views of others but make their own decisions of what is right — 35%
Use a democratic and collaborative style of leadership in achieving their vision — 33%
Dare to be different and willing to challenge general opinion — 29%
Listen to find middle ground in the face of opposing viewpoints to preserve harmony — 24%
Remain firm in their course of action despite feedback and resistance — 22%
Take incremental steps to cautiously implement their vision — 19%
Rely on consensus and support from others to make a difference — 17%
Enlist everyone's approval and acceptance to an idea before moving ahead — 10%

■ Top-down/ Bold (T)   ▨ Shared (D+T)   ▩ Democratic (D)

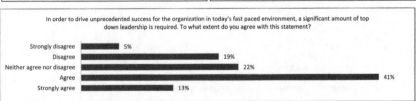

In order to drive unprecedented success for the organization in today's fast paced environment, a significant amount of top down leadership is required. To what extent do you agree with this statement?

Strongly disagree — 5%
Disagree — 19%
Neither agree nor disagree — 22%
Agree — 41%
Strongly agree — 13%

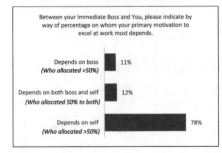

Between your Immediate Boss and You, please indicate by way of percentage on whom your primary motivation to excel at work most depends.

Depends on boss (Who allocated >50%) — 11%
Depends on both boss and self (Who allocated 50% to both) — 12%
Depends on self (Who allocated >50%) — 78%

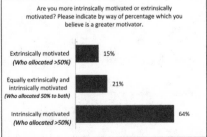

Are you more intrinsically motivated or extrinsically motivated? Please indicate by way of percentage which you believe is a greater motivator.

Extrinsically motivated (Who allocated >50%) — 15%
Equally extrinsically and intrinsically motivated (Who allocated 50% to both) — 21%
Intrinsically motivated (Who allocated >50%) — 64%

FIGURE A.17 Netherlands

PORTUGAL (n=315)

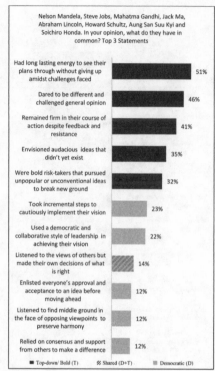

Nelson Mandela, Steve Jobs, Mahatma Gandhi, Jack Ma, Abraham Lincoln, Howard Schultz, Aung San Suu Kyi and Soichiro Honda. In your opinion, what do they have in common? Top 3 Statements

- Had long lasting energy to see their plans through without giving up amidst challenges faced — 51%
- Dared to be different and challenged general opinion — 46%
- Remained firm in their course of action despite feedback and resistance — 41%
- Envisioned audacious ideas that didn't yet exist — 35%
- Were bold risk-takers that pursued unpopular or unconventional ideas to break new ground — 32%
- Took incremental steps to cautiously implement their vision — 23%
- Used a democratic and collaborative style of leadership in achieving their vision — 22%
- Listened to the views of others but made their own decisions of what is right — 14%
- Enlisted everyone's approval and acceptance to an idea before moving ahead — 12%
- Listened to find middle ground in the face of opposing viewpoints to preserve harmony — 12%
- Relied on consensus and support from others to make a difference — 12%

■ Top-down/ Bold (T) ⌀ Shared (D+T) ▨ Democratic (D)

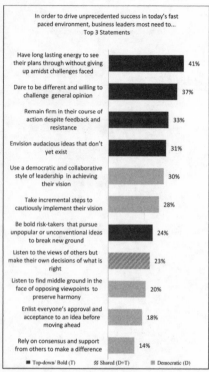

In order to drive unprecedented success in today's fast paced environment, business leaders most need to... Top 3 Statements

- Have long lasting energy to see their plans through without giving up amidst challenges faced — 41%
- Dare to be different and willing to challenge general opinion — 37%
- Remain firm in their course of action despite feedback and resistance — 33%
- Envision audacious ideas that don't yet exist — 31%
- Use a democratic and collaborative style of leadership in achieving their vision — 30%
- Take incremental steps to cautiously implement their vision — 28%
- Be bold risk-takers that pursue unpopular or unconventional ideas to break new ground — 24%
- Listen to the views of others but make their own decisions of what is right — 23%
- Listen to find middle ground in the face of opposing viewpoints to preserve harmony — 20%
- Enlist everyone's approval and acceptance to an idea before moving ahead — 18%
- Rely on consensus and support from others to make a difference — 14%

■ Top-down/ Bold (T) ⌀ Shared (D+T) ▨ Democratic (D)

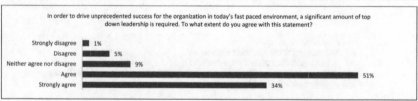

In order to drive unprecedented success for the organization in today's fast paced environment, a significant amount of top down leadership is required. To what extent do you agree with this statement?

- Strongly disagree — 1%
- Disagree — 5%
- Neither agree nor disagree — 9%
- Agree — 51%
- Strongly agree — 34%

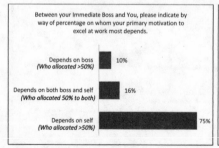

Between your Immediate Boss and You, please indicate by way of percentage on whom your primary motivation to excel at work most depends.

- Depends on boss *(Who allocated >50%)* — 10%
- Depends on both boss and self *(Who allocated 50% to both)* — 16%
- Depends on self *(Who allocated >50%)* — 75%

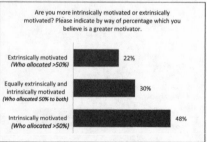

Are you more intrinsically motivated or extrinsically motivated? Please indicate by way of percentage which you believe is a greater motivator.

- Extrinsically motivated *(Who allocated >50%)* — 22%
- Equally extrinsically and intrinsically motivated *(Who allocated 50% to both)* — 30%
- Intrinsically motivated *(Who allocated >50%)* — 48%

FIGURE A.18 Portugal

RUSSIA (n=595)

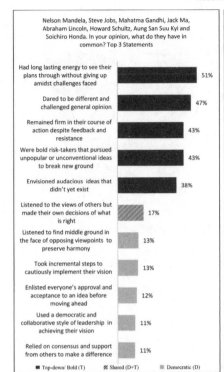

Nelson Mandela, Steve Jobs, Mahatma Gandhi, Jack Ma, Abraham Lincoln, Howard Schultz, Aung San Suu Kyi and Soichiro Honda. In your opinion, what do they have in common? Top 3 Statements

Had long lasting energy to see their plans through without giving up amidst challenges faced	51%
Dared to be different and challenged general opinion	47%
Remained firm in their course of action despite feedback and resistance	43%
Were bold risk-takers that pursued unpopular or unconventional ideas to break new ground	43%
Envisioned audacious ideas that didn't yet exist	38%
Listened to the views of others but made their own decisions of what is right	17%
Listened to find middle ground in the face of opposing viewpoints to preserve harmony	13%
Took incremental steps to cautiously implement their vision	13%
Enlisted everyone's approval and acceptance to an idea before moving ahead	12%
Used a democratic and collaborative style of leadership in achieving their vision	11%
Relied on consensus and support from others to make a difference	11%

■ Top-down/ Bold (T)   ▨ Shared (D+T)   ▧ Democratic (D)

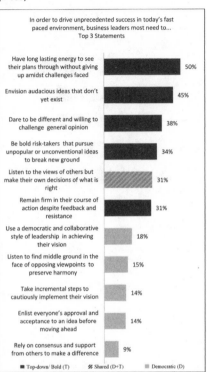

In order to drive unprecedented success in today's fast paced environment, business leaders most need to... Top 3 Statements

Have long lasting energy to see their plans through without giving up amidst challenges faced	50%
Envision audacious ideas that don't yet exist	45%
Dare to be different and willing to challenge general opinion	38%
Be bold risk-takers that pursue unpopular or unconventional ideas to break new ground	34%
Listen to the views of others but make their own decisions of what is right	31%
Remain firm in their course of action despite feedback and resistance	31%
Use a democratic and collaborative style of leadership in achieving their vision	18%
Listen to find middle ground in the face of opposing viewpoints to preserve harmony	15%
Take incremental steps to cautiously implement their vision	14%
Enlist everyone's approval and acceptance to an idea before moving ahead	14%
Rely on consensus and support from others to make a difference	9%

■ Top-down/ Bold (T)   ▨ Shared (D+T)   ▧ Democratic (D)

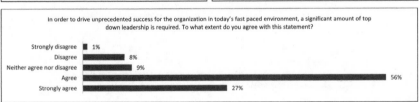

In order to drive unprecedented success for the organization in today's fast paced environment, a significant amount of top down leadership is required. To what extent do you agree with this statement?

Strongly disagree	1%
Disagree	8%
Neither agree nor disagree	9%
Agree	56%
Strongly agree	27%

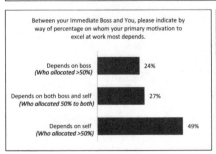

Between your Immediate Boss and You, please indicate by way of percentage on whom your primary motivation to excel at work most depends.

Depends on boss (Who allocated >50%)	24%
Depends on both boss and self (Who allocated 50% to both)	27%
Depends on self (Who allocated >50%)	49%

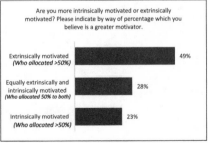

Are you more intrinsically motivated or extrinsically motivated? Please indicate by way of percentage which you believe is a greater motivator.

Extrinsically motivated (Who allocated >50%)	49%
Equally extrinsically and intrinsically motivated (Who allocated 50% to both)	28%
Intrinsically motivated (Who allocated >50%)	23%

FIGURE A.19 Russia

SINGAPORE (n=322)

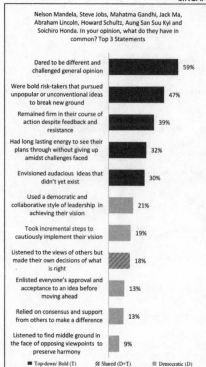

Nelson Mandela, Steve Jobs, Mahatma Gandhi, Jack Ma, Abraham Lincoln, Howard Schultz, Aung San Suu Kyi and Soichiro Honda. In your opinion, what do they have in common? Top 3 Statements

Statement	%
Dared to be different and challenged general opinion	59%
Were bold risk-takers that pursued unpopular or unconventional ideas to break new ground	47%
Remained firm in their course of action despite feedback and resistance	39%
Had long lasting energy to see their plans through without giving up amidst challenges faced	32%
Envisioned audacious ideas that didn't yet exist	30%
Used a democratic and collaborative style of leadership in achieving their vision	21%
Took incremental steps to cautiously implement their vision	19%
Listened to the views of others but made their own decisions of what is right	18%
Enlisted everyone's approval and acceptance to an idea before moving ahead	13%
Relied on consensus and support from others to make a difference	13%
Listened to find middle ground in the face of opposing viewpoints to preserve harmony	9%

■ Top-down/ Bold (T)   ▨ Shared (D+T)   ▧ Democratic (D)

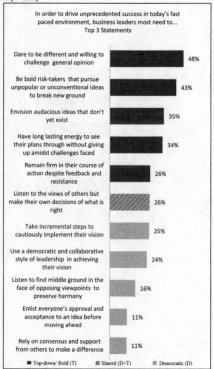

In order to drive unprecedented success in today's fast paced environment, business leaders most need to... Top 3 Statements

Statement	%
Dare to be different and willing to challenge general opinion	48%
Be bold risk-takers that pursue unpopular or unconventional ideas to break new ground	43%
Envision audacious ideas that don't yet exist	35%
Have long lasting energy to see their plans through without giving up amidst challenges faced	34%
Remain firm in their course of action despite feedback and resistance	26%
Listen to the views of others but make their own decisions of what is right	26%
Take incremental steps to cautiously implement their vision	25%
Use a democratic and collaborative style of leadership in achieving their vision	24%
Listen to find middle ground in the face of opposing viewpoints to preserve harmony	16%
Enlist everyone's approval and acceptance to an idea before moving ahead	11%
Rely on consensus and support from others to make a difference	11%

■ Top-down/ Bold (T)   ▨ Shared (D+T)   ▧ Democratic (D)

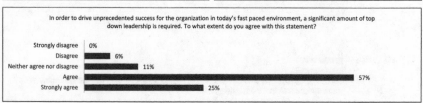

In order to drive unprecedented success for the organization in today's fast paced environment, a significant amount of top down leadership is required. To what extent do you agree with this statement?

	%
Strongly disagree	0%
Disagree	6%
Neither agree nor disagree	11%
Agree	57%
Strongly agree	25%

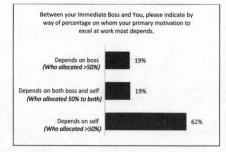

Between your Immediate Boss and You, please indicate by way of percentage on whom your primary motivation to excel at work most depends.

	%
Depends on boss *(Who allocated >50%)*	19%
Depends on both boss and self *(Who allocated 50% to both)*	19%
Depends on self *(Who allocated >50%)*	62%

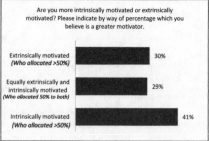

Are you more intrinsically motivated or extrinsically motivated? Please indicate by way of percentage which you believe is a greater motivator.

	%
Extrinsically motivated *(Who allocated >50%)*	30%
Equally extrinsically and intrinsically motivated *(Who allocated 50% to both)*	29%
Intrinsically motivated *(Who allocated >50%)*	41%

FIGURE A.20 Singapore

SOUTH AFRICA (n=274)

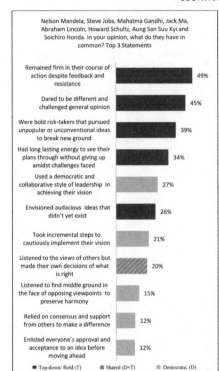

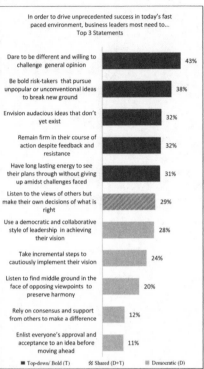

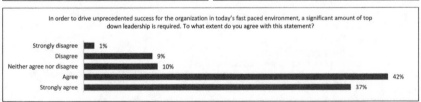

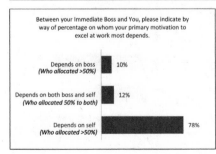

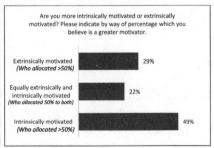

FIGURE A.21 South Africa

SOUTH KOREA (n=596)

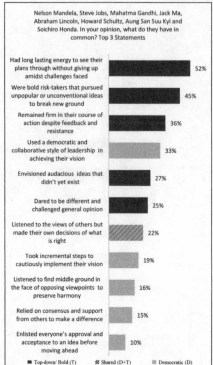

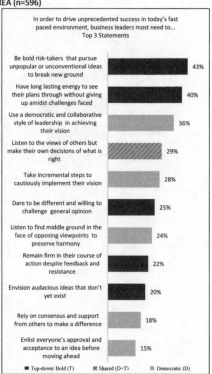

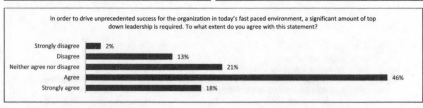

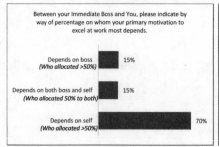

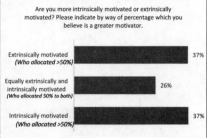

FIGURE A.22 South Korea

SPAIN (n=591)

Nelson Mandela, Steve Jobs, Mahatma Gandhi, Jack Ma, Abraham Lincoln, Howard Schultz, Aung San Suu Kyi and Soichiro Honda. In your opinion, what do they have in common? Top 3 Statements

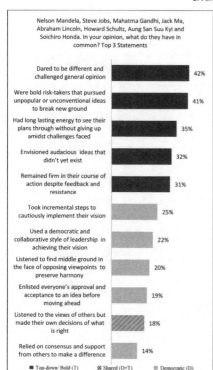

In order to drive unprecedented success in today's fast paced environment, business leaders most need to... Top 3 Statements

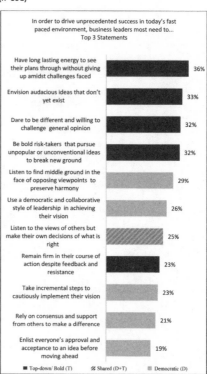

In order to drive unprecedented success for the organization in today's fast paced environment, a significant amount of top down leadership is required. To what extent do you agree with this statement?

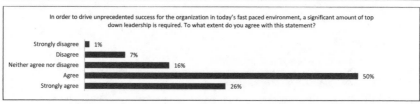

Between your Immediate Boss and You, please indicate by way of percentage on whom your primary motivation to excel at work most depends.

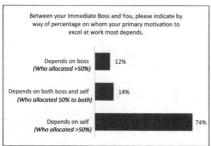

Are you more intrinsically motivated or extrinsically motivated? Please indicate by way of percentage which you believe is a greater motivator.

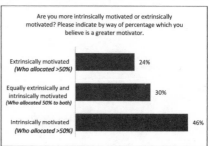

FIGURE A.23 Spain

SWEDEN (n=317)

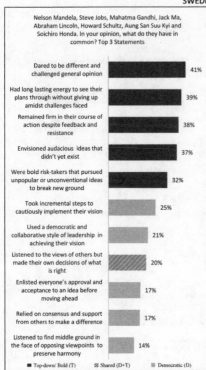

Nelson Mandela, Steve Jobs, Mahatma Gandhi, Jack Ma, Abraham Lincoln, Howard Schultz, Aung San Suu Kyi and Soichiro Honda. In your opinion, what do they have in common? Top 3 Statements

Statement	%
Dared to be different and challenged general opinion	41%
Had long lasting energy to see their plans through without giving up amidst challenges faced	39%
Remained firm in their course of action despite feedback and resistance	38%
Envisioned audacious ideas that didn't yet exist	37%
Were bold risk-takers that pursued unpopular or unconventional ideas to break new ground	32%
Took incremental steps to cautiously implement their vision	25%
Used a democratic and collaborative style of leadership in achieving their vision	21%
Listened to the views of others but made their own decisions of what is right	20%
Enlisted everyone's approval and acceptance to an idea before moving ahead	17%
Relied on consensus and support from others to make a difference	17%
Listened to find middle ground in the face of opposing viewpoints to preserve harmony	14%

■ Top-down/ Bold (T)   ▨ Shared (D+T)   ▦ Democratic (D)

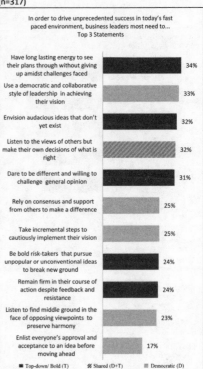

In order to drive unprecedented success in today's fast paced environment, business leaders most need to... Top 3 Statements

Statement	%
Have long lasting energy to see their plans through without giving up amidst challenges faced	34%
Use a democratic and collaborative style of leadership in achieving their vision	33%
Envision audacious ideas that don't yet exist	32%
Listen to the views of others but make their own decisions of what is right	32%
Dare to be different and willing to challenge general opinion	31%
Rely on consensus and support from others to make a difference	25%
Take incremental steps to cautiously implement their vision	25%
Be bold risk-takers that pursue unpopular or unconventional ideas to break new ground	24%
Remain firm in their course of action despite feedback and resistance	24%
Listen to find middle ground in the face of opposing viewpoints to preserve harmony	23%
Enlist everyone's approval and acceptance to an idea before moving ahead	17%

■ Top-down/ Bold (T)   ▨ Shared (D+T)   ▦ Democratic (D)

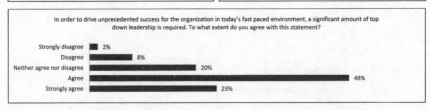

In order to drive unprecedented success for the organization in today's fast paced environment, a significant amount of top down leadership is required. To what extent do you agree with this statement?

	%
Strongly disagree	2%
Disagree	8%
Neither agree nor disagree	20%
Agree	48%
Strongly agree	23%

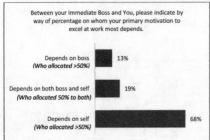

Between your Immediate Boss and You, please indicate by way of percentage on whom your primary motivation to excel at work most depends.

	%
Depends on boss *(Who allocated >50%)*	13%
Depends on both boss and self *(Who allocated 50% to both)*	19%
Depends on self *(Who allocated >50%)*	68%

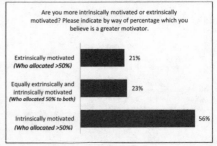

Are you more intrinsically motivated or extrinsically motivated? Please indicate by way of percentage which you believe is a greater motivator.

	%
Extrinsically motivated *(Who allocated >50%)*	21%
Equally extrinsically and intrinsically motivated *(Who allocated 50% to both)*	23%
Intrinsically motivated *(Who allocated >50%)*	56%

FIGURE A.24 Sweden

THAILAND (n=321)

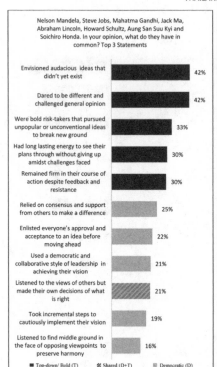

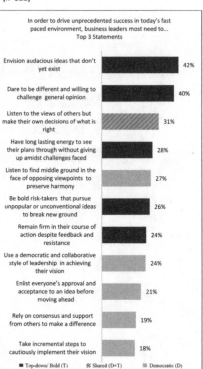

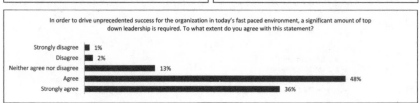

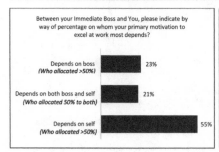

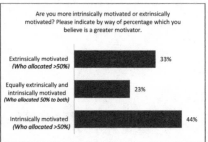

FIGURE A.25 Thailand

UK (n=588)

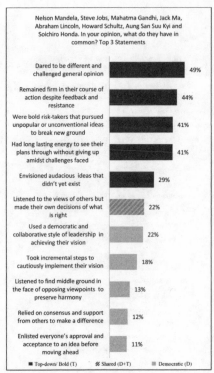

Nelson Mandela, Steve Jobs, Mahatma Gandhi, Jack Ma, Abraham Lincoln, Howard Schultz, Aung San Suu Kyi and Soichiro Honda. In your opinion, what do they have in common? Top 3 Statements

Statement	%
Dared to be different and challenged general opinion	49%
Remained firm in their course of action despite feedback and resistance	44%
Were bold risk-takers that pursued unpopular or unconventional ideas to break new ground	41%
Had long lasting energy to see their plans through without giving up amidst challenges faced	41%
Envisioned audacious ideas that didn't yet exist	29%
Listened to the views of others but made their own decisions of what is right	22%
Used a democratic and collaborative style of leadership in achieving their vision	22%
Took incremental steps to cautiously implement their vision	18%
Listened to find middle ground in the face of opposing viewpoints to preserve harmony	13%
Relied on consensus and support from others to make a difference	12%
Enlisted everyone's approval and acceptance to an idea before moving ahead	11%

■ Top-down/ Bold (T)   ▨ Shared (D+T)   ▪ Democratic (D)

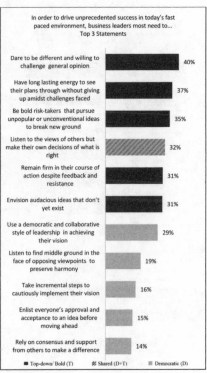

In order to drive unprecedented success in today's fast paced environment, business leaders most need to... Top 3 Statements

Statement	%
Dare to be different and willing to challenge general opinion	40%
Have long lasting energy to see their plans through without giving up amidst challenges faced	37%
Be bold risk-takers that pursue unpopular or unconventional ideas to break new ground	35%
Listen to the views of others but make their own decisions of what is right	32%
Remain firm in their course of action despite feedback and resistance	31%
Envision audacious ideas that don't yet exist	31%
Use a democratic and collaborative style of leadership in achieving their vision	29%
Listen to find middle ground in the face of opposing viewpoints to preserve harmony	19%
Take incremental steps to cautiously implement their vision	16%
Enlist everyone's approval and acceptance to an idea before moving ahead	15%
Rely on consensus and support from others to make a difference	14%

■ Top-down/ Bold (T)   ▨ Shared (D+T)   ▪ Democratic (D)

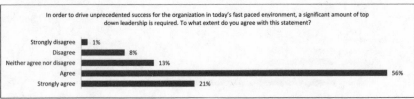

In order to drive unprecedented success for the organization in today's fast paced environment, a significant amount of top down leadership is required. To what extent do you agree with this statement?

	%
Strongly disagree	1%
Disagree	8%
Neither agree nor disagree	13%
Agree	56%
Strongly agree	21%

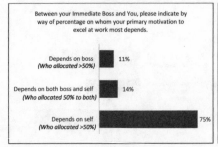

Between your Immediate Boss and You, please indicate by way of percentage on whom your primary motivation to excel at work most depends.

	%
Depends on boss (Who allocated >50%)	11%
Depends on both boss and self (Who allocated 50% to both)	14%
Depends on self (Who allocated >50%)	75%

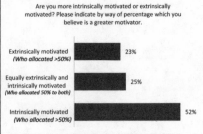

Are you more intrinsically motivated or extrinsically motivated? Please indicate by way of percentage which you believe is a greater motivator.

	%
Extrinsically motivated (Who allocated >50%)	23%
Equally extrinsically and intrinsically motivated (Who allocated 50% to both)	25%
Intrinsically motivated (Who allocated >50%)	52%

FIGURE A.26   United Kingdom

USA (n=709)

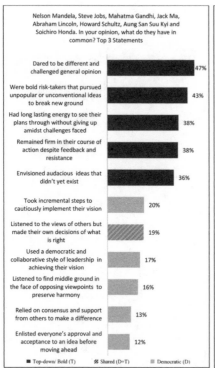

Nelson Mandela, Steve Jobs, Mahatma Gandhi, Jack Ma, Abraham Lincoln, Howard Schultz, Aung San Suu Kyi and Soichiro Honda. In your opinion, what do they have in common? Top 3 Statements

Statement	%
Dared to be different and challenged general opinion	47%
Were bold risk-takers that pursued unpopular or unconventional ideas to break new ground	43%
Had long lasting energy to see their plans through without giving up amidst challenges faced	38%
Remained firm in their course of action despite feedback and resistance	38%
Envisioned audacious ideas that didn't yet exist	36%
Took incremental steps to cautiously implement their vision	20%
Listened to the views of others but made their own decisions of what is right	19%
Used a democratic and collaborative style of leadership in achieving their vision	17%
Listened to find middle ground in the face of opposing viewpoints to preserve harmony	16%
Relied on consensus and support from others to make a difference	13%
Enlisted everyone's approval and acceptance to an idea before moving ahead	12%

■ Top-down/ Bold (T)   ▨ Shared (D+T)   ▩ Democratic (D)

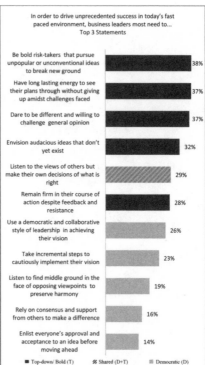

In order to drive unprecedented success in today's fast paced environment, business leaders most need to... Top 3 Statements

Statement	%
Be bold risk-takers that pursue unpopular or unconventional ideas to break new ground	38%
Have long lasting energy to see their plans through without giving up amidst challenges faced	37%
Dare to be different and willing to challenge general opinion	37%
Envision audacious ideas that don't yet exist	32%
Listen to the views of others but make their own decisions of what is right	29%
Remain firm in their course of action despite feedback and resistance	28%
Use a democratic and collaborative style of leadership in achieving their vision	26%
Take incremental steps to cautiously implement their vision	23%
Listen to find middle ground in the face of opposing viewpoints to preserve harmony	19%
Rely on consensus and support from others to make a difference	16%
Enlist everyone's approval and acceptance to an idea before moving ahead	14%

■ Top-down/ Bold (T)   ▨ Shared (D+T)   ▩ Democratic (D)

In order to drive unprecedented success for the organization in today's fast paced environment, a significant amount of top down leadership is required. To what extent do you agree with this statement?

	%
Strongly disagree	2%
Disagree	11%
Neither agree nor disagree	13%
Agree	48%
Strongly agree	26%

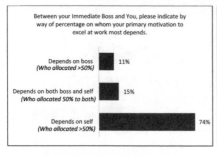

Between your Immediate Boss and You, please indicate by way of percentage on whom your primary motivation to excel at work most depends.

	%
Depends on boss (Who allocated >50%)	11%
Depends on both boss and self (Who allocated 50% to both)	15%
Depends on self (Who allocated >50%)	74%

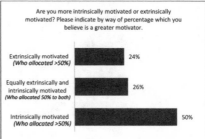

Are you more intrinsically motivated or extrinsically motivated? Please indicate by way of percentage which you believe is a greater motivator.

	%
Extrinsically motivated (Who allocated >50%)	24%
Equally extrinsically and intrinsically motivated (Who allocated 50% to both)	26%
Intrinsically motivated (Who allocated >50%)	50%

FIGURE A.27   United States

VIETNAM (n=268)

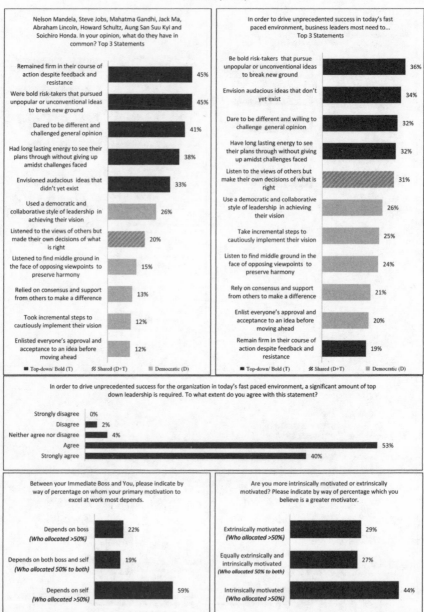

Nelson Mandela, Steve Jobs, Mahatma Gandhi, Jack Ma, Abraham Lincoln, Howard Schultz, Aung San Suu Kyi and Soichiro Honda. In your opinion, what do they have in common? Top 3 Statements

Statement	%
Remained firm in their course of action despite feedback and resistance	45%
Were bold risk-takers that pursued unpopular or unconventional ideas to break new ground	45%
Dared to be different and challenged general opinion	41%
Had long lasting energy to see their plans through without giving up amidst challenges faced	38%
Envisioned audacious ideas that didn't yet exist	33%
Used a democratic and collaborative style of leadership in achieving their vision	26%
Listened to the views of others but made their own decisions of what is right	20%
Listened to find middle ground in the face of opposing viewpoints to preserve harmony	15%
Relied on consensus and support from others to make a difference	13%
Took incremental steps to cautiously implement their vision	12%
Enlisted everyone's approval and acceptance to an idea before moving ahead	12%

■ Top-down/ Bold (T)   ▨ Shared (D+T)   ▦ Democratic (D)

In order to drive unprecedented success in today's fast paced environment, business leaders most need to... Top 3 Statements

Statement	%
Be bold risk-takers that pursue unpopular or unconventional ideas to break new ground	36%
Envision audacious ideas that don't yet exist	34%
Dare to be different and willing to challenge general opinion	32%
Have long lasting energy to see their plans through without giving up amidst challenges faced	32%
Listen to the views of others but make their own decisions of what is right	31%
Use a democratic and collaborative style of leadership in achieving their vision	26%
Take incremental steps to cautiously implement their vision	25%
Listen to find middle ground in the face of opposing viewpoints to preserve harmony	24%
Rely on consensus and support from others to make a difference	21%
Enlist everyone's approval and acceptance to an idea before moving ahead	20%
Remain firm in their course of action despite feedback and resistance	19%

■ Top-down/ Bold (T)   ▨ Shared (D+T)   ▦ Democratic (D)

In order to drive unprecedented success for the organization in today's fast paced environment, a significant amount of top down leadership is required. To what extent do you agree with this statement?

	%
Strongly disagree	0%
Disagree	2%
Neither agree nor disagree	4%
Agree	53%
Strongly agree	40%

Between your Immediate Boss and You, please indicate by way of percentage on whom your primary motivation to excel at work most depends.

	%
Depends on boss (Who allocated >50%)	22%
Depends on both boss and self (Who allocated 50% to both)	19%
Depends on self (Who allocated >50%)	59%

Are you more intrinsically motivated or extrinsically motivated? Please indicate by way of percentage which you believe is a greater motivator.

	%
Extrinsically motivated (Who allocated >50%)	29%
Equally extrinsically and intrinsically motivated (Who allocated 50% to both)	27%
Intrinsically motivated (Who allocated >50%)	44%

FIGURE A.28 Vietnam

UAE (n=181)

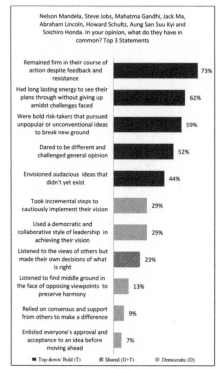

Nelson Mandela, Steve Jobs, Mahatma Gandhi, Jack Ma, Abraham Lincoln, Howard Schultz, Aung San Suu Kyi and Soichiro Honda. In your opinion, what do they have in common? Top 3 Statements

- Remained firm in their course of action despite feedback and resistance — 73%
- Had long lasting energy to see their plans through without giving up amidst challenges faced — 62%
- Were bold risk-takers that pursued unpopular or unconventional ideas to break new ground — 59%
- Dared to be different and challenged general opinion — 52%
- Envisioned audacious ideas that didn't yet exist — 44%
- Took incremental steps to cautiously implement their vision — 29%
- Used a democratic and collaborative style of leadership in achieving their vision — 29%
- Listened to the views of others but made their own decisions of what is right — 23%
- Listened to find middle ground in the face of opposing viewpoints to preserve harmony — 13%
- Relied on consensus and support from others to make a difference — 9%
- Enlisted everyone's approval and acceptance to an idea before moving ahead — 7%

■ Top-down/ Bold (T)   ⌗ Shared (D+T)   ■ Democratic (D)

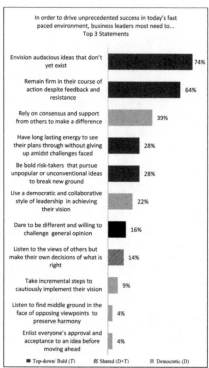

In order to drive unprecedented success in today's fast paced environment, business leaders most need to... Top 3 Statements

- Envision audacious ideas that don't yet exist — 74%
- Remain firm in their course of action despite feedback and resistance — 64%
- Rely on consensus and support from others to make a difference — 39%
- Have long lasting energy to see their plans through without giving up amidst challenges faced — 28%
- Be bold risk-takers that pursue unpopular or unconventional ideas to break new ground — 28%
- Use a democratic and collaborative style of leadership in achieving their vision — 22%
- Dare to be different and willing to challenge general opinion — 16%
- Listen to the views of others but make their own decisions of what is right — 14%
- Take incremental steps to cautiously implement their vision — 9%
- Listen to find middle ground in the face of opposing viewpoints to preserve harmony — 4%
- Enlist everyone's approval and acceptance to an idea before moving ahead — 4%

■ Top-down/ Bold (T)   ⌗ Shared (D+T)   ■ Democratic (D)

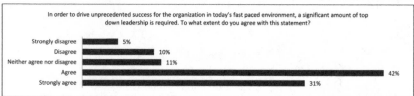

In order to drive unprecedented success for the organization in today's fast paced environment, a significant amount of top down leadership is required. To what extent do you agree with this statement?

- Strongly disagree — 5%
- Disagree — 10%
- Neither agree nor disagree — 11%
- Agree — 42%
- Strongly agree — 31%

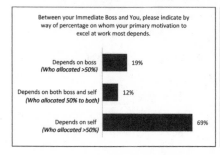

Between your Immediate Boss and You, please indicate by way of percentage on whom your primary motivation to excel at work most depends.

- Depends on boss (Who allocated >50%) — 19%
- Depends on both boss and self (Who allocated 50% to both) — 12%
- Depends on self (Who allocated >50%) — 69%

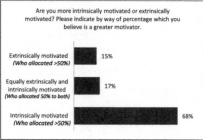

Are you more intrinsically motivated or extrinsically motivated? Please indicate by way of percentage which you believe is a greater motivator.

- Extrinsically motivated (Who allocated >50%) — 15%
- Equally extrinsically and intrinsically motivated (Who allocated 50% to both) — 17%
- Intrinsically motivated (Who allocated >50%) — 68%

FIGURE A.29   United Arab Emirates

REFERENCES

INTRO

1. Global population doubled from three billion . . . : United Nations, Department of Economic and Social Affairs, Population Division. (2017). World Population Prospects: The 2017 Revision, Key Findings and Advance Tables. Retrieved from: https://esa.un .org/unpd/wpp/Publications/Files/WPP2017_KeyFindings.pdf.
2. Picasso quote—Computers are useless: Pablo Picasso. Brainy Quote.com. Retrieved from: https://www.brainyquote.com/quotes /authors/p/pablo_picasso.html.

CHAPTER 1

1. In 1900, much of the Western workforce was still defiantly agricultural . . . : Fisk, Donald M. (2003, January 30). "American Labor in the 20th Century." U.S. Bureau of Labor Statistics. Retrieved from: http://www.bls.gov/opub/mlr/cwc/american-labor -in-the-20th-century.pdf.
2. Women's participation in the U.S. workforce . . . : Anitha, S., and Pearson, R. (2013). "World War I: 1914–1918," Striking Women. Lincoln: University of Lincoln. [Online]. Retrieved from: http:// www.striking-women.org/module/women-and-work/world-war-i -1914-1918.
3. Services, at 11 percent, were a small but soon to be rapidly growing sector of the employment market . . . : Kutscher, Ronald. (1993, November). "The American Workforce, 1992–2005." *Monthly Labor Review*. Retrieved from: http://www.bls.gov/mlr/1993/11/ art1full.pdf.
4. Telephones were limited to one-on-one discussion . . . : Odlyzko, Andrew. (2000, June 16). "The History of Communications and Its Implications for the Internet." AT&T Labs—Research. Retrieved from: http://www.dtc.umn.edu/~odlyzko/doc/history .communications0.pdf.
5. Only 0.11 of every 1,000 Americans owned a car . . . : Dudley, Geoff. (2014, November). "Future Demand: The Motor Car and the Construction of a New World." Ministry of Transport, New Zealand. Retrieved from: http://www.transport.govt.nz/assets/

Uploads/Our-Work/Documents/fd-car-and-the-construction-of-a
-new-world.pdf.

6. Hamel, in fact, believes that management as a concept may
have been the greatest invention . . . : Hamel, Gary. (2011, May
20). "Gary Hamel: Reinventing the Technology of Human
Accomplishment." Retrieved from: https://www.youtube.com
/watch?v=aodjgkv65MM&index=4&list=PLowtqNzwm1fFo
noI9ErTw1F-uIWM5jyeG.

7. Ford's Model T brought automobiles to the masses . . . : The
Saylor Foundation. "Scientific Management Theory and the Ford
Motor Company." Retrieved from: http://www.saylor.org/site/
wp-content/uploads/2013/08/Saylor.orgs-Scientific-Management
-Theory-and-the-Ford-Motor-Company.pdf.

8. In 1956, workers in white-collar roles outnumbered blue-collar
workers . . . : Hill, Roger. B. (1992, 1996). "History of Work
Ethic: The Work Ethic in the Information Age." Retrieved from:
http://workethic.coe.uga.edu/hia.html.

9. It took 76 years for the telephone to reach half of the U.S.
population . . . : PwC United Kingdom. "Megatrends:
Technological Breakthroughs." Retrieved from: http://www.pwc
.co.uk/issues/megatrends/technological-breakthroughs.html.

10. In contrast, the smartphone achieved the same coverage in under
10 years . . . : Ernst and Young. (2015). "Megatrends 2015:
Making Sense of a World in Motion." Retrieved from: http://www
.ey.com/Publication/vwLUAssets/ey-megatrends-report-2015
/$FILE/ey-megatrends-report-2015.pdf.

11. Fast running out of cash . . . IBM laid off 60,000 members of
its global workforce . . . .: Bobkoff, Dan. (2016, June 14). "IBM
Refused to Lay Off Workers for Decades, and Then America Had
to Rethink Its Entire Corporate Strategy." *The Business Insider*,
Australia. Retrieved from: http://www.businessinsider.com.au/
ibm-corporate-america-history-2016-6?r=US&IR=T.

12. By 2014, the United States had 28 million temporary workers . . . :
Greenhouse, Steven. (2014, August 31). "The Changing Face of
Temporary Employment." *New York Times*. Retrieved from: http:
//www.nytimes.com/2014/09/01/upshot/the-changing-face-of
-temporary-employment.html.

13. By 2012, some 20 percent of short-term assignments . . . : PwC.
(2012) "Talent Mobility—2020 and Beyond." Retrieved from:
https://www.pwc.com/gx/en/managing-tomorrows-people/future
-of-work/pdf/pwc-talent-mobility-2020.pdf.

14. An estimated 2.1 million U.S. manufacturing jobs were
eliminated . . . : Scott, Robert E. (2012, August 23). "The China
Toll." Economic Policy Institute. Retrieved from: http://www.epi
.org/publication/bp345-china-growing-trade-deficit-cost/.

15. In recent years, 13 out of every 100 computer programming jobs have shifted offshore . . . : The Week Staff. (2011, March 18). "Where America's Jobs Went." Retrieved from: http://theweek.com/articles/486362/where-americas-jobs-went.

16. Mobile phone sales are outpacing seemingly old fashioned PC or laptop purchases six to one . . . : Davidson, Jacob. (2015, May 26). "Here's How Many Internet Users There Are." TimeInc/ *Money.* Retrieved from: http://time.com/money/3896219/internet-users-worldwide/.

17. Could it be that in only a decade or two Internet connectivity is considered a basic human right?: World Economic Forum. (2015, September). "Deep Shift: Technology Tipping Points and Societal Impact." Retrieved from: http://www3.weforum.org/docs/WEF_GAC15_Technological_Tipping_Points_report_2015.pdf.

18. Who you are in "real life" . . . : World Economic Forum. (2015, September). "Deep Shift: Technology Tipping Points and Societal Impact." Retrieved from: http://www3.weforum.org/docs/WEF_GAC15_Technological_Tipping_Points_report_2015.pdf.

19. Organizations both public and private are going to have to find ways of building public trust . . . : World Economic Forum. (2015, September). "Deep Shift: Technology Tipping Points and Societal Impact." Retrieved from: http://www3.weforum.org/docs/WEF_GAC15_Technological_Tipping_Points_report_2015.pdf.

20. If that isn't startling enough, robots are . . . : World Economic Forum. (2015, September). "Deep Shift: Technology Tipping Points and Societal Impact." Retrieved from: http://www3.weforum.org/docs/WEF_GAC15_Technological_Tipping_Points_report_2015.pdf.

21. Robots already account for 80 percent . . . : World Economic Forum. (2015, September). "Deep Shift: Technology Tipping Points and Societal Impact." Retrieved from: http://www3.weforum.org/docs/WEF_GAC15_Technological_Tipping_Points_report_2015.pdf.

22. While most people expect to retire by 65 . . . : Boschna, Janie. (2015, June 23). "When Do Americans Think They'll Actually Retire?" *The Atlantic.* Retrieved from: http://www.theatlantic.com/business/archive/2015/06/ideal-retirement-age-work/396464/.

23. The entrepreneurs and free agents of today . . . : Ernst and Young. (2015). "Megatrends 2015: Making Sense of a World in Motion." Retrieved from: http://www.ey.com/Publication/vwLUAssets/ey-megatrends-report-2015/$FILE/ey-megatrends-report-2015.pdf.

24. Entrepreneurship is particularly popular in rapid growth markets . . . : Ernst and Young. (2015). "Megatrends 2015: Making Sense of a World in Motion." Retrieved from: http://www

.ey.com/Publication/vwLUAssets/ey-megatrends-report-2015
/$FILE/ey-megatrends-report-2015.pdf.

25. Growth in key developing markets is expected to taper . . . : Ernst
and Young. (2015). "Megatrends 2015: Making Sense of a World
in Motion." Retrieved from: http://www.ey.com/Publication/
vwLUAssets/ey-megatrends-report-2015/$FILE/ey-megatrends
-report-2015.pdf.

26. Additionally, almost 50 percent of managers . . . are allowed
to work remotely: The Economist Intelligence Unit. (2015,
February). "Engaging and Integrating a Global Workforce."
SHRM Foundation. Retrieved from: http://whitepaper-admin
.eiu.com/futurehrtrends/wp-content/uploads/sites/2/2015/03/
Engaging-and-Integrating-a-Global-Workforce-June2015.pdf.

27. Many of the jobs that people will be doing in 5 to 10 years . . . :
Ernst and Young. (2015). "Megatrends 2015: Making Sense
of a World in Motion." Retrieved from: http://www.ey.com/
Publication/vwLUAssets/ey-megatrends-report-2015/$FILE/ey
-megatrends-report-2015.pdf.

28. The Indian subcontinent will jump from 1.6 billion people . . . :
Larsen, Janet. (2014, February 4). "Eco-economy Indicators:
Global Temperature. Earth Policy Institute." Retrieved from:
http://www.earth-policy.org/indicators/C51.

29. Countries like Yemen, Somalia . . . : Larsen, Janet. (2014,
February 4). "Eco-economy Indicators: Global Temperature.
Earth Policy Institute." Retrieved from: http://www.earth-policy
.org/indicators/C51.

30. However, a 2014 report . . . world population stabilization was
unlikely . . . .: Gerland, P., Raftery, A., et al. (2014, October
10). "World Population Stabilization Unlikely This Century."
Science 346 (issue 6206): 234–237. Retrieved from: http://science
.sciencemag.org/content/346/6206/234.full.

31. Currently 54 percent of the global population lives in cities . . . :
Ernst and Young. (2015). "Megatrends 2015: Making Sense
of a World in Motion." Retrieved from: http://www.ey.com/
Publication/vwLUAssets/ey-megatrends-report-2015/$FILE/ey
-megatrends-report-2015.pdf.

32. Again, the vast majority of urban growth . . . : Ernst and Young.
(2015). "Megatrends 2015: Making Sense of a World in Motion."
Retrieved from: http://www.ey.com/Publication/vwLUAssets/ey
-megatrends-report-2015/$FILE/ey-megatrends-report-2015.pdf.

33. In 2014, nearly one billion people lived in urban slums . . . : Ernst
and Young. (2015). "Megatrends 2015: Making Sense of a World
in Motion." Retrieved from: http://www.ey.com/Publication/
vwLUAssets/ey-megatrends-report-2015/$FILE/ey-megatrends
-report-2015.pdf.

34. From 1990 to 2010 the gross enrollment . . . : Taylor, P., and Kochlar, R. et al. (2009, September 3). "Recession Turns a Graying Office Grayer." Pew Research Centre. Retrieved from: http://www.pewsocialtrends.org/2009/09/03/recession-turns-a-graying-office-grayer/#prc-jump.

35. Between 1979 and 2014, China's annual real GDP . . . : Morrison, Wayne M. (2015, October 21). "China's Economic Rise: History, Trends, Challenges and Implications for the United States." Congressional Research Service. Retrieved from: https://www.fas.org/sgp/crs/row/RL33534.pdf.

36. China's economic growth . . . : Scott, Robert E. (2012, August 23). "The China Toll." Economic Policy Institute. Retrieved from: http://www.epi.org/publication/bp345-china-growing-trade-deficit-cost/.

37. In 2010 China overtook the United States . . . : Kamrany, N. M., and Jiang, F. (2015, February 2). "China's Rise to Global Economic Superpower." *The Huffington Post*. Retrieved from: http://www.huffingtonpost.com/nake-m-kamrany/chinas-rise-to-global-eco_b_6544924.html.

38. However, China's demographics . . . are changing: Morrison, Wayne M. (2015, October 21). "China's Economic Rise: History, Trends, Challenges and Implications for the United States." Congressional Research Service. Retrieved from: https://www.fas.org/sgp/crs/row/RL33534.pdf.

39. It is no longer "cheap China" . . . : Booz & Co. (2010, March 30). "Serving the China Market Emerges as Primary Strategy of Multinational Manufacturers in New AMCHAM Shanghai/Booz & Company Study." Retrieved from: http://www.strategyand.pwc.com/global/home/press/displays/47818590.

40. The rise of Chinese organizations like Huawei . . . : De Silva, Jan. (2012, September/ October). "The War for Talent in China." *Ivey Business Journal*. Retrieved from: http://iveybusinessjournal.com/publication/the-war-for-talent-in-china/.

41. At present, Bangladesh, Kenya, Morocco, and Nigeria will contribute a third of the estimated growth in the labor force . . . : Dobbs, R., and Lund, S., et al. (2012, November). "Talent Tensions Ahead: A CEO Briefing." *McKinsey Quarterly*. Retrieved from: http://www.mckinsey.com/global-themes/employment-and-growth/talent-tensions-ahead-a-ceo-briefing.

42. Since 1980 collective human demands on our natural resources . . . : Brown, Lester. (2009, July 30) "Learning from Past Civilizations." *Grist*. Retrieved from: http://grist.org/article/2009-07-29-learning-from-past-civilizations/.

43. During the last half of the twentieth century the irrigated land used for food production tripled . . . : Brown, Lester. R. (2013,

April 12). "Peak Water: What Happens When the Wells Go Dry?" Retrieved from: http://blogs.worldbank.org/water/peak-water -what-happens-when-wells-go-dry.

44. According to the World Bank, 175 million Indians are being fed . . . : Brown, Lester. R. (2013, April 12). "Peak Water: What Happens When the Wells Go Dry?" Retrieved from: http://blogs .worldbank.org/water/peak-water-what-happens-when-wells-go -dry.

45. In India, the states of Tamil Nadu and Karnataka are already fighting over the Cauvery river . . . : Mallet, Victor. (2016, April 14). "India: Water Wars." *Financial Times*. Retrieved from: https: //www.ft.com/content/96687242-009b-11e6-ac98-3c15a1aa2e62.

46. Demand for agricultural land is predicted to double . . . : Monbiot, George. (2015, November 19). "There's a Population Crisis All Right. But Probably Not the One You Think." *The Guardian*. Retrieved from: https://www.theguardian.com/commentisfree /2015/nov/19/population-crisis-farm-animals-laying-waste-to -planet.

47. Clearing or weakening half the Amazon rainforest . . . : Brown, Lester. R. (2009, July 30). "Learning from Past Civilizations." Grist. Retrieved from: http://grist.org/article/2009-07-29-learning -from-past-civilizations/

48. These alarming statistics are at least in part the result of the massive diversion of grain to fuel the ethanol industry: Brown, Lester. R. (2010, June 29). "Book Bytes: The Population-Poverty Connection." Earth Policy Institute. Retrieved from: www.earth -policy.org/book_bytes/2010/pb4ch07_ss1.

49. At the same time 80 percent of the world's oceanic fisheries are being fished at or beyond their sustainable yields: Brown, Lester. R. (2013, September 15). "The Ecology of Population Growth." *Pop!ulation Press*. Retrieved from: https://populationpress.org /2013/09/15/the-ecology-of-population-growth-by-lester-r-brown/.

50. According to *The Guardian* . . . : Monbiot, George. (2015, November 19). "There's a Population Crisis All Right. But Probably Not the One You Think." *The Guardian*. Retrieved from: https://www.theguardian.com/commentisfree/2015/nov/19/ population-crisis-farm-animals-laying-waste-to-planet.

51. Monbiot also notes that our urban transport needs will similarly rise . . . : Monbiot, George. (2015, November 19). "There's a Population Crisis All Right. But Probably Not the One You Think." *The Guardian*. Retrieved from: https://www.theguardian .com/commentisfree/2015/nov/19/population-crisis-farm-animals -laying-waste-to-planet.

52. If Asia followed American consumption patterns . . . : Nair, Chandran. (2011). *Consumptionomics: Asia's Role in Reshaping Capitalism and Saving the Planet*. Singapore: John Wiley & Sons.

53. This financial speed accelerates the speed at which decisions can be taken to exploit resources . . . : Nair, Chandran. (2011). *Consumptionomics: Asia's Role in Reshaping Capitalism and Saving the Planet.* Singapore: John Wiley & Sons.

CHAPTER 2

1. What happened to Kodak will . . . : Seiler, Marco Ronnie. (2016, April 28). "Everything Is Changing Faster Than Ever Before." LinkedIn. Retrieved from: https://www.linkedin.com/pulse/everything-changing-faster-than-ever-before-marco-ronnie-seiler.

2. The digital camera was invented at Eastman Kodak . . . : Wikipedia. "Steven Sasson." Retrieved from: https://en.wikipedia.org/wiki/Steven_Sasson.

3. As Seiler rightly points out in his post . . . : Seiler, Marco Ronnie. (2016, April 28). Everything is changing faster than ever before. Retrieved from: https://www.linkedin.com/pulse/everything-changing-faster-than-ever-before-marco-ronnie-seiler.

4. John Chambers of Cisco agrees . . . : *Fortune.* "Cisco's John Chambers Explains How Leaders Can Cross the Digital Divide." Retrieved from: http://fortune.com/2016/09/14/cisco-john-chambers-digital-age/.

5. According to Vivek Wadhwa, Disney, Ford . . . : Wadhwa, Vivek. (June 7). "Democracy Is a Great Thing, Except in the Workplace." *The Washington Post.* Retrieved from: https://www.washingtonpost.com/news/innovations/wp/2016/06/07/democracy-is-a-great-thing-except-in-the-workplace/.

6. Uber CEO with tears in his eyes . . . : NDTV. (2017, February 22). Uber CEO, With Tears in His Eyes, Apologises for Company Culture. Retrieved from: http://www.ndtv.com/world-news/uber-ceo-apologizes-for-company-culture-after-harassment-claims-1662213.

7. Uber CEO apologizes . . . : Bloomberg. (2017, February 22). Uber CEO Apologizes for Company Culture After Harassment Claims. Retrieved from: https://www.bloomberg.com/news/articles/2017-02-21/uber-ceo-apologizes-in-staff-meeting-after-harassment-allegations

8. Of the original Fortune 500 list published in 1955 . . . : csinvesting. (2012, January 6). "Fortune 500 Extinction." Retrieved from: http://csinvesting.org/2012/01/06/fortune-500-extinction/.

9. Abraham Lincoln was another leader who understood forgiveness . . . : Symphonyofdissent. (2014, May 18). "Forgiving Others: The Example of Abraham Lincoln." Retrieved from: https://symphonyofdissent.wordpress.com/2014/05/18/forgiving-others-the-example-of-abraham-lincoln/.

10. Sanduk was born in 1955 to uneducated parents in Olanchungola, northeast Nepal . . . : Traveller. (2012, April 7). "The Barefoot

Surgeon." Retrieved from: http://www.traveller.com.au/the
-barefoot-surgeon-1w7a6.

11. It was here that Ruit knew cataract surgery would restore their
humanity . . . : Cure Blindness, Himalayan Cataract Project.
"Dare The Impossible." Retrieved from: http://www.cureblindness
.org/our-story/transformative.

12. He provides cheap, efficient, and, more importantly, world-class
eye care to the people . . . : Lak, Daniel. (2003, October 28).
"Nepal's Unique Eye Care Centre." BBC News. Retrieved from:
http://news.bbc.co.uk/2/hi/south_asia/3218471.stm.

13. Both husband and wife have walked for two days through the
foothills of the Himalaya . . . : The Fred Hollow's Foundation.
"Sudip's Story." Retrieved from: http://www.hollows.org/au/what
-we-do/our-stories/sudip-s-story.

14. His efficient model of eye care is now practiced in many parts of
the world . . . : Mero Gulf. (2016, December 15). "Dr. Sanduk Ruit
for CNN Heroes 2011." Retrieved from: http://www.meroguff
.com/2011/03/dr-sanduk-ruit-for-cnn-heroes-2011.html.

15. Slicing through someone's eyeball with steady hands was hard . . . :
Aljazeera. (2014, July 20). "The Gift of Sight." Retrieved from:
http://www.aljazeera.com/programmes/101east/2014/07/gift
-sight-201471574440164234.html.

16. Establishing Tilganga Institute of Ophthalmology in 1994 . . . :
Protagonisten. "Out of the Darkness." Retrieved from: http://
www.outofthedarkness-film.com/protagonisten/.

17. Sushma Limbu was only eight years old when she hurt her eye . . . :
Newar, Naresh. (19 March 2004–25 March 2004). "An Eye for an
Eye." Nepali Times, issue 188. Retrieved from: http://nepalitimes
.com/news.php?id=3804#.WDvFyeT_pjo.

18. Fifty-year-old Thuli Maya Thing has struggled with life and caring
for the needs of her family since losing her eyesight . . . .: Kristof,
Nicholas. (2015, November 7). "In 5 Minutes, He Lets the Blind
See." New York Times. Retrieved from: http://www.nytimes.com
/2015/11/08/opinion/sunday/in-5-minutes-he-lets-the-blind-see
.html?_r=0.

19. The maverick who refused to allow a skeptical medical
establishment to get in the way of his dream . . . : Levy, Megan.
(2016, November 5). " 'It's A Whole New World': Nepalese
Doctor Who Studied Under Fred Hollows Is Changing Lives for
Thousands." The Sydney Morning Herald. Retrieved from: http:
//www.smh.com.au/national/its-a-whole-new-world-nepalese
-doctor-who-studied-under-fred-hollows-is-changing-lives-for
-thousands-20161024-gs9pnc.html.

20. Hollows was also a pillar of support in battling resistance from
the international medical fraternity . . . : Melhem, Yaara Bou.
(2014, September 2). "Nepal's Very Own 'Fred Hollows' Is on a

Mission to Eradicate Curable Blindness." SBS. Retrieved from: http://www.sbs.com.au/news/article/2014/09/02/nepals-very-own -fred-hollows-mission-eradicate-curable-blindness.

CHAPTER 3

1. Powerful Victims for Forbes.com . . . : Peshawaria, Rajeev. (2015, May 11). "Powerful Victims." *Forbes.* Retrieved from: http://www .forbes.com/sites/rajeevpeshawaria/2015/05/11/powerful-victims /#3c8a17044e6b.
2. Research by Professor Adam Grant . . . : Grant, Adam M. "Rethinking the Extraverted Sales Ideal: The Ambivert Advantage." The Wharton School, University of Pennsylvania. Retrieved from: https://faculty.wharton.upenn.edu/wp-content/ uploads/2013/06/Grant_PsychScience2013.pdf.
3. Sales revenue by levels of extraversion . . . : Priceonomics. (2013, November 29). "Do Extraverts Make the Best or Worst Sales People?" Retrieved from: https://priceonomics.com/do-extraverts -make-the-best-or-worst-sales-people/.
4. As Barbara Kellerman of Harvard and Jeffrey Pfeffer of Stanford agree . . . : Kellerman, Barbara. (2012). *The End of Leadership.* Harper Collins.
5. As Barbara Kellerman of Harvard and Jeffrey Pfeffer of Stanford agree . . . : Pfeffer, Jeffrey. (2015). *Leadership BS.* Harper Business.
6. As Barbara Kellerman of Harvard and Jeffrey Pfeffer of Stanford agree . . . : Wakefield, Nicky. (2016, February 29). "Leadership Awakened." Deloitte University Press. Retrieved from: https:// dupress.deloitte.com/dup-us-en/focus/human-capital-trends/2016/ identifying-future-business-leaders-leadership.html#endnote-sup-1.
7. In 2014, she crushed the world record for the longest triathlon in history . . . :"Be Relentless: A Documentary About Norma Bastidas." *Indiegogo.* Retrieved from: https://www.indiegogo.com /projects/be-relentless-a-documentary-about-norma-bastidas#/.
8. I have a son who's losing his sight . . . :"Be Relentless." Retrieved from: http://www.normabastidas.com/.
9. Norma's father passed away when she was 11 and left her mother alone with a family of five children . . . : Coorlim, Leif. (2016, May 17). "Human Trafficking Survivor Who Smashed Triathlon World Record." CNN. Retrieved from: http://edition.cnn.com /2016/05/16/world/human-trafficking-norma-bastidas-triathlon -record/.
10. Some family members took advantage of Norma's vulnerability . . . : Heilpern, Will. (2016, July 12). "How a Human Trafficking Survivor Smashed a Record-Breaking 3,762- Mile Triathlon." *Business Insider UK.* Retrieved from: http:// uk.businessinsider.com/norma-bastidas-the-human-trafficking -survivor-who-broke-a-world-record-triathlon-2016-7/?IR=T.

11. He was diagnosed with cone-rod dystrophy . . . : Parkes, Melenie. (2013, May 6). "Extraordinary Moms: Norma Bastidas." Retrieved from: https://au.be.yahoo.com/lifestyle/a/17029301/extraordinary -moms-norma-bastidas/#page1.

12. The news was unbearable for 38-year-old Norma, then a struggling single parent in Calgary . . . : Newsner. (2016, 31 May). "She Was Raped and Sold as a Sex Slave. 36 Years Later, She Crushes the Triathlon World Record and Inspires Us All." Retrieved from: http://en.newsner.com/she-was-raped-and-sold-as-a-sex-slave-36 -years-later-she-crushes-the-triathlon-world-record-and-inspires -us-all/about/news,gender-en,sports.

13. Norma's reason for pushing through her physical limits is also fueled by the desire to send a message to other survivors of human trafficking . . . : Fuhrmaneck, Jessika. (2016, June 27). "The Story of Norma Bastidas." *Two Wings.* Retrieved from: http:// withtwowings.org/the-story-of-norma-bastidas/.

14. She never gave up and pushed forward to send a message . . . : Bernstein, Lenny. (2014, May 2). "Norma Bastidas Is About to Complete the Longest Triathlon Ever." *Washington Post.* Retrieved from: https://www.washingtonpost.com/news/to-your -health/wp/2014/05/02/norma-bastidas-is-about-to-complete-the -longest-triathlon-ever/.

15. Adversity has been a recurring theme in Norma's life, . . . : Nazarian, Angella. (2015, May 14). "An Interview with Norma Bastidas: Pursuing Dreams." *Positively Positive.* Retrieved from: http://www.positivelypositive.com/2015/05/14/an-interview-with -norma-bastidas-pursuing-dreams/.

16. Running became a form of release . . . : WR, Team. (2014, November 21). "Inspiration Awards: Norma Bastidas." *Women's Running.* Retrieved from: http://womensrunning.competitor .com/2014/11/inspiration/inspiration-awards-norma-bastidas _32941#qhWmAK1UjVbCkRMZ.97.

17. When we want to help the poor, . . . : "Muhammad Yunus Quotes." Retrieved from: https://www.goodreads.com/author/ quotes/1254841.Muhammad_Yunus.

18. To the amazement of the world, in 2016 the United Arab Emirates established two new ministries . . . .: *Gulf News,* Dubai.

19. William has defied all odds, turning adversity into advantage . . . : Virtue, R., and Millington, B. (2016, May 30). "Cancer Survivor Dr. William Tan Eyes Final Paralympics Performance." ABC News. Retrieved from: http://www.abc.net.au/news/2016-05 -30/cancer-survivor-dr-william-tan-eyes-final-paralympics -performan/7459500.

20. William's resilience was tested like never before with the diagnosis of end-stage leukemia . . . : Tee, Karen. "Against All Odds."

Singapore International Foundation. Retrieved from: http://singaporemagazine.sif.org.sg/against-all-odds.

21. Topping the class in his fourth year, he also won two year-long scholarships . . . : HSBC Bank (Singapore) Limited. "Why No Journey Is Too Tough for Paralympian William Tan." Retrieved from: https://www.hsbc.com.sg/1/2/hsbcpremier/live-richer/plan-my-retirement/william-tan-journey/.

22. He was determined to excel in his studies . . . : Dunlap, Tiare. (2016, June 3). "Dr. William Tan Was Told He Had 12 Months to Live with Stage 4 Cancer—Seven Years Later, He's Gearing Up for the Rio Paralympics." People.com. Retrieved from: http://people.com/sports/dr-william-tan-was-told-he-had-12-months-to-live-with-stage-4-cancer-seven-years-later-hes-gearing-up-for-the-rio-paralympics/.

23. He finished at Raffles with flying colors and joined the prestigious . . . : Chan, Wilson, et al. "The Doctor in a Wheelchair." *Rafflesian Times*. Retrieved from: https://rafflesiantimes.wordpress.com/2015/10/13/the-doctor-in-a-wheelchair/.

24. William was born in Singapore in 1957 . . . : Celebrity Speakers. "Exclusive Gold Elite Speaker: Dr William Tan." Retrieved from: http://www.celebrityspeakers.co.nz/dr-william-tan/.

25. Dedicated his race to the Children's Hospital fund-raising program . . . : YouTube. (2007, November 9). "Dr William Tan "(video). Retrieved from: http://www.youtube.com/watch?v=p_q90gJ7Nbc&feature=related.

26. William's athletic endeavors weren't purely for self-fulfillment or for the sake of competition alone . . . : Tan, William. (2006). "No Journey Too Tough; My Record Breaking Attempt To Race in 10 Marathons in 65 Days Across 7 Continents." National University of Singapore.

27. He eventually caught hold and bit the bullying hands . . . : Singapore Heroes. "Dr William Tan." Retrieved from: http://singaporeheroes.weebly.com/william-tan.html.

CHAPTER 4

1. A widely used example is that of U.S. airline Southwest, that challenged its staff to bring the plane turnaround time on the tarmac down to only 10 minutes . . . : Dean, Michael. (2016, July 28). "The Pros & Cons of Stretch Goals." Peakon. Retrieved from: https://peakon.com/blog/post/the-pros-and-cons-of-stretch-goals.

2. We set ourselves goals we know we can't reach . . . : "Ten Things We Know To Be True." Google Company. Retrieved from: https://www.google.com/about/company/philosophy/.

3. Stretch goals have also come in for a share of criticism . . . : Ordóñez, L., and Schweitzer, M., et al. (2009, February 11). "Goals

Gone Wild: The Systematic Side Effects of Over-Prescribing Goal Setting." Harvard Business School Working Paper Summaries. Retrieved from: http://hbswk.hbs.edu/item/goals-gone-wild-the -systematic-side-effects-of-over-prescribing-goal-setting.

4. Organization-wide stretch goals can also backfire, simply because the wrong companies are setting them . . . : Sitkin, Sim. (2010). "The Paradox of Stretch Goals: Organizations in Pursuit of the Seemingly Impossible." *The Academy of Management Review.*

5. Microsoft, in fact, discovered Pareto applied to both product features . . . : Rooney, Paula. (2002, October 3). "Microsoft's CEO: 80-20 Rule Applies To Bugs, Not Just Features." Retrieved from: http://www.crn.com/news/security/18821726/microsofts -ceo-80-20-rule-applies-to-bugs-not-just-features.htm.

6. Welch believed that rigorous differentiation between employees was critical . . . : *Business Insider Australia.* (2015, September 28). "Tips from the Very Top: 10 Leadership Insights from Legendary GE CEO Jack Welch." Retrieved from: http://www .businessinsider.com.au/jack-welch-leadership-insights-2015-9.

7. Welch's enthusiasm (and spectacular results) at GE were at least part of the reason why the 20:70:10 model became so widespread across the 1980s and 1990s . . . : Murray, Alan. "Should I Rank My Employees?" *The Wall Street Journal Asia Edition*, adapted from *The Wall Street Journal Guide to Management.* Retrieved from: http://guides.wsj.com/management/recruiting-hiring-and -firing/should-i-rank-my-employees/.

8. An Uber driver is not required to work a certain amount of hours . . . : Huet, Ellen. (2015, January 22). "Uber's Ever- Renewing Workforce: One-Fourth of Its US Drivers Joined Last Month." *Forbes.* Retrieved from: http://www.forbes.com/sites/ ellenhuet/2015/01/22/uber-study-workforce/#315fac361244.

9. Contract grading comes in several different formats . . . : Harvard University. (2012, June 17). "Making Your Own Grade II: Contract Grading in the 21st Century." Retrieved from: http:// bokcenter.harvard.edu/blog/making-your-own-grade-ii-contract -grading-21st-century.

10. Professors Jane Danielewicz and Peter Elbow at the University of Massachusetts sign a contract with their students . . . : Volk, Steve. (2016, March 27). "Contract Improv: Three Approaches to Contract Grading." Oberlin College. Retrieved from: http:/ /languages.oberlin.edu/blogs/ctie/2016/03/27/contract-improv -three-approaches-to-contract-grading/.

11. A study by professor of psychology and psychiatry at Ohio State University Stephen Reiss . . . : Grabmeier, Jeff. (2000, June 28). "New Theory of Motivation Lists 16 Basic Desires That Guide Us." Ohio State University. Retrieved from: https://news.osu.edu/ news/2000/06/28/whoami/.

12. General Electric, Grant Thornton, Grubhub, Netflix, LinkedIn, Virgin Group, and HubSpot are already allowing unlimited vacation . . . : Frohlich, Thomas C. (2015 December 19). "7 Companies with Unlimited Vacation." *USA Today*. Retrieved from: http://www.usatoday.com/story/money/business/2015/12/19/24-7-wall-st-companies-unlimited-vacation/77422898/.

13. Managers are doing such a poor job in motivating and measuring their workers . . . : Snyder, Benjamin. (2015, April 2). "Half of Us Have Quit Our Jobs Because of a Bad Boss." *Fortune*. Retrieved from: http://fortune.com/2015/04/02/quit-reasons/.

14. Companies fail to choose the right manager for the job 82 percent of the time . . . : Beck, R., and Harter, J. (2014, March 25). "Why Great Managers Are So Rare." Gallup. Retrieved from: http://www.gallup.com/businessjournal/167975/why-great-managers-rare.aspx.

CHAPTER 5

1. As Cy Wakeman says on Forbes.com . . . : Wakeman, C. (2013, January 14). "It's Time to Rethink Employee Engagement." *Forbes*. Retrieved from: http://www.forbes.com/sites/cywakeman/2013/01/14/its-time-to-rethink-employee-engagement/#2fdfa6293983.

2. By its own admission, only 13 percent of the global workforce is engaged . . . : Crabtree, Steve. (2013, October 8). "Worldwide, 13% of Employees Are Engaged at Work." Gallup. Retrieved from: http://www.gallup.com/poll/165269/worldwide-employees-engaged-work.aspx.

3. As Bloomberg writer Elizabeth Ryan says . . . : Ryan, Elizabeth. (2012, October 5). "The Employee Engagement Racket." *Bloomberg*. Retrieved from: https://www.bloomberg.com/news/articles/2012-10-05/the-employee-engagement-racket.

4. As George Serafeim at Harvard and Claudine Gartenberg at Stern found out in their research . . . : Serafeim, G., and Gartenberg, C. (2016, October 21). "The Type of Purpose That Makes Companies More Profitable." *Harvard Business Review*. Retrieved from: https://hbr.org/2016/10/the-type-of-purpose-that-makes-companies-more-profitable.

5. A quick Google on the words "Corporate Culture." . . . : Investopedia. Retrieved from: http://www.investopedia.com/terms/c/corporate-culture.asp.

6. The Small Business Encyclopedia defines . . . : "Corporate Culture." *Entrepreneur*. Retrieved from: https://www.entrepreneur.com/encyclopedia/corporate-culture.

7. Hoffman, Casnocha, and Yeh use the story of John Lasseter . . . : Hoffman, R., and Casnocha, B., et al. (2014, July 8). "The Alliance: Managing Talent in the Networked Age." *Harvard Business Review*. Retrieved from: https://hbr.org/product/the

-alliance-managing-talent-in-the-networked-age/an/14046-HBK
-ENG.

CHAPTER 6

1. Stephen van Vuuren lives in Greensboro . . . : Vuuren, Stephen van. (2016, October 10). Personal interview.
2. As originally described by McKinsey & Co. . . . : Chambers, Elizabeth G., Fouldon, Mark, Handfield-Jones, Helen, Hankin, Steven M., Michaels, Edward G., the War for Talent, McKinsey Quarterly, retrieved from: http://www.executivesondemand.net/managementsourcing/images/stories/artigos_pdf/gestao/The_war_for_talent.pdf
3. In 2013, The Economist even questioned . . . : *The Economist.* (2013, January 12). "Has the Ideas Machine Broken Down?" Retrieved from: http://www.economist.com/news/briefing/21569381-idea-innovation-and-new-technology-have-stopped-driving-growth-getting-increasing/.
4. This graphic is adapted from . . . : Brabham, Daren C. (2013)." Using Crowdsourcing in Government." IBM Center for The Business of Government. Collaborating Across Boundaries Series.
5. Per Howe, crowdsourcing is . . . : Howe, Jeff. (2006, June 2). "Crowdsourcing: A Definition." Retrieved from: http://crowdsourcing.typepad.com/cs/2006/06/crowdsourcing_a.html.
6. In a personal interview, Jason C. Crusan . . . : Crusan, Jason C., Director, Advanced Exploration Systems Division, NASA Human Exploration and Operations Mission Directorate, (2016 September 15). Personal Interview.
7. Wikipedia is another example . . . : Wikipedia. "Statistics." Retrieved from: https://en.wikipedia.org/wiki/Wikipedia:Statistics.
8. According to eYeka . . . : eYeka. "The State of Crowdsourcing in 2016." Retrieved from: https://en.eyeka.com/resources/reports. In its annual Mobility Report . . . : Ericsson. (2015, June). "Ericsson Mobility Report." Retrieved from: http://www.ericsson.com/res/docs/2015/ericsson-mobility-report-june-2015.pdf.
9. It's technology, not business or governments . . . : Sean Parker, quoted in David Kirkpatrick, "With a Little Help from His Friends," *Vanity Fair,* October 2010. Retrieved from: http://www.vanityfair.com/culture/2010/10/sean-parker-201010.
10. Another example of this is the pharmaceutical company Merck . . . : "Using the Crowd as an Innovation", Boudreau, Kevin J., Lakhani, Karim R., Harvard Business Review, April 2013.
11. Polaris Industries . . . partnered with Spigit . . . : "Case Study of Polaris Industries: Driving Breakthrough Innovation Through Crowd Sourcing." Retrieved from: http://go.spigit.com/rs/123-ABC-801/images/Spigit_Polaris_Case_Study.pdf.

12. Take the pharmaceutical company Pfizer as an example . . . : Kreutz, Christian. (2016, January 19). "36 Great Examples of Crowdsourcing." WE THINQ. Retrieved from: https://www .wethinq.com/en/blog/2014/08/12/39-Great-Crowdsourcing -Examples.html.

13. United Airlines learned the hard way . . . : Sonsofmaxwell. (2009, July 6). "United Breaks Guitars" (video). YouTube. Retrieved from: https://www.youtube.com/watch?v=5YGc4zOqozo

14. United Airlines learned the hard way . . . : Wikipedia. "United Breaks Guitars." Retrieved from: https://en.wikipedia.org/wiki/ United_Breaks_Guitars.

15. Using the crowd for innovation did not catch on at Procter & Gamble until . . . : Huston, L., and Sakkab, N. (2006, March). "Connect and Develop: Inside Procter & Gamble's New Model for Innovation." *Harvard Business Review*. Retrieved from: https: //hbr.org/2006/03/connect-and-develop-inside-procter-gambles -new-model-for-innovation.

16. According to IMPACT Hiring Solutions . . . : Deutsch, Barry. (2012, October 16). "IMPACT Hiring Solutions." Retrieved from: http://www.barrydeutsch.net/impact-hiring-solutions/.

17. On October 24, 2016, a *New York Times International Edition* article . . . : Farrell, Christopher. (2016, October 22). "Very Mobile Work Force, Never Far from Home." *New York Times*, International Edition.

18. The 2014 State of the Industry report . . . : The International Association of Outsourcing Professionals (IAOP), "New York. 2014 Key Findings from the State of the Industry Report." Retrieved from: https://webcache.googleusercontent.com/search?q=cache:p-Fuh82WIFkQJ:https://www.iaop.org/Download/Download .aspx%3FID%3D2532%26AID%3D3999%26SID%3D34%26S-SID%3D175%26RP%3D%252FSOTI%252F2014+&cd=1&hl= en&ct=clnk.

19. In his book *The Ownership Quotient* . . . : Heskett, J., and Sassare Jr., et al. (2008, December 9). "The Ownership Quotient: Putting the Service Profit Chain to Work for Unbeatable Competitive Advantage." Harvard Business Press.

20. A study by Undercover Recruiter found . . . : Hebbard, Laurence. (2015). "Why Employee Referrals Are the Best Source of Hire." The Undercover Recruiter. Retrieved from: http:// theundercoverrecruiter.com/infographic-employee-referrals -hire/.

21. Zappos, the online shoe . . . : Sullivan, Dr. John. (2014, June 2). "Examining Zappos's 'No Job Postings' Recruiting Approach— Innovation or Craziness?" Blog Post, Ere Media. Retrieved from: https://www.eremedia.com/ere/examining-zapposs-no-job -postings-recruiting-approach-innovation-or-craziness/.

22. New recruitment platforms, such as the one hosted by Reflik . . . :
    Reflik. (2015, September 22). "Why Crowdsourcing Works for
    Recruiting." Retrieved from: https://www.reflik.com/blog/why
    -crowdsourcing-works-recruiting/.
23. In 1997, Steven Hankin of McKinsey & Co. . . . : Chambers,
    Elizabeth G., Fouldon, Mark, Handfield-Jones, Helen, Hankin,
    Steven M., Michaels, Edward G., the War for Talent, McKinsey
    Quarterly, retrieved from: http://www.executivesondemand.net/
    managementsourcing/images/stories/artigos_pdf/gestao/The_
    war_for_talent.pdf.

In addition to the direct references cited above, my thoughts and
recommendations in this chapter were informed by the following
articles and books:

1. Abrahamson, S., and Ryder, P., et al. (2013, January). *Crowdstorm:
   The Future of Innovation, Ideas, and Problem Solving*. John
   Wiley & Sons, Inc., Hoboken, New Jersey.
2. Board of Innovation. List of open innovation crowdsourcing
   platforms. Retrieved from: http://www.boardofinnovation.com/
   list-open-innovation-crowdsourcing-examples/.
3. Brabham, Daren C. (2013). "Crowdsourcing." MIT Press.
   Retrieved from: https://mitpress.mit.edu/books/crowdsourcing.
4. Bratvold, David. "What Is Crowdsourcing." Daily Crowdsource.
   Retrieved from: https://dailycrowdsource.com/content/crowd
   sourcing.
5. Chrum, Alex. (2012, September 11). "Learning from the
   Crowdsourcing Efforts at Netflix." CrowdSource. Retrieved
   from: http://www.crowdsource.com/blog/2012/09/learning-from
   -the-crowdsourcing-efforts-at-netflix/.
6. Cirujano, Ron. (2014, March 19). "Crowdsourcing: A Shift in
   Talent Acquisition." Crowdsourcingweek.com. Retrieved from:
   http://crowdsourcingweek.com/blog/crowdsourcing-a-shift-to
   -talent-acquisition/.
7. Deloitte LLP UK. (2016). "The Three Billion Enterprise
   Crowdsourcing and the Growing Fragmentation of Work."
8. Fuller, Johann. (2012, July 9). "The Dangers of Crowdsourcing."
   Harvard Business Manager. Retrieved from: http://www
   .harvardbusinessmanager.de/blogs/a-840963.html.
9. Gardner, James. (2015, December 7). "How to Succeed at
   Crowdsourcing Innovation." Techonomy Exclusive. Retrieved from:
   http://techonomy.com/2015/12/how-to-succeed-at-crowdsourc
   ing-innovation/.
10. Gardner, James. "Innovation as a Science: Predicting the
    Value of Ideas." Daily Crowdsource. Retrieved from: https://
    dailycrowdsource.com/content/open-innovation/1459-innovation
    -as-a-science-predicting-the-value-of-ideas.

11. Gasca, Peter. (2013, February 14). "6 Reasons to Use Crowdsourcing." *Inc.* Retrieved from: http://www.inc.com/peter -gasca/6-reasons-to-use-crowdsourcing.html.

12. Gaudino, Laura. (2014, April 28). "Crowdsourcing Benefits, Limitations and How to Avoid Failure." Crowdsourced Testing. Retrieved from: https://crowdsourcedtesting.com/resources/ crowdsourcing-benefits/.

13. Hancock, Bill. (2015, June). "Sixth Rock from the Sun." *O. Henry Magazine 5*, no. 6.

14. Heskett, James. (2016, November 2). "Are Employees Becoming Job 'Renters' Instead of 'Owners'?." Harvard Business School. Retrieved from: http://hbswk.hbs.edu/item/are-employees -becoming-job-renters-instead-of-owners.

15. Horthon, Karen. (2015, June 4). "NASA Uses Crowdsourcing for Open Innovation Contracts." NASA TV Press Release. Release J15-010. Retrieved from: https://www.nasa.gov/press-release/nasa -uses-crowdsourcing-for-open-innovation-contracts.

16. Howe, Jeff. (2008, 2009). *Crowdsourcing. Why the Power of the Crowd Is Driving the Future of Business.* Three Rivers Press, New York.

17. Howe, Jeff. (2006, June 1). The Rise of Crowdsourcing. Retrieved from https://www.wired.com/2006/06/crowds/.

18. "In Saturn's Rings Blog." Retrieved from: http://insaturnsrings .com/blog/.

19. Intuit Investor Relations. (2015, August 13). "Intuit Forecast: 7.6 Million People in On-Demand Economy by 2020" (press release). Retrieved from: http://investors.intuit.com/press-releases/press -release-details/2015/Intuit-Forecast-76-Million-People-in-On -Demand-Economy-by-2020/default.aspx.

20. Kass, A., and Dubey, A. (2016, February 22). "Putting Crowdsourcing to Work for the Enterprise." *Accenture*, Technology Labs Blog. Retrieved from: https://www.accenture .com/us-en/blogs/blogs-putting-crowdsourcing-work-enterprise.

21. Kearns, Kathryn. (2015, October 7). "9 Great Examples of Crowdsourcing in the Age of Empowered Consumers." Tweak Your Biz.com. Retrieved from: http://tweakyourbiz.com/ marketing/2015/07/10/9-great-examples-crowdsourcing-age -empowered-consumers/.

22. Kickstarter.com. "About us." Retrieved from: https://www .kickstarter.com/about?ref=nav.

23. Kickstarter.com. "Funding Project: In Saturn's Rings." Retrieved from: https://www.kickstarter.com/projects/sv2/adagio-in-space -the-greensboro-symphony-in-saturns?ref=nav_search.

24. Ladime, Kazim. (2014, June 13). "Should You Start Crowdsourcing Talent?" Recruiter. Retrieved from: https://www.recruiter.com/i/ should-you-start-crowdsourcing-talent/.

25. Lindegaard, Stefan. (2012, August 9). "40 Examples of Open Innovation and Crowdsourcing." Innovation Excellence. Retrieved from: http://innovationexcellence.com/blog/2012/08/13/40-examples-of-open-innovation-crowdsourcing/.
26. Morton, Michael. (2014, August 12). "Driving Innovation with Crowdsourcing." Retrieved from: https://www.entrepreneur.com/article/236418.
27. Neumann, Michel. (2014, April 17). "Open Innovation vs. Crowdsourcing vs. Co-creation." Retrieved from: https://www.wazoku.com/blog/open-innovation-vs-crowdsourcing-vs-co-creation/.
28. Noble, C., and Durmusoglu, S., et al. (2014, October). *Open Innovation, Product Development and Management Association.* John Wiley & Sons, Inc., Hoboken, New Jersey.
29. Shellshear, Evan. (2016, July 16). "Innovation Tools: The Most Successful Techniques to Innovate Cheaply and Effectively." 7 Publishing.
30. Silverman, Rachel E. (2012, January 17). "Big Firms Try Crowdsourcing." *Wall Street Journal.* Retrieved from: http://www.wsj.com/articles/SB10001424052970204409004577157493201863200.
31. Simperl, Elena. (2015). "How to Use Crowdsourcing Effectively: Guidelines and Examples." *Liber Quarterly* 25, issue 1.
32. Sloane, Paul. (2011). *A Guide to Open Innovation and Crowdsourcing: Advice from Leading Experts.* Kogan Page Limited, United Kingdom.
33. Speier, Kim. (2016, January 7). "4 Examples of Clever Crowdsourcing Campaigns." Mainstreethost Blog Post. Retrieved from: http://www.mainstreethost.com/blog/four-examples-of-clever-crowdsourcing-campaigns/.
34. SPIGIT. "6 Ways to Create a Successful Innovation Program." Retrieved from: https://www.spigit.com/project/6-ways-to-create-a-successful-innovation-program/.
35. Stevens, Darren. "Crowdsourcing: Pros, Cons, and More." Hongkait.com. Retrieved from: http://www.hongkiat.com/blog/what-is-crowdsourcing/.
36. Talentsbay. "A Case for Talent Crowdsourcing." Retrieved from: http://talentsbay.com/downloads/talent-crowdsourcing.pdf.
37. Thiel, Peter. (2014). *Zero to One: Notes on Startups, or How to Build the Future.* Virgin Books, London.
38. Wagorn, Paul. (2014, April 8). "The Problems with Crowdsourcing and How to Fix Them." IdeaConnection. Retrieved from: https://www.ideaconnection.com/innovation-articles/the-problems-with-crowdsourcing-and-how-to-fix-them-00574.html.
39. West, Harry. (2015, August 21). "How Crowdsourcing Can Solve Your Toughest Talent Gaps." REWORK. Retrieved from: https:

//www.cornerstoneondemand.com/rework/how-crowdsourcing
-can-solve-your-toughest-talent-gaps.

40. Wheeler, Kevin. (2013, May 2). "5 Ways to Build a Crowdsourcing Strategy to Uncover Hard-to-Find Talent." ERE Media. Retrieved from: https://www.eremedia.com/ere/5-ways-to-build-a -crowdsourcing-strategy-to-uncover-hard-to-find-talent/.

41. Wladawsky-Berger, Irving. (2013, January 27). "Innovation May Be Slowing, Threatening Great Stagnation." *Wall Street Journal.*

42. Zhou, Wynn. (2015, October 22). "Crowdsourcing: How to Get the Best Global Talent to Work for Your Startup." Tech.Co. Retrieved from: http://tech.co/crowdsourcing-get-best-global -talent-work-startup-2015-10.

43. Zoref, Lior. (2015). *Mindsharing: The Art of Crowdsourcing Everything.* Penguin Publishing Group, New York, New York.

INDEX

ABOUT THE AUTHOR

CEO of the Iclif Leadership and Governance Centre, author of *Too Many Bosses, Too Few Leaders*, and a contributor for Forbes.com, Rajeev Peshawaria has extensive global experience in leadership and human capital consulting. He began his professional life as a banker and currency trader. Very soon thereafter he became disillusioned with the fact that a lot of young people joined the workforce full of hope and enthusiasm, only to be crushed into cynicism by bosses who don't care to develop and nurture them. He could not understand the work-life balance debate, and struggled with questions like: Why are work and life considered so different and opposite from each other? Why don't people feel a sense of excitement coming to work every day? He also noticed that while technological advances were changing life and work at a pace never experienced before, management practice was still stuck in the 1930s.

Unable to discard these thoughts from his mind, Rajeev began to educate himself on the mysteries of human behavior, and eventually abandoned the highly lucrative field of trading for a career in human resources—something that was considered suicidal at that time. He concluded that many people and organizations underachieve their potential because of poor leadership, or no leadership at all. He has since dedicated his life to redefining leadership, thereby helping individuals in enriching their lives, and organizations in achieving their full potential.

Rajeev provides speaking and consulting services globally to organizations in both the public and private sectors. Prior to joining Iclif, he was Chief Learning Officer of both Coca-Cola and Morgan Stanley, and has held senior positions at American Express and Goldman Sachs.

A TEDx talk based on one of the themes of this book can be viewed at https://www.youtube.com/watch?v=Y6bTquxTC-c.